Thriving in the Knowledge Age

Thriving in the Knowledge Age

*New Business Models for Museums
and Other Cultural Institutions*

JOHN H. FALK AND BEVERLY K. SHEPPARD

ALTAMIRA
PRESS

A Division of
ROWMAN & LITTLEFIELD PUBLISHERS, INC.
Lanham • New York • Toronto • Oxford

ALTAMIRA PRESS
A Division of Rowman & Littlefield Publishers, Inc.
A wholly owned subsidary of The Rowman & Littlefield Publishing Group, Inc.
4501 Forbes Boulevard, Suite 200
Lanham, MD 20706
www.altamirapress.com

PO Box 317, Oxford, OX2 9RU, UK

British Library Cataloguing in Publication Information Available

Library of Congress Cataloguing-in-Publication Data Available

ISBN-13: 978-0-7591-0757-1 (cloth : alk. paper)
ISBN-10: 0-7591-0757-2 (cloth : alk. paper)
ISBN-13: 978-0-7591-0758-8 (pbk. : alk. paper)
ISBN-10: 0-7591-0758-0 (pbk. : alk. paper)

Printed in the United States of America

♾ The paper used in this publication meets the minimum requirements of American National Standard for Information Sciences—Permanence of Paper for Printed Library Materials, ANSI/NISO Z39.48-1992.

Contents

Preface   vii

PART I. Doing Business in the Knowledge Age

1   A World in Transition   3

2   Creating a New Business Model   17

PART II. An Environmental Scan: Yesterday, Today and Tomorrow

3   Business in the Industrial Age   29

4   The Brave New World of the Knowledge Age   48

PART III. Building a Knowledge Age Business Model

5   Experiences That Matter   83

6   Understanding What's Important   106

7   Being Community   135

8   Attending to the Bottom Line   161

PART IV. Implementing and Sustaining a Knowledge Age Business Model

9   Strategies for Success   185

10 Putting It All Together: Thriving in the Knowledge Age   221

References   245

Index   253

About the Authors   263

Preface

The impetus for this book began in the late 1990s. Everything was going great for museums—so great that it made John nervous. It's not that he's a worrier. Quite the contrary. He's by nature an optimist. His training is in ecology, however, and what he was seeing was an exponential growth curve in museums—exponential growth in the number of people visiting museums, exponential growth in the expansion of existing museums, and exponential growth in the numbers of new museums being created. As any ecologist will tell you, exponential growth cannot be sustained. So, as he looked around at this booming industry, what he saw concerned him.

As much as John respected the dedication and hard work of museum professionals, it was his opinion that the overwhelming recent successes of museums were largely the result of forces outside of the museum community. As described in *Learning from Museums*,[1] John believed that large-scale societal changes brought about by the dawning of the Knowledge Age were largely responsible for the ever-increasing public interest and use of museums, rather than anything specific museums themselves were doing. Nothing wrong with that, though. Many of the most successful individuals and organizations owe their achievement largely to being in the right place at the right time.

What concerned John was the lack of recognition by many in the museum community about what it was that they owed their success to. Even more problematic, there appeared to be a widespread lack of awareness about how continuing societal change might adversely impact their organizations. Everyone seemed to be caught up in their current success and involved in planning elaborate expansions so that they could continue doing exactly what they had always done, just on a larger scale. In short, John became increasingly concerned about the long-term sustainability of museums and the business models on which they were based. He began to talk casually with friends about his concerns, including Beverly, who shared a similar concern from her perspective at the Institute of Museum and Library Services. Beverly, too, believed that museums should be instituting changes and new relationships to respond to the accelerating needs of a totally new Knowledge Age.

By the early years of the twenty-first century, both of us, Beverly and John were beginning to share our concerns more publicly and trying to explain what we felt were the challenges the museum community faced. We did not have long to wait until others, too, shared our concerns.

The atrocities of September 11, 2001, and the following period of economic and social instability clearly initiated a very difficult period for museums. Indeed, cultural and nonprofit institutions across the United States and around the world suffered dramatic declines in audience and funding during this time. It was alarming to see how many museum professionals seemed willing to blame their woes exclusively on these short-term events rather than exploring whether current conditions were merely catalysts, exacerbating a series of trends already underway. As is often the case, it's hard to see problems coming when times are good, and when times are bad, who has the time to think about it? We believe that now, when things are beginning to look a little better, is exactly the right time to address the serious challenges the museum community will face in the years ahead.

At a time when many people all over the world feel that their core institutions are failing them, we should be increasingly attuned to the dramatic changes taking place in society. The familiarity of an Industrial Age, the time in which museums as we know them were born, is yielding to the new challenges of a Knowledge Age. No institution, however cherished, will be untouched by the economic, social, and political changes that are sweeping old ways aside. This new Knowledge Age could and should be a time in which museums thrive, but whether they will is anyone's guess at the moment.

As observers and practitioners in the world of museums, we share a deep admiration and passion for museums and a strong conviction that they are critical institutions for the twenty-first century. We also share an anxious concern that the financial condition of museums is becoming increasingly fragile. The business models of the past appear to be dangerously out of sync with the rapid changes taking place around us. The public of this new century has changing needs and expectations, and most museums are woefully ill-prepared to meet these. Although museums should be among the resource-rich leaders in this expanding era of learning, they are in danger of residing on the sidelines or quietly disappearing—unless they can reexamine old assumptions and make dramatic changes in practice.

In writing this book we have tried to bring together two strands of knowledge—a deep understanding of museums past and present and a comprehensive awareness of business practices and ideas. We have tried, whenever possible, to intertwine these two strands into a single, unified story about how to rethink, dare we say, reinvent the business of museums. Although far from a "how-to," we hope this book provides sufficient tangible ideas to enable museum professionals to begin the long and difficult task of forging new business models, business models suited to this new age in which we now find ourselves. At the very least, we hope this book will challenge all museum professionals—educators, curators, marketers, evaluators, administrators, volunteers, funders, and trustees—to reflect seriously on the current business models of the institutions they support and attempt to envision how those models might need to change in light of the new realities of the twenty-first century.

Above all, our goal in writing this book is to help forge a dialogue among our colleagues, to encourage a reappraisal of the way we currently run our institutions and a reevaluation of what we consider success. We hope that this book provokes not only conversation, but outright debate, since we know that not everyone in the community will agree with all of the ideas we've put forward. In order to aid these conversations we have ended each chapter with a series of discussion questions. Debate and reappraisal are exactly what the museum community, all communities, need now. For no institution of any kind will long survive in the Knowledge Age without engaging in serious and continuous appraisal of its business model. That said, a few qualifications are worth noting.

First, although we've focused this book on museums, we do not believe that the ideas presented here apply exclusively to museums. It is our belief that the basic business model framework we've proposed could equally apply to any nonprofit organization, or perhaps even to a for-profit one. The specifics would of course vary depending upon the nature of the organization, but the big ideas would hold. It is because of the specifics that we focused on museums. The richness of any story is in the details, and so in order to tell this story well, we felt it best to highlight the single type of organization we know best, museums.

A similar qualification relates to our focus on the U.S. situation. Although we occasionally make reference to institutions and situations outside of the United States, the clear focus here is on the American context. We took this approach not because we felt that these ideas applied only to the United States or that American museums are somehow more important than other museums, but rather because each country, each region of the world, has its own specific and unique realities. The U.S. reality was the reality we knew best and could most authoritatively address.

So, please feel free to apply these ideas to institutions beyond museums and to countries other than the United States, but do so with caution and thoughtfulness. We believe the basic suit will fit a wide diversity of bodies, but it undoubtedly will require some tailoring to fit well.

Finally, as is always the case, the ideas in this book are not exclusively ours. We are particularly grateful to a number of individuals who helped us think about these issues over the past several years, some explicitly, some through their writings, and some just through their inspiration. We begin by thanking Lynn Dierking, who invested many hours not just in conversation, but in the hard and often thankless work of editing and commenting on this text. We are forever grateful for the ideas of Stephen Weil and Roy Schafer, whom we will miss dearly. We also wish to thank all the individuals we talked to and interviewed for this book, including and particularly Al DeSena, Emlyn Koster, David Chesebrough, Katherine Lee Reid, Mamie Bittner, John Jacobsen, Lou Cassagrande, and Lesley Lewis. Special thanks to reviewers we know—Peter Anderson, Bill Booth, Desmond Griffin, Colin Johnson, and Ellen Rosenthal— as well as to a couple we do not; your comments were invaluable in helping to shape, and reshape the book. We were influenced by a wide array of business writers, but particularly those of Peter Drucker, Shoshana Zuboff and James

Maxmin, Fred Crawford and Ryan Mathews, James Collins and Jerry Porras, and Robert Kaplan and David Norton. Finally, we thank AltaMira Press for supporting our effort to write this book and in so doing, helped to ensure that these ideas will be read and discussed by many.

John H. Falk
Beverly Sheppard
August 2005

NOTE

1. J. H. Falk and L. D. Dierking, *Learning from Museums* (Walnut Creek, CA: AltaMira Press, 2000).

I

Doing Business in the Knowledge Age

1

A World in Transition

Not everything that is faced can be changed, but nothing can be changed until it is faced.
—James Baldwin

William and Maria Rodriquez and their three children, William Jr. (nine), Lupe (seven), and Esta (six), arrived at the Alabaster Natural History Museum around 10:30 Saturday morning as was their habit. Waiting at the door to greet them was museum staffer Frances. An outsider would have thought that Frances was welcoming long-lost friends—she hugged each of the Rodriquezes in turn, commenting on Lupe's dress, Esta's hair ribbon, and Willy's (William Jr.) new haircut. Then, without missing a beat, she went to the shelf and pulled out a bin with the Rodriquez family name on it. She handed the bin to Maria and, with a parting call of "have a great visit, Maria," scurried off to greet a new family that was just walking in the door.

Maria took the bin and placed it on the table in the greeting area and helped the children take off their coats and hang them up in the special locker area that had been set aside for them. Once everyone was settled, Maria opened up the bin. The bin contained five hand-held personal computers, each one labeled with one of their names. Maria passed out the hand-held devices to each person, helping Esta and Lupe with the strap so that they wouldn't lose or drop them. When everyone was ready, the family set out on their visit.

As they proceeded through the building, the family members used their personal hand-held computers to guide their curiosity and answer their questions. Each of their hand-held devices contained a record of what they were interested in, what their ability level was, and what was an age-appropriate strategy for engaging them in the content of the museum. Over the months of working with the devices, each had become quite comfortable, in fact, attached to these technological guides. Yet, throughout their visit, they also continued to talk with each other, pointing out items in the exhibits or referring to something on their computers that they wanted to share. As they walked through the museum they were greeted by name by the museum's staff, several of whom made a point of engaging them in conversation and asking them about their specific interests and questions. It was clear that this was a family who had built a personal relationship with the staff and the institution through repeated and continuous use of the facility.

About thirty minutes into their visit, the family split into two groups. William and Willy headed off for the gems and minerals section while the "girls" set off for their favorite section of the museum, the Discovery Room.

Willy had good reason to want to visit the gems and minerals section of the museum. He had been conducting an experiment on radioactive decay in the hall for weeks now. Inside the exhibit area was an exhibit of a radioactive rock, complete with a Geiger counter. Using his hand-held computer as a research guide, as well as data entry and analysis device, Willy had been following the radioactive decay process and calculating how long it would take for the rock to stop being radioactive. He had made some predictions the previous week and he was eager to see if they were accurate. Mr. Rodriquez could hardly keep up with Willy as he ran to the back corner of the exhibit hall. But he had no fear of him getting lost and no concern about his well-being. He knew that Frank would be waiting there, as if he'd known that Willy would be there at just this time. It wasn't that Frank was totally prescient. As soon as the Rodriquez family had logged onto their hand-helds, Frank had been sent a note that the family was in the building. Frank's hand-held computer provided him with a picture of each member of the family, an update on their whereabouts in the building, and a reminder of the interests and experiments they were working on. Frank did not require a reminder about the appearance of the Rodriquezes or their experiment. He was a nuclear chemist who worked as a docent on weekends at the museum. For the past two months he had been working with Willy on this particular experiment. He was as excited to see Willy as Willy was to see him; the opportunity to work one on one with this child was what made volunteering worthwhile. Only after fifty-five minutes of engrossed dialogue, looking, and entering of information into his hand-held did Willy feel like moving on, and then it was just about time to meet back up with his mother and sister.

Meanwhile, William Rodriquez didn't just sit there; he, too, had been hard at work with his own hand-held in the exhibition. There was a reason beyond just chaperoning Willy that he was eager to head to this particular exhibition area! William was an amateur rock collector and a member of the local Rockhounds Club. He was using the collection to help identify some new specimens that he had recently purchased from one of his fellow club members after the latter's return from a rock-hunting expedition in Arizona. William had scanned the images of his new specimens into his computer and e-mailed them to the museum for help in identification. The museum had uploaded the location of the type specimens for him on a map of the gems and minerals hall so that he could easily find them. He was using his hand-held device's GPS to help find the specimens and the hand-held's database was providing him with additional information on each type of rock. Occasionally, William would write in questions, some of which could be immediately answered by the device's database Others would need to be answered later by the museum's staff and e-mailed back to him.

An hour into his musings, a message flashed on William's hand-held; his wife said that she and the girls were heading to lunch and that Willy and he should join them there as soon as possible. She let him know that they had picked an "insect table" for lunch today. [*Note*: Every week the museum put a new series of collections into their specially built dining area tables and wall cubicles. On each table were laminated interpretive materials that allowed diners to examine and learn more about the museum's collection while they ate.]

Upon entering the museum foodservice area William and Willy were greeted by name by the restaurant hostess and immediately shown to the Rodriquezes' "insect" table. As soon as she had gotten into the museum, Maria had used her hand-held device to inform the restaurant that she and her family were planning on having lunch at around 12:00. Although this particular area was primarily self-service, good customers like the Rodriquez family were given preferential treatment, which meant that even on the busiest days they would be guaranteed a table. Although it was not really necessary, the hostess took it upon herself to take their drink orders before escorting them to the special cafeteria-style line reserved for Elite Members. Each family member selected their food and headed to the cashier. The cashier tallied up their items but no money was exchanged; their bill was automatically charged to their account (including their membership discount).

Based upon their experiences, their hand-held devices made recommendations for items in the museum shop that directly related to what they had seen and done so far that day. Usually the museum shop was an important and regular component of their visit. The family had other plans this particular afternoon, so after lunch they prepared to leave. They returned to the area where they had been originally greeted by Frances. Frances was not there, but her replacement, Bill, also immediately recognized the Rodriquez family and inquired how their visit had been and if he could do anything for them. He also remarked to Maria and William how thankful the museum was that they had brought their children to the museum this day and what great parents they were. Maria and William thanked Bill. Esta proceeded to tell Bill all about what she had done in the Discovery Room. Eventually, everyone had retrieved and put on their coats and Bill had collected their hand-held computers. Before placing them back into their container and shelving them, he inserted them into a special docking station. The docking station recharged the hand-held devices' batteries so that they would be fresh and ready for the Rodriquezes' next visit, plus it connected the devices' memories to the museum's central computer. The hand-held computers had noted all of the interactions each of the Rodriquez family members had with their devices—their track through the museum as recorded by sensors throughout the institution, the questions posed by the machines and the responses given, the questions posed by the individual family members and responses given by the hand-helds—and all of this data was downloaded for analysis and reactions by the museum. The museum's main computer was programmed to analyze automatically most of this information, to note the individual learning path taken by each family member, and to add the data to the museum's assessment program that was monitoring the personal growth of each of its members. This information was part of a large-scale effort by the museum to track its impact on the community, an effort designed to measure the in-depth and longitudinal learning the museum helped to support in its visiting public.

The museum's computer was also programmed to note if any member of the family had posted any questions or concerns that could not be answered by their personal devices, or if anything occurred that fell sufficiently outside the norm anticipated by the assessment program. A summary of the Rodriquezes' visit, plus any of the additional notes, would be sent off to a staff member for review to ensure that any specific questions or concerns were dealt with. They would route questions to an appropriate staff member for reply and a note would be sent to the Rodriquez family via e-mail letting them know the status of their questions. In this way, they could make sure that they remained in contact with the family. But that's not all that was sent to the Rodriquez family via e-mail. Based upon what each member of the family did and saw that day, they would also be sent suggestions for additional things they could do— when television shows on the topics they were interested were airing in the next week or two; suggestions for age-, ability-, and interest-level-appropriate articles and books for each family member (there was also a notation about which of these were currently on the shelf at their neighborhood library or bookstore); links to websites; an occasional personal note from one of the staff suggesting things to see, do, or think about over the next few days; and occasionally even the e-mail addresses of other individuals in the community who shared similar interests. In this way, the Rodriquez family's experience with the museum was more than just a weekly visit; it was really an ongoing personal journey, a journey in which the museum played the role of personal learning guide and coach. Through this relationship, each family member's unique interests and curiosities were supported and encouraged, and the museum was able to forge an educationally and financially rewarding partnership with not only the Rodriquez family, but all of the similarly interested individuals in the community.

The Alabaster Natural History Museum had not always been like this. For years the museum had seen declining visitation and falling revenues. Like many institutions of its size and content, the museum had tried various strategies to turn things around. For years it had invested in renting blockbuster exhibitions in order to bring in new audiences. Yet each year the costs of these exhibitions rose higher and higher and it got increasingly difficult to attract new audiences; in fact, despite greater expenditures, audience numbers stayed about the same and the new audiences did not return and become frequent visitors. Then in the wake of September 11, even the blockbuster exhibitions no longer seemed to attract the crowds. Although the museum knew that it should increase marketing dollars so that it could increase visitation, with decreasing revenues the marketing budget was the first to be reduced. After all, better to reduce marketing dollars than money for collections and staff! The other thing that suffered was maintenance of the building. All of this was beginning to feel like a death spiral—a deteriorating facility with no monies for advertising and promotion, resulting in declining attendance and revenues; lower revenues resulting in greater deterioration of facilities and even less money for advertising and promotion, which in turn led to even greater declines in attendance and revenues. Everyone agreed something had to be done. But what?

Like so many institutions at the beginning of the twenty-first century, the Alabaster Natural History Museum realized that continuing to do business the way it always had was just not going to work. Something radically new had to be tried, something that allowed the museum to get out of the downward spiral it seemed to be in. Then one of the board members who was head of a consumer electronics company suggested that the key change they had to make was to change their focus; they needed to move away from their historic approach of trying to serve "the masses" with "one size fits all" experiences to a new approach that emphasized intensive, long-term, customized, quality relationships with a more limited number of key constituencies. He said that his industry had been in a similar decline several years ago, and this was what it had taken to turn it around.

This required a huge leap of faith on the part of the museum, its board and staff, and, in particular, the community. To implement this new approach fully would require more than just another Band-Aid solution but a radical realignment in priorities and fundamental changes in staffing and funding—changing behaviors and mind-sets that had served the museum well for more than fifty years! On the surface, the solution seemed "old school"—increase earned revenues by increasing visitor numbers, but the "below the surface" strategy for doing so was anything but old school. The new institutional goal was to become known as *the* place in Alabaster County where families and organizations with science interests could satisfy those interests, not just once and superficially, but *repeatedly and richly*. The museum would be the preeminent "Science Experience" institution in Alabaster County, offering not just a fluffy, cheap-thrills kind of experience, but a deeply engaging, long-lasting kind of experience. It wanted to create a perception among core users that it could anticipate and satisfy its users' every need related to the topics of interest to them—not just once but repeatedly over many years. What was radical about the approach was that the museum wanted to convert 15,000 annual visits into 20,000 annual visits not by convincing thousands of new people to visit the museum, but by convincing a core group of "best customers" to come repeat-edly—ideally ten to fifteen or more times per year—and to pay full price each time they came! That was radical!

Take the Rodriquez family, for example. Before this new approach was ini-tiated, the Rodriquez family had been members; they came to the museum about eight or ten times over the course of a year. Instead of paying the usual entrance fee of $44.00 ($11.50 per adult and $7 per child); they had bought a membership for $100; this obviously made great financial sense to the Rodriquezes, but was a net financial loss for the museum. Now, as "Elite Mem-bers" of the museum (which cost $20 to join), the Rodriquezes pay $35 each time they come to the museum, but they get much more value for their money than before. Before, all they got was free admission each year; now they get highly personalized experiences and premium service. They end up paying more, but they also end up getting more. The experience has proven suffi-ciently rewarding for the Rodriquez family that they are willing to pay the $35 entrance fee to the museum; $35 every time they come (plus food and items at the shop)! The Rodriquezes still get a modest discount on admissions and pur-chases, but they do not get a free ride. Over the course of the year, the museum now earns roughly twelve times more revenue from this family than it did before, while at the same time providing a more satisfying experience for each family member. And the Rodriquez family is not the only family who has become "Elite Members." Elite Members pay a slightly reduced entrance fee each time they visit (a 20 percent discount), they are able to have this fee auto-matically billed to their credit card account, and they do not wait in line for tickets; they just walk in, pick up their hand-held devices, and put anything they do not want to carry with them in their personal lockers. Although the cost of going to the museum so frequently represents a significant percentage of the Rodriquez family's working income, William and Maria Rodriquez say it is a price they are more than happy to pay. What price, personal growth and learning for their children, and for them as well? They've seen both Willy's and Lupe's interest in school increase and William has seen his own interest in his rock collecting hobby soar. Where else in a community like Alabaster County could they get this level of personalized attention and service? Where else could their children be challenged and encouraged to stretch themselves intel-lectually? What is $35 per week if it gives each of their children a significant advantage in life, a chance to become successful in the future? And where else could they go and do all of this as a family in a safe, comfortable, and support-ive environment?

That the Rodriquezes along with several hundred other families in the com-munity would feel this way and thus make this kind of financial investment is fundamental to the business model of the Alabaster Natural History Museum. The museum thoroughly researched the needs and interests of families in the community and determined that it could provide a quality, personalized, science-rich experience that families, even moderate-income families like the Rodriquezes, would want to participate in. Over a period of four years, the Alabaster built up its Elite Membership numbers. What it promised Elite Mem-bers was that they would each receive the highest-quality, most personalized experiences the museum could possibly provide; however, it did not promise their Elite Members that they would get steeply discounted prices. The hunger in the community was sufficient to build the core constituency that the museum needed to make this experiment financially viable—the break-even point was roughly 125 families, enough money to not only cover the cost of hardware but also the extra employees required. The museum now has 335 families enrolled in the Elite Membership program. The Alabaster is not a large natural history museum, but it currently is a financially sound institution.

The amazing part of this whole change in approach was that the benefits of the Elite Members program rippled through every part of the institution's finances. Now, as before, the institution depends upon earned revenues to keep its doors open. Although it used to receive about a quarter of its operat-ing funds from the county, and could usually count upon another quarter coming from various fundraisers and gifts, fully half of its income historically was derived from fees charged for admission, sales at the gift shop, and pro-ceeds from its food services. Interestingly, even with the introduction of the new business model this basic formula has not changed, but what has changed are the total revenues generated. Although total annual attendance has re-mained relatively flat over the course of this three-year experiment—about 15,000 visits per year—earned revenues have climbed nearly 200 percent.

In fact, the Alabaster's total operating budget has climbed from $400,000 per year to over $750,000 per year. One-shot visitor admissions and spending still contribute about the same amount—roughly $120,000 annually—but the con-tribution of members (fees and spending on food and gift shop items) has climbed from about $30,000 per year to roughly $300,000 per year. But this new program has not merely increased earned revenues; it has also significantly increased other sources of income. Gift income from the community has grown as a result of the partnerships the Alabaster has now forged with various interest groups such as the Rockhounds Club. In return for club members doing volunteer work with museum scientists, the museum provides club members with free advice and consultation. The museum has forged similar partnerships with a wide assortment of community groups ranging from local hobbyists like birders, herpetologists, and archeologists, to community groups like churches, boys' and girls' clubs, and the YWCA and the YMCA. The goal was to ensure that there was a seamless relationship between the museum's areas of interest and those in the community who shared those interests; plus this quid pro quo arrangement has resulted in a net financial benefit to the museum because of the personnel savings generated by the volunteer workers (as the Baby Boom generation enters retirement age, the ranks of qualified individuals ready and willing to serve as volunteers have begun to once again swell). These collaborations have resulted not only in increased contributions of volunteer time, but increased financial donations as well. The local birding club stands out. Last year the Alabaster County Audubon Society donated $50,000 to the museum—an unheard of sum of money from a local group. Perhaps in response to the museum's elevated profile in the community, the excitement generated by this new initiative resulted in a number of major articles in the local newspaper and a feature on the local evening news and as a result the county government also doubled the museum's annual budget allotment despite funding pressures in the county. Everyone in the community seems to be noticing the museum and wants to support the good works it's doing for local families.

Certainly, change was not immediate. Once the museum shifted its focus from the inside-out to the outside-in, from a sole focus on its expertise to a focus on matching the needs of its public with its expertise, however, everything began to fall into place. It took more than a year for the staff and board of the museum to buy into this new business model, to accept the profound changes it would mean for the institution. But ultimately most did; those that could not left and were replaced by those who did buy into the new model. In fact, it was a particularly enthusiastic board member who helped the museum secure a major grant from a local bank that made the whole effort possible. The grant allowed the museum to not only buy the hardware, program the software, hire a volunteer coordinator, and recruit and train the cadre of new volunteers necessary to make the personalized experience possible, but it allowed the museum to work with faculty from the local college to interview current and potential members about their needs and interests. Once additional revenues began to come in, the museum added additional part-time staff to help support personalized visitor experiences and it was also able to add another scientist to the staff. It was able to identify a public-oriented scientist who was eager to have as part of his duties responding to members' and community partners' questions and needs. The museum has also created a separate fund for hardware replacement so that it can continue to keep all of its hand-held machines operative and up-to-date. In short, this new way of thinking about why it exists, whom it serves, and how best to serve them has transformed the museum. It has adopted a business strategy that emphasizes high-quality learning experiences and totally personalized service; there is no one else in Alabaster County that comes close in these two areas. It is widely recognized as a science learning leader in the community. And although the number of families it currently serves in this way is relatively limited, it has just been approached by a major national funder and encouraged to apply for a grant that will allow it to expand dramatically these types of experiences to a much wider percentage of the community, particularly those with limited financial means. In short, the museum has adopted a new business model that appears to be working. This new model emphasizes personalized, high-quality learning experiences. Although exhibits and collections are still important, their role in the institution is now secondary to creating first-rate public education experiences. The model is supported by staff, by the board, by the local government, and by collaborations within the community. The model has been made possible by a combination of new technologies and an ever-expanding cadre of dedicated volunteer staff that enable the museum to provide a level of personalized learning facilitation never before possible. Equally important, the Alabaster museum is systematically collecting feedback from their Elite Members that allows the institution to get ever better at meeting Elite Members' needs. It doesn't hurt that this data also provides evidence that demonstrates to funders and the public alike that the museum is accomplishing its mission and fulfilling its institutional promise to the community.

If this all sounds too good to be true, perhaps it is. Unfortunately, the Alabaster Museum of Natural History is not a real museum. Although we would love to be able to say that a family like the Rodriquez family really had the kind of experiences we described and that the scenario we created really exists, this is not the case. Business models resembling the one presented above do not exist in any museum we are aware of, although pieces of such a model are beginning to creep into a number of institutions. It is not that it couldn't, it is just that it does not. We chose to take a very high-technology approach in this opening scenario, but we could have just as easily created a more low-tech version. It wouldn't have mattered. Low-tech versions of this kind of ongoing, totally customized, high-quality learning experience are equally hard to find in today's mass-produced museum world. Across the land, most museum visitors, including longtime members, are treated by most museums as just another nameless, faceless entity, statistics in the museum's numerical accounting system of success. A first-time visitor or fiftieth-time visitor normally gets the same treatment; the likelihood of being recognized by staff as an individual typically depends more upon the persistence and personality of the visitor rather than upon the business strategy and mission of the institution. Museum visitors are rarely treated as long-lost friends or given special recognition or high-quality service; their learning experiences outside the museum are infrequently supported or even encouraged, and their personal learning growth is normally neither catered to nor monitored.

The model for how to run today's museum, from content to finances, was forged by the realities and needs of the Industrial Age of the twentieth century. In the Industrial Age organizations were run as top-down, paternalistic, mass-market, and mass-production businesses; the business models that evolved from this approach were applied to everything from making automobiles to French fries, from schooling to government, and, yes, to the running of museums. This is, and has been, the prevailing business model of museums for many years. For this reason, a typical individual visiting a typical museum today can expect a visitor experience that feels mass-produced and impersonal. Although the quality of museum exhibitions has improved, staff become more professional, the amount of merchandise in gift shops expanded, the food in the cafe less institutional, and in some institutions the guards friendlier, the fundamental nature of the museum experience has changed little over the past few decades because the underlying business model of museums has not changed.

As we find ourselves immersed in a new age, a Knowledge Age, museums of all kinds need to readjust their ways of doing business. This new age screams out for new approaches, for new business models better attuned to the rapidly evolving realities of the marketplace and society. In short, museums need to create new business models that are bottom-up rather than top-down, business models that match the needs and desires of their publics with the needs and desires of the institution. Museums need to figure out how to use the assets they possess to build long-term, meaningful relationships with their publics. They need to seek out kindred organizations within their community in order to build mutually supportive collaborations of organizations that share their values and interests. No longer can or should museums strive to be all things to all people; no longer can museums operate as if they exist in isolation. In the twenty-first century, museums will need to invest in relationships, bringing to those relationships those things that they alone as institutions do best. Museums also need to invest in themselves financially, developing sustainable and profitable revenue streams that can support development and growth. In short, museums need to fundamentally rethink for whom they exist and how they exist in order to build new business models appropriate to this new age in which we now live.

THIS BOOK

There is unlikely a museum director, trustee, or senior staff member who has not appreciated that the world is changing and that the museums they work for need to change. As we look around at our colleagues, however, we see few that seem to grasp fully how these changes are affecting their institutions, few who seem to completely understand what they must do to accommodate these changes. In short, we see few who have really understood the full scope and scale of the crisis that increasingly besets the museum industry. And as is often the case, many of those who were most successful in the twentieth century seem the most unwilling and least able to change. In writing this book, we hope to provide guidance to those seeking new directions, to provide a new vision for how to lead a museum in the Knowledge Age. This book is designed to help museums create business models designed to ensure that they will not merely survive, but *thrive* in the twenty-first century.

This involves a big leap—for many, a scary and hazardous leap. But not to leap will be even more dangerous. In this book we try to provide a guide to this new way of thinking. We outline what a business model is and then describe the basic structure of the current business models of museums, framing it within prevailing Industrial Age realities from which it sprang. We also outline what we think should be a framework for a new business model, one that is responsive to the Knowledge Age changes in society. Because it is so important, we spend some time reviewing where we as a society have come from and where we think we as a society are heading, all with museums in mind. Against this background, we apply the ideas of this new approach to business models, using real world examples to illustrate how changes might be applied to building a Knowledge Age museum. Our goal is to support a rethinking of the roles and functioning of these unique institutions we call museums—their audiences, their assets, and their business potential. Using all of this information, we attempt to provide a framework for rethinking the business of museums, one that better aligns the strengths and abilities of museums with the changing realities of society. We hope this book will provide a vision for how museums can begin to face the challenges of this new century, challenges that will demand a whole range of novel intellectual, social, and economic solutions.

As will become increasingly clear, we do not believe that there is a single pathway to success. For just as there cannot be a single description of what it means to be a museum, there can not be a single prescription for how to do business as a museum. We believe the frameworks we provide make it clear that there is not one, but dozens if not hundreds upon hundreds of strategies and tactics that might enable a museum to be successful in the Knowledge Age. We do, however, believe that most of these strategies and tactics will tend to converge upon a few basic premises. A key passageway into the Knowledge Age will involve transitioning from the mass-production, object-centered models of the twentieth century into something more closely resembling the individualized and personalized learning-focused model described at the beginning of this chapter. We believe that the vast majority of successful Knowledge Age museums will be those that increasingly embrace a quality-first business model. We believe this transformation will open up a world of opportunity to museums, opportunities rapidly closing to those that resist these changes. Is this the only opening through the wall that separates the twentieth and twenty-first centuries, the Industrial and the Knowledge Ages? Perhaps not, but currently it is the entryway that we can best imagine. If we are to pass through the gate in the wall, we must first see the wall; we must see that museums are businesses with business models.

DISCUSSION QUESTIONS

- Is your institution doing business fundamentally the same way it was ten to fifteen years ago? What's stayed the same and what's changed?
- What is the evidence of success you use to justify continuing to keep doing things the same way?
- What were the reasons you changed the way you do business? What evidence do you have that these changes improved your success?

NOTE

Epigraph: James Baldwin, *The Fire Next Time* (New York: Dell, 1962), 140.

2

Creating a New Business Model

I repeat, this is not a test. This is the beginning of a crisis that won't remain quiet for long. And as the Stanford economist Paul Romer so rightly says, "A crisis is a terrible thing to waste."
—Thomas L. Friedman

In a recent conversation, Katherine Lee Reid reflected on her fifteen distinguished years leading two of the largest art museums in the country, including most recently the Cleveland Museum of Art. We specifically asked her to talk about what was different about directing a museum today from the past. Katherine has a particularly unique perspective on this question. Both Katherine and her father, Sherman Lee, directed the same museum, the Cleveland Museum of Art, separated by a period of roughly twenty years.

> The major challenge an art museum director faces today is running a museum in a world that has so many options, a world where people feel less of a connection to the past. Today, a museum must work to bring to life the original works of art because we are surrounded by images and surrogates. We need to figure out how to make art an urgently needed part of people's lives. Although not for everybody, the art museum must become a critical part of the education system.
>
> Today the focus of the museum is on audience and the relationship of art to people. In my father's day, when he ran the museum, the focus was almost exclusively on the idea of art. This is a fundamental shift. We've become very motivated about audience, starting with the person rather than starting with the subject matter.

The key thing now is less on acquisition and much more on interpretation. My father's generation was operating on the Victorian model of venerating knowledge, but they were still in the stage of categorizing things. Today we know so much more. Today our goal is to use our knowledge, to interpret what we know so that people can benefit from what we've learned.

Without doubt, the business of running a museum is not only different but arguably a far more difficult task than it was a generation ago. In an interview some years ago, the director of the Metropolitan Museum of Art in New York noted, "All a director needs is administrative ability, knowledge of art, communication skills, international connections, languages, a blue suit and dinner with the trustees."[1] By contrast, today's director experiences complex splits in expectations, balancing new responsibilities for entrepreneurial management, team building, business acumen, vision, and leadership with the traditional requirements for fundraising, subject matter specialty, and a high degree of public visibility. There are now so many more things to deal with, so many more levels of complexity, not the least of which is a rapidly changing world. Steering a fragile ship through reef-filled waters is a lot easier if you not only have a rudder but a chart to show where the reefs lie. Without an overall strategy, without a business model, even if you are the most intrepid of captains, it is hard to get where you are going, or even know where you are going.

BUSINESS MODEL DEFINED

Business model is a term that emerged rather recently in the business vernacular and is sometimes disparaged because it has often been used in a fast and loose manner. But when defined and used properly, it is a term that can provide valuable insights. Whereas business plans are primarily focused on the overall strategic positioning of a business within the business ecosystem, the term *business model* also includes key structural and operational characteristics of a business. In other words, when used properly, *business model* is a broader description of a business than just its plan or strategy.

In brief, a business model is a description of the operations of a business, including the purpose of the business, components of the business, the functions of the business, the core values of the business, and the revenues and expenses that the business generates. Nonprofits, like museums, have business models just as certainly as do for-profits; it's just that they are not always aware of it. A business model is the mechanism by which a business intends to manage its costs and generate its outcomes—in the case of for-profits, the outcomes are primarily revenues earned, and in the case of nonprofits, the outcome is primarily the public good created. In either case, though, a business model is a summary of how an organization plans to serve the needs of its customers. It involves both strategy and implementation. According to a business encyclopedia,[2] a business model is the totality of how a business:

1. selects its customers
2. defines and differentiates its product offerings
3. creates [benefit] for its customers
4. attracts and keeps customers
5. goes to the market (promotion strategy and distribution strategy)
6. defines the tasks [and services] to be performed
7. configures and optimizes its resources
8. captures profit [or enhances public good]

The business model has accurately been described as the engine of the business, the framework upon which all activities are based. According to businessman and university lecturer Bruce M. Firestone, "If you get the business model right, then the harder you work, the more money you make (Google is an example here). If you get it wrong, then the harder you work, the more money you lose (Napster is an example here)."[3]

Museums seemed to have once live in a rarified world, a world free from the tawdry demands of the marketplace. No longer do museums live in that world. Today, museums must compete for audience, publicity, and resources. Increasingly, museum boards and directors have embraced the language of business. Over the past twenty years museums have created vision and mission statements, strategic plans, and marketing plans. Now we're saying that they have to have a business model. Well, museums have always had business models; every business—large or small, manufacturing or service, for-profit or not-for-profit—operates with a business model. That model can be implicit or explicit, but either way it exists.

A business model requires a well-articulated vision and mission statement, but these are only one piece of a business model. Developing a strategic plan, including setting BHAGs (Big, Hairy, Audacious Goals), is part of the process too. BHAGs is a concept first made popular in the business bestseller *Built to Last: Successful Habits of Visionary Companies* by Jim Collins and Jerry Porras,[4] but as stated above, a business model requires a strategy, but a strategy is not a business model. Every business has products (goods and services for sale), but products are only one of many concrete and visible manifestations of a business model. Every business has assets. An asset management plan is an excellent idea, which should also be part of any good business model. A business model is all of these things. A business model is the theory that undergirds how, why, and in what ways an organization conducts its business. It defines the realities of the environment in which the organization exists and the strategies the organization needs to adopt in order to thrive within that environment.

To be successful, every business must create a business model designed to address and answer four key questions.

1. Why do you exist? Whom are you serving? In the case of museums, who is your public and what specific needs do they have that you are uniquely positioned to satisfy?
2. What assets do you bring to the table? What are the internal assets your institution brings to its business, such as the human resources of staff, board, and supporters; also the assets of collections, building, and brand?
3. How will you forge and maintain partnerships and collaborations with like-minded organizations in the community in order to leverage your impact?
4. How will you support your business? What is your business strategy? What is the unique combination of products and services you can provide in order to satisfy specific public needs and generate sufficient revenues to keep your doors open?

The answers to these four questions cannot be made in a vacuum; the answers must always be situated within the context of the larger world or ecosystem. Each business must understand the realities of the economic, social, and political context in which it operates, both the ever evolving marketplace of the business world but equally the changing values, needs, and desires of the larger society in which the organization exists.

Finally, a business model is a dynamic not a static thing; it must always be evolving and changing because the world in which a business operates is constantly changing. At the heart of any successful business model is a strategy for judging the marketplace, evaluating current successes and failures, and predicting the future so the institution can keep one step ahead of the competition. In today's world the strategy for acquiring this kind of knowledge is research—market research, evaluation research, and basic research. These kinds of research provide data about the internal and external assets and strategies that a business needs in order to sustain itself into the future. Thus it is in the context of all these realities that a business model prescribes how an organization will operate; what its products and services will be; the relationships it will create, both inside and outside of the organization; and finally how it measures success and failure.

Figure 2.1 shows how these elements were traditionally organized by museums into a business model; this is a typical Industrial Age business model. This

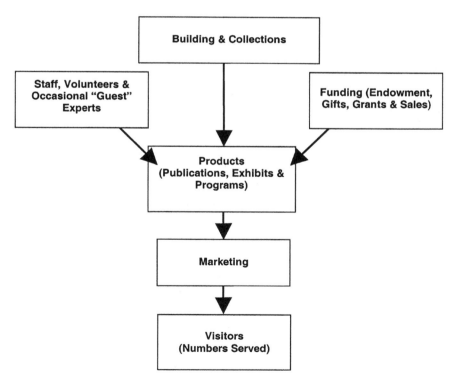

FIGURE 2.1
Industrial Age Business Model (for Museums).

model is top-down and linear. Ideas flow from the "head" of the organization (director and curators) down to the "consumers" (both general public and scholarly peers). There are essentially no feedback loops from the consumers back to the director and curators. Evidence of success is that people use the products or services; the quantity of units "delivered" (e.g., exhibitions mounted, catalogues printed) are sufficient evidence of success. The most important assets of the organization are tangible resources like collections and buildings. Other assets such as human resources and finances are important but secondary. Importantly, this model suggests that the organization is only tangentially, if at all, dependent upon those outside the organization—collaborators, competitors, economic cycles, and the like. The museum intersects with the outside world through guest curators, fundraising, and marketing. Otherwise it functions essentially as an island separate from the larger world. This is a classic "build it and they will come" approach to doing business.

By contrast we would offer a new model (Figure 2.2). The Knowledge Age business model shows the interaction and interrelationship of all these factors with particular reference to the nonprofit business context of museums. Rather than being *top-down*, the model is *bottom-up*—it emphasizes that the business model must begin with the consumer. Each museum needs to start with figuring how it, given its unique assets, can best understand and meet the needs of the public. Also figuring prominently in this new model is that it is situated within the ecosystem of the larger society. Rather than a linear model, this new model takes a systems approach—all pieces interact and feed back upon each other. When all of these pieces work together and become an integrated whole, then and only then will museums have constructed a business model that will allow them to thrive in the Knowledge Age.

Every nonprofit, every museum, has a business model. As we've pointed out, too often these business models are implicit rather than explicit. As a community, museums have only recently begun to appreciate that they need to be more explicit about their business models, that they need to attend to the details of their business model as much as do businesses in the for-profit world. For just as in the for-profit world, a poor business model for a not-for-profit organization spells troubles.

CHANGING MODELS

As alluded to above, business models do not exist in a vacuum. In fact, the essence of a good business model is that it is a plan for how to succeed within

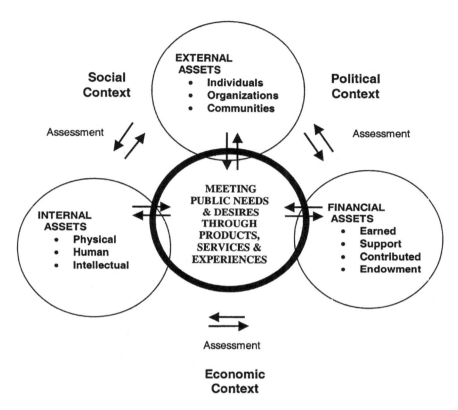

FIGURE 2.2
Museum Knowledge Age Business Model.

the world, a plan that requires a theory of how the world is. Problems arise when business models do not fully accommodate to the realities of the world—both the internal world of the institution and the external world of the community and larger society. And the world of today is definitely not like the world in which most museums forged their current business models. Most museums today still operate with some variation of the mass-production model forged during the Industrial Age of the twentieth century. By contrast, the scenario presented at the beginning of the previous chapter describes a museum with a very different model for how to do business, one utilizing aspects of the new Knowledge Age business model described above. The old business models of museums worked fabulously during the twentieth century, particularly in the last quarter of the century. Yet these old models, like the

Industrial Age from which they developed, are increasingly out of step with the realities of the new century. Just as Katharine Lee Reid described how her job at the Cleveland Museum of Art was different from that of her father when he directed the same institution twenty years before, so, too, all of us now live in a world with different needs and expectations.

Change has always been a part of our world. In fact, every generation of Americans has felt that their world was fundamentally different than that of their parents—and by and large they were right. Yet the changes we're seeing today are not evolutionary in nature, they are revolutionary. Everyone seems to agree that we are living through one of the greatest periods of economic and social upheaval in recorded history. Why should we assume that evolutionary changes in the ways we do business are what will be required in these revolutionary times?

In order for museums to become Knowledge Age businesses, they must first abandon the Industrial Age models they currently use. This will not be easy since it will require abandoning many of the attributes that are currently near and dear to many in the museum community. For example, it will probably mean abandoning the paternalistic attitude that the museum can and should be the arbitrator of quality and knowledge. It probably will require abandoning the idea that success can be achieved without knowing anything at all about the publics the museum claims to serve, knowing little or nothing about what they actually want and need. The current business models used by museums dictate that success can be measured by the quantity of individuals served; the greater the attendance, the greater the assumed accomplishment. As was appropriate in the twentieth century, the assumption is that high visitor attendance indicates that something good is happening. We believe that museums will ultimately be forced to reject this approach. We suspect that museum professionals will need to radically rethink why museums exist and how they go about meeting their public mandates. For many this will mean redefining the purpose of the museum as a free-choice learning resource rather than as a tourist destination, a place devoted to people rather than things, a place where success is measured in terms of the quality of the transactions that occur rather than in the quantity of people that move through the gates. But we're getting ahead of our story here.

Like any good narrative, the story of business models we're trying to tell here is situated within a context. In order to understand how to build a Knowledge

Age business model, museums must understand the context in which they have existed, the context in which they currently exist, and, as much as possible, the context they will soon be existing within. In strategic planning language, this is what is called an Environmental Scan. We would like to provide a business-oriented Environmental Scan for the museum community. We begin this Environmental Scan by taking a journey back in time, back to the golden age of museums as we now know them, back to the twentieth century.

DISCUSSION QUESTIONS

- Does your organization have an explicit or implicit business model?
- What is your institution's current business model? Is it closer to an Industrial Age or a Knowledge Age model?
- What business are you in? What are your organization's main products and services?

NOTES

Epigraph: Thomas L. Friedman, *The World Is Flat: A Brief History of the Twenty-First Century* (New York: Farrar, Straus & Giroux, 2005), 306.

1. Kent Lydecker, interview with Sherene Suchy, in *Leading With Passion: Change Management in the 21st Century* (Walnut Creek, CA: AltaMira Press, 1996), 75.

2. 3 January 16, 2004, www.en.wikipedia.org, "business model."

3. Bruce M. Firestone, Business Model—A definition. www.dramtispersonae .org/BusinessModel, 2002, accessed February 20, 2004.

4. Jim Collins and Jerrry L. Porras, *Built to Last* (New York: Harper Business, 1994).

II

An Environmental Scan

Yesterday, Today, and Tomorrow

Business in the Industrial Age

History is a guide to navigation in perilous times.
History is who we are and why we are the way we are.
—David McCullough

The crowd gathered long before the doors were to open. The line of waiting people snaked around the building. In the early morning fog the couples and families happily chatted among themselves as they waited, eager to see this new exhibition. Season after season, year after year, this scene was repeated. For fifteen straight years visitor numbers increased annually. The museum was celebrated in the community and the director was viewed as a savior, the man who had turned around a dying icon. The board eagerly participated in a capital campaign to raise money to renovate the building and add a new wing. In record time, $35 million was raised, an architect hired, and the job completed. Numbers increased again as the crowds flooded in to see the newly installed exhibitions and the shining new wing. Press and public alike claimed it as a testimonial to the value and stature of the community, an emblem of the community's growing success and culture. But the story doesn't end here.

As the new millennium arrived plans were already on the drawing board to start another capital campaign, to expand once again. Yet now the lines of people did not snake around the building. Rather than increased numbers every year, numbers were down—initially a little, then dramatically. With decreasing attendance came decreasing revenues. The economy was stagnating and sources of monies were drying up. The capital campaign was quietly shelved. First the temporary exhibition budget had to be drastically reduced, then the marketing budget, then staff, and finally the museum needed to cut back its hours. The economy revived, but not attendance. The director, once heralded as the savior of the institution, was quietly removed and a new director, someone with a strong business and marketing background, was brought in to revive the museum. Still the woes continued. What went wrong? How could something so good, for so long, go so bad, so quickly?

"Boom times for museums!" the articles in the *New York Times, Washington Post, Newsweek,* and *Museum News* proclaimed as the twentieth century ended.[1] Boom times, indeed! The museum community experienced unprecedented growth during the last quarter of the twentieth century—museums of all kinds grew in numbers, size, and popularity. Every year, the statistics on how many people visited museums seemed to climb. Although there were a few valleys and plateaus, the overall trend was steadily up. So why, as we arrive at the midpoint of the first decade of the new millennium, are so many within the museum community nervous? What has changed?

For one thing, many established museums are experiencing stagnant attendance. Even though the dire years following September 11, 2001, seem to be behind us, the recovery is anything but robust. This flattening out of visitor numbers is making many within the museum community extremely concerned, and for good reason. Attendance is at the heart of the current museum business model. Today everything begins and ends with visitor numbers. In the current business models of museums, attendance drives budgets—either directly through the revenues generated by gate, merchandising, and food service or indirectly as a key part of the grant and contribution formula. Like most organizations in our society, for-profit and nonprofit alike, museums operate on a growth model. Given that the yardstick of success is visitor numbers, annual growth in attendance figures indicates success; declines or even steady state suggest failure. What, then, is to be made of the recent attendance problems, and who is to blame?

Rather than "who," we are asking "what". We suggest that the "what" is the current business model of museums, a model with its roots firmly planted in the twentieth century. We believe the museum community's business model needs a drastic overhaul. What is this current business model? How did it become so prevalent? Where will change begin? These are the questions we address in this chapter.

FRAMING THE ISSUE

"I remember it as if it was yesterday. It was so exciting to see these treasures, to be part of the experience. There were literally thousands of people; all of us lined up. Slowly, the line snaked past the exhibits. We really couldn't pause very long in front of any of the exhibits because of the crowds; we had to keep moving because there were so many people behind us who also wanted to see the beautiful gold objects and the amazing workmanship of the Egyptians."[2]

This is one woman's recollection of the King Tut Exhibition, often referred to as the first of the "blockbuster" exhibitions. The exhibition, organized by the Metropolitan Museum of Art in 1974, toured the United States for several years; in all, more than 8 million people waited in line to see the exhibition. Arguably the most important exhibition of the twentieth century, the exhibition had a profound impact on the museum community. Ever since King Tut, a string of blockbusters became news stories and media events, drawing huge crowds. They brought in new members, attracted corporate sponsors, contributed fresh income, and demonstrated the museum's capacity to attract visitors from far beyond the traditional museum constituencies.

With the blockbuster era, museums were emerging from an inward-looking focus on collections to an outward-looking focus on the public. The museum's role as an essential educator came front and center, and a new concern for understanding and marketing to public interests took hold. Museums experienced new energy, drama, and newsworthiness. They added more commercial amenities—more high-end restaurants and retail shops. If in mid-century, many in the public thought of museums as old and dusty, by the end of the century, more of the public found them educational and entertaining.

Museums were a hot commodity! Over the course of a century, museums and the experiences they offered had become bigger, sexier, more diverse, more populist, and designed to attract millions. As the century progressed, museums had been increasingly pressured to create larger constituencies of supporters and increase their sale of goods and services to maintain the escalating costs of operations. These changes and additions were part of an explicit effort to revamp the public perceptions of museums, to revamp the business of museums.

Accordingly, museums have incrementally adapted their business models in recent years. Like all businesses, museums responded to the changes in the world around them. Arguably, much of the fabulous success museums enjoyed in the latter part of the twentieth century reveals the ability of museums to adapt and to accommodate a growing public hunger for knowledge, learning, and experience at the dawn of the Knowledge Age.

Yet, as the twenty-first century brings ever more changes, museums now seem to be falling behind. Despite surface changes to accommodate an idea-driven public, the underlying structure and functioning of museums—their business models—have not changed. The modern museum, with its underlying business framework, remains a product of the twentieth century, the period when museums rose to their current position of importance and prominence as public institutions. Thus, for better or worse, the history of today's museums, including and particularly the business models on which they operate, is inextricably enmeshed with the history and business practices of the twentieth-century Industrial Age. A brief analysis of the origins and structure of this business model will inform this assertion.

A BRIEF HISTORY OF THE TWENTIETH-CENTURY INDUSTRIAL AGE AND ITS BUSINESS MODELS

The Industrial Revolution in America also created the Consumer Revolution. The twentieth century was marked by unprecedented levels of public affluence and consumption. Economist J. Bradford DeLong, credited with one of the most comprehensive studies of the U.S. economy for this period, believes that the most salient characteristic of the time was the "broad upward sweep" of increase in the wealth of individuals.[3] According to DeLong, the average family in the United States enjoyed a six- to sevenfold increase in annual buying power. But more impressive still, according to DeLong, is that even this striking figure understates the buying power of today's family as compared with their counterpart a century ago. The average family in 1900 was forced to spend virtually all their income on food, clothing, and shelter, which today accounts for only about a third of our expenses. Nearly half of what middle-class consumers purchase today wasn't even invented or available at the turn of the century—things like quality medical care, health insurance, higher education, air travel, unlimited access to music, films, and entertainment, year-round fruits and vegetables, beauty aids—and the list goes on. Using all of these criteria, DeLong concludes that the actual growth in economic capacity of families over the course of the twentieth century was a whopping sixteenfold increase![4]

More and more workers produced goods and services at better and better wages. The rising affluence of the masses, combined with the wide availability of affordable goods and services, fueled mass consumption of goods and services—which in turn fueled demand—which in turn fueled more jobs and greater affluence.

The business models of the twentieth-century Industrial Age helped create these realities. Most of these models were predicated on three fundamental tenets of the Industrial Age:

1. Mass production allowed a business to provide abundant goods and/ or services to a large public at competitive prices; this led to mass consumption.
2. Maintaining such mass consumption could only be accomplished by manipulation of demand through mass marketing.
3. Mass production and mass marketing required larger-scale enterprises than ever before (which led to the creation of the corporation), which in turn required whole new processes of organizing and managing people and technology.

Collectively, these three changes in the way the world worked revolutionized the way all of us lived and worked. What follows is a brief explanation of each these three changes.

Mass Production and Mass Consumption

For most of human history, both production and consumption of goods and services was a very small-scale, personal event. If I needed a new pair of boots, I went to the town cobbler—who made only one style. It might take a week for me to get my boots, but that was okay. I had plenty of time. If I was lucky, my boots might last several years. In fact, since boots were expensive, I would try my best to ensure that they did. In a small town, I might have waited for a traveling cobbler to come by or perhaps I would have journeyed to a larger town for his services. And so it was for hundreds of years. The Industrial Revolution changed all of that.

Industrialization of services began in the late eighteenth century as water-powered mills drew labor from the farms and applied the forces of nature to running simple machinery. By the early nineteenth century, even small towns were served by neighborhood mills that took over many of the most tedious of hand tasks. In quick order, steam power and faster transportation further eroded rural economies, and the handmade world of the past yielded to the more efficient, organized, and economical production of a new industrial era. Gradually, middle-class individuals found they could afford to buy merchandise and services that previously only the wealthiest enjoyed.[5] And, soon, these new habits of consumption spread to the working classes, too. The impact of industrialization had brought the cost and availability of many goods and services within their financial reach.

Despite the early origins of industrialization, the mass production of goods and services that we take for granted today was almost wholly a product of the twentieth century. For example, although the automobile was invented in the nineteenth century, for the first quarter of the twentieth century nearly all cars were custom-made, high-end products, designed for the elite. It was the Ford Motor Company that first committed to building affordable cars for the masses. As a businessman, Henry Ford was convinced that the greatest economic potential rested with ordinary working people. He understood that huge numbers of moderate-income consumers, factory workers, farmers, and shopkeepers, were just as desirous of mobility and independence as were the wealthy. Ford was the first to apply the principles of mass production to large-scale manufacturing. He was also the first to pay high enough wages to his workers that they, too, could buy his automobiles. The processes he put in place changed the nature of the world forever.

As Ford's innovations were increasingly adopted by more and more manufacturers, an ever-escalating spiral of inexpensively produced consumer goods set in motion the relationships between mass production, increased consumer demand, more production, and higher wages. So successful was this model that almost overnight (in historical terms), all previous ways of creating goods virtually disappeared. Before Henry Ford's automobile, cars had been highly diverse, catering to the whims and fancies of their individual wealthy patrons. By 1924, Ford Motor Company had produced 1.5 million identical, black Model Ts; each selling for $260, the lowest price in history for a four-cylinder automobile.[6]

The Mass Production of Services

Whereas the application of mass production ideas to the creation of goods was well established by the time of World War II, it was only after the war that the concept of mass production was effectively applied to services. The two pioneers of mass-produced service were Ray Kroc and Walt Disney.

Ray Kroc bought a hamburger stand from the McDonald brothers and figured out how to apply the principles of mass production to the food service industry. Like Ford, Ray Kroc limited variety and standardized "assembly" in such a way so that he could provide huge numbers of consumers the kinds of food they desired, at a moderate price and at a consistent level of quality. Kroc's model of mass-produced services followed the traditional models of mass production—eliminate variability by focusing on a few identical, highly desirable services; reduce labor costs by streamlining the process so that each individual in the system does only a single, tightly specified task; and then, through economies of scale, bring the cost of raw materials down to minimal levels. This is the business model used today by businesses as diverse as 7-Eleven, The Hair Cuttery, Wal-Mart, and Blue Cross/Blue Shield.

The mass entertainment model utilized and perfected by Walt Disney and most eloquently exemplified by Disneyland is yet another model. In this model, the service isn't replicated hundreds or thousands of times in many places, but rather is perfected in a single location so that not hundreds but millions of people can participate in it—each experiencing the same thing. It's like creating the mother of all McDonald's and having everyone in the world drive through a single set of Golden Arches.

Disney came of age during the birth of mass consumption of goods; what he helped to pioneer was the mass consumption of entertainment. Disneyland is a one-of-kind mass entertainment experience that is always there. Its operation is designed so that one size fits all. Every trip through the *Pirates of the Caribbean* or the *Mad Hatters' Tea Party* is exactly the same; *It's a Small, Small World* sounds exactly the same every time you visit. And, unlike the challenges of thousands of McDonald's spread around the world, there is only one place to maintain, one staff to hire and train, and one experience to "imagineer."

Creating Mass Demand

Now travel back to the middle of the twentieth century. The year is 1950, and life is full of choices, or so it seems. Need a new car? You can purchase either a Ford, GM, or Chrysler. You can select between four, five, or six different movies to watch at the cinema if you live in a reasonable-sized town. In the evening you can choose between watching CBS, NBC, or that new station, ABC. You can read either the popular weekly *Look* or *Life,* and you can get your weekly news from either *Time* or *Newsweek.* Life is good! So many options! Like mass production, mass marketing was born in the twentieth century.

Most Americans who were adults in the 1950s came of age during a time of unprecedented shortage and deprivation. Following the scarcities of the Great Depression and the years of rationing brought on by World War II, Americans at mid-century reveled in their new abundance. The machinery of mass production was turned from war products to consumer products and the machinery of mass marketing from patriotic propaganda to public consumption. Advertising agencies flourished, using both the traditional and new vehicles of mass communication. In his presidential address to the American National Council on Family Relations in the late 1940s, sociologist Clark Vincent explained that "the family could now be regarded less as a 'production' unit and more as a 'viable consuming unit.'"[7]

By the 1950s, a whole class of business professionals had emerged, ready for the challenges of mass consumption—enter the advertising and marketing executives of Madison Avenue. The professionalization of advertising and the birth of marketing both occurred in the twentieth century. Marketing and advertising became the connecting link between industry and mass consumption.

Much of the nature of twentieth-century marketing owes its beginnings to J. B. Watson. Watson, one of the leading social scientists of the time and a proponent of the psychology of behaviorism, left his professorship at Johns Hopkins University in 1920 and went to work on Madison Avenue for J. Walter Thompson, one of the largest advertising agencies in the United States. Watson introduced psychology to advertising, selling image, and appeal. He and his contemporaries revolutionized advertising, but, more important, they changed forever the nature of consumption—changing consumption from its historical basis in *need* to its contemporary basis in *desire.* Advertising now was evocative rather than informative, and great emphasis was placed upon affecting the buyer's identity with the product, in effect, creating an emotional bond with the product. This was no trivial change. From Watson's day forward, all advertising campaigns have been predicated on the assumption that mass demand was best accomplished through the heart rather than the head.

Neither Ray Kroc nor Walt Disney could have achieved their successes without the help of mass marketing; successful mass production of both goods and services requires mass consumption. The growth of mass communications also made mass advertising feasible, especially in an era when there were fewer choices in magazines and television channels. A well-placed ad in *Life* magazine or aired during the Ed Sullivan Show would reach millions with the same message.

Something amazing, however, happened in the latter part of the twentieth century. Ultimately the success of mass production and communications created the conditions for its own undoing. Things kept getting more and more plentiful, people kept getting more and more affluent, and, equally important, communications kept getting better and better. The result was that there were now too many products, too many choices, and too many ways to get information; the effectiveness of mass marketing began to wane. By the end of the century there weren't just three television stations, but several hundred. There weren't just a handful of cinemas but hundreds to choose from. There wasn't just one mainstream type of music or fashion, but there were dozens if not hundreds. As the century closed, a variety of strategies were applied to try and deal with this increasing fragmentation of consumer demand, but most businesses still clung to the ideals of mass markets, albeit segmented into a number of "small masses."

What's essential to appreciate here is the continuation of the idea that demand for a mass-produced product can, in fact, *must* be created through marketing and advertising. In this model, the locus of control begins and ends with the organization. The organization decides what it wants to produce and then uses marketing to create demand for that product. The only thing that has changed among those who persist in using this Industrial Age model is that the approach must now be segmented to appeal to niche markets as opposed to being pitched to a full mass market. The essential, top-down logic of the model, though, has changed little.

The Corporation

The twentieth century not only gave birth to the modern practices of mass production and mass marketing, it also gave birth to a whole new way in which to run a business, the modern corporation. Henry Ford's innovations described earlier were not only innovations of machines; they were also innovations in the use of people, creating systems that relied on people being interchangeable parts. Work itself was standardized, with control being in the hands of engineers and managers.

Eventually, Alfred Sloan of General Motors invented the system that established vertical integration and a centralized bureaucracy to oversee and coordinate decentralized operations. Every level of the hierarchy, from the lowest-level employee to the CEO, was expected to fulfill their part of the business. What set this approach apart was its relentless and total reliance upon the control and measurement of product and distribution.

The new managerial class, often graduates of schools of business, frequently went directly from the classroom into the board room, never interacting directly with the consumer. This style of corporation set in place a top-down management that has become the norm for organizing and running an organization in both the for-profit and nonprofit sectors. It is evident not only in businesses, but also in the running of schools, hospitals, government, civic organizations, and, yes, museums. Though the pressures of a changing society and the prevalence of myriad management fads have twisted and refined this model, most organizations still hold fast to the construct of an organization run by a management team. Historically, that team based its decisions on reports and statistics, but far too often knew next to nothing about the actual individuals they purported to serve.

The Twentieth-Century Industrial Business Model
The twentieth century spawned millions of businesses, each with its own unique business model based upon its unique combination of mission, products, services, and realities. The most successful ones, certainly the ones whose names we recognize, converged on an approach to doing business modeled along the lines described above, and this is equally true for both the for-profit and nonprofit realms. Products, goods, and services were designed for mass audiences. Businesses focused on only a few standardized, highly desirable products or services. They reduced labor costs by streamlining the process so that each individual in the system did only a single, tightly specified task. Then, through economies of scale and control of raw materials, they minimized the per unit cost. The underlying assumption was that the world was well served, and thus would reward the organization for supplying large numbers of goods and services at such a low price.

Management of the business was top-down, with layers of authority designed to engineer results at each level. Meanwhile, consumers, the individuals for whom the goods and services were designed, were functionally outside of the organization. The only parts of the organization charged with knowing anything about the customer were the marketing department and the sales department.

THE BUSINESS MODELS OF MUSEUMS

Coming back to the present with this little history lesson under our belts, we can now begin to describe and understand the current underlying assumptions of most museum business models—models that sound strikingly like the ones described above. As with our examination of the Industrial Age business model, we take a brief look at the history of the modern museum and then its contemporary business structure and relationship to the three tenets of the Industrial Age business model: mass production; mass marketing; and a corporate, top-down structure.

A Brief History of American Museums

A brief history of museums in America offers some insight, for even though American museums are changing, vestiges of our history stubbornly remain. The nineteenth century was America's first great era of museum founding. Buoyed by Victorian exuberance and belief in public improvement, museums became handsome symbols of a new civic pride. In large cities and small towns, historical societies lauded their community's founders and collected local icons of accomplishment. Private collections opened to the public, and great art collections, housed in magnificent urban temples, showed the world that American cities could compete as centers of world-class culture. As was the nature of intellectual inquiry at the time, collections became the cornerstones of museums, and caring for, studying, housing, and exhibiting them were the primary tasks of the great museums.

Many museums of this era also embraced education as a key mission. The Smithsonian Institution, dedicated to "the increase and diffusion of knowledge," was founded in 1846. The first American zoo opened in Philadelphia in 1854, the first botanical garden in Washington, D.C., in 1850, and the first children's museum in Brooklyn in 1899. In the twentieth century, the emphasis on museums as educators continued to grow. The school field trip became a popular and enduring form of such education. Students lined up to walk through the great halls, receiving an encyclopedic tour of wondrous things. It was wholly agreed that encounters with museum collections had ennobling purposes, opening new worlds to all who visited.

For many, the art museum became the dominant museum image. The 1870s witnessed the founding of such great institutions as the Metropolitan Museum of Art, the Museum of Fine Arts in Boston, and the Philadelphia Museum of Art—offering a model of the museum as a glorious treasure house. This model focused on collections, scholarship, and cultural authority, and, in turn, developed world standards in collecting, researching, conserving, and managing collections. It also established a model of governance and operations that continues today, one dependent upon private subsidies from wealthy patrons for the majority of the museum's support. Enormous personal philanthropy built America's great collections and museums and continues to play a vital role in maintaining them today. It also set in motion a fundamental business model for museums that relied heavily on private support and endowments, a fragile model that began to undergo considerable change in the twentieth century.

Two threads of interest in American museums—the focus on the sublime and the rare and the interest in the vernacular and everyday—give us an amazingly diverse set of museums. The Institute of Museum and Library Services recognizes such diverse entities as "aquariums, arboreta and botanical gardens, art museums, youth museums, general museums, historic houses and sites, history museums, nature centers, natural history and anthropology museums, planetariums, science and technology centers, specialized museums and zoological parks" as museums. For many it is difficult to see the relationships between such a broad spectrum of institutions, and their differences fuel debates about changing missions and purposes. This very diversity, however, suggests that Americans care deeply about establishing places that offer new ways of encountering and understanding their complex world.

Americans clearly love their museums—or at least building them. Museum building was vigorous again in the late twentieth century. As many as half of the nation's museums have been started since 1960. These include a variety of special-purpose and special-interest museums—museums of African American, Latino, Asian, Native American, and gay and lesbian history and culture—a fascinating statement about museums as places for validation. Science and technology–based museums and children's museums have been particularly popular, providing new ideas about interactive and experience-based learning. They suggest public interest and concern about science literacy, early learning opportunities, and learning outside the classroom. The era of museum building is not over and may become even more diverse as many in society have come to see museums as the perfect venues for preserving and telling the nation's stories—from the history of steelmaking to the atrocities of the Armenian holocaust to America's fascination with the secrets of spies.

It is here, however, that we return to the development of the business model of museums that so clearly emerged out of this history. Each period of museum building, though responding to different needs, has maintained consistent patterns of balancing the budget, relying heavily on personal and private philanthropy and on attendance-related revenue. For years, museums have invited visitors into the great halls to walk past exotic treasures, re-created historic moments, taxidermied animals, and the cultural icons of the world. Each carefully researched and mounted exhibition expressed the expertise of the scholars and curators of the institution. From the inside out, exhibitions were created for mass audiences, presenting the museum's expertise in a static and unchanging manner.

Thus, the primary product of the museum community has been the encounter and experience it provides the public with its collections or areas of expertise—art, history, science, the natural world, and so on. Their expectation has been to serve as many members of the public as possible. This goal is usually reflected in the museum's mission statement. For many years, the mission statements of museums have focused on what they do: "Our mission is to collect, interpret, research, exhibit . . . (fill in the blank)." Many also provide a generic sense of the good they hope to accomplish—usually statements that fall within the broad domain of education. Some use active language like "experience," "discover," and "explore," but many use more passive language like "disseminate," "view," and "share." Increasingly mission statements define their intended audience, usually in broad swipes—"all visitors," "the public," or occasionally more narrowly, "all children." In other words, like others with their roots in the Industrial Age, most museums are still defining themselves as being in the business of creating products for mass audiences.

Although museums employ a wide assortment of products and services for accomplishing their mass education mission, most converge on a single dominant strategy—the exhibition. The museum exhibition, too, represents a highly refined, well-crafted artifact of the Industrial Age. As we currently know them, exhibitions are designed to accommodate large numbers of people and to provide everyone with a comparable quality experience. The best-researched and finest designed exhibition is still a singular experience presented with few opportunities, if any, for visitor input. Using the Disney model, the goal is to craft an experience that everyone can enjoy and learn from, but one that essentially never changes and lacks the capacity to accommodate the individualized needs of the user.

Although there have been attempts lately to make exhibitions more personalized and more sharply targeted to niche audiences, the results still represent a "twiddling with the dials" approach to the problem—small refinements rather than fundamental change. For example, some efforts in the direction of personalization may be seen in the recent use of interactive computer technologies and the new generation of audio-guides. Except for the very newest, twenty-first-century versions, however, most permit only a limited amount of choice and control, and only to the extent the visitor chooses something designed into the system by the exhibit developers. In other words, the number of available choices has increased from a couple to a couple dozen, but the model remains, basically, a mass marketing one.

Meanwhile, as competition has increased, merely creating "high-quality" exhibitions on important topics has not been sufficient to make ends meet. Originally, most American museums were supported by funds from one of two sources, either private philanthropists or direct government subsidies. By the mid-twentieth century, these sources of funding began eroding or became insufficient; museums responded by turning to their publics. They expanded their educational roles, enhanced their entertainment quality, added to their commercial enterprises, and began charging admission. In so doing, they became increasingly dependent upon audience numbers for support—either directly through admission fees and gift shop revenues or as evidence to public, corporate, and private funders of the public good they performed. In the Industrial mass-market world of the twentieth century what was important were inputs (exhibitions/products produced) and outputs (visitors served/ products consumed). Museums became very good at generating both.

As an antidote to continuing financial pressures, the museum community latched onto the same solution other Industrial Age pioneers such as Disney and McDonald's have used to generate increased numbers—change. Just as McDonald's and Disney have sought to retain their past customers and keep generating new ones by developing a constant string of new menu items, promotions, and experiences—relying heavily on extraordinarily expensive mass advertising—museums have sought to retain their past audiences and keep generating new ones by creating a never-ending string of compelling new exhibitions, buildings, and experiences. The blockbuster was the museum's version of a high-profile new theme park experience.

Inspired in large part by the success of the King Tut Exhibition and its successors, a clear trend has been the creation of themed, often short-lived, and often traveling exhibitions, designed first and foremost to attract audiences. Promotional and fundraising priorities have come to dominate this approach to selecting exhibition themes. Topics deemed too mundane or narrow to attract a large, diverse audience have often been rejected regardless of their educational merit. Such practices may cause controversy—as in the recent decision of the Museum of Science in Boston to cancel the tricentennial exhibition on the life and accomplishments of Benjamin Franklin in favor of a Star Wars exhibition—but the need to drive large numbers of people through the front door has become an increasing imperative in today's museum world.

Furthermore, keeping the theme narrowly focused on a single, widely recognized topic makes it easier to sell. Mirroring the lessons learned by the Madison Avenue mass marketers of the twentieth century, if you can't explain the topic in a sound bite, then you shouldn't select that topic in the first place. Promotional and fundraising concerns need to be considered from the very beginning.

Marketing, thus, has become an increasingly important part of the museum's core business strategy. Driven by the need to attract ever-growing numbers of visitors, museums have built strong marketing and public relations departments, developing "the message" and delivering it with all the finesse and sophistication of a for-profit business. Museum marketers, working with far smaller budgets than their for-profit peers, have also become masters of collaborative business ventures, building partnerships with hotels, tour agencies, retailers, and others who can assist in making the museum a "hot" destination. "Museum facades began to resemble movie theater marquees, more and more of them sporting banners that proclaimed current temporary exhibitions."[8]

Similar marketing tactics have created whole lines of merchandise to accompany the new headline exhibition. Everything from mugs and posters, books and catalogues, reproduction jewelry, clothing accessories, toys and games, postcards, and crafts fill the shelves of the museum shop (or, more likely, a special exhibition shop that one must go through to exit the exhibition). While these have the potential of extending the museum experience, they are making the whole experience a very complex commercial venture—one that will disappear when the exhibition ends. The tie-ins with airlines and railroads, restaurants, and hotels will also come to an end, until the whole process begins anew. While these ventures have the advantage of drawing the life of the museum into the larger economic life of the community, they also become intense and exhausting efforts, frequently more than a few steps away from the museum's avowed mission.

These advertising strategies have done little to disabuse the public of the view that the museum is a short-term consumable. The museum ads in newspapers and on the sides of buses tout "New Exhibition!" and often the public responds. If it wasn't for the new thing, though, would the public see a reason to return? The combination of constantly changing, flashy (and expensive) new exhibitions and the strong voice of marketing has driven many museums down a costly, one-way path. Depending on novelty to keep attendance steady creates a constant need to support change rather than reinvest in fundamental institutional needs.

Thus, as the blockbuster exhibitions have become an increasingly important and complex part of the museum's success, they have created many significant problems. Designed to entice new audiences, they are often enormously popular, filling galleries to capacity and creating experiences very unlike the leisurely museum stroll of the past. Stimulating, crowded, and noisy, many such exhibitions are actually inhospitable to prolonged intellectual engagement. They may create environments of complexity and novelty, but not necessarily of meaningful engagement and contemplation. Ironically, the buzz they create may actually inhibit the learning they are trying to promote. One can almost compare the interactive-rich museum exhibition with the quickly changing visuals of present-day television programming. In both cases, the changes have resulted in significantly increased viewer attention but significantly decreased cognition and learning.[9] The end result (getting people through the door) can collide with the mission itself.

The constant quest for sufficient funding also challenges the fine ethical lines that museums must walk, as well as their intellectual autonomy. Corporate support of exhibitions and programs, for example, has increased dramatically over the past twenty-five years,[10] but these monies often come with significant strings attached, not the least of which is a pressure to ensure maximal exposure to the largest possible audience.[11] Even public monies come with expectations that may force the museum to meet external demands tangential to its goals. Grant programs often set their own stringent criteria, requiring expenditures and emphases that take the museum down a different path than it truly seeks. The whole system, it seems, has become self-reinforcing.

Corporate structure is the third component of the Industrial Age business model, one that is seen in today's museum as clearly as in today's business world. The fundraising components of the museum alone require specialization of a sort unheard of when American museums were first established. From the director on down, a significant infrastructure is required to vie for monies in our ever-more competitive fundraising marketplace. Numerous subspecialties tackle corporations, foundations, big donors, little donors, members, and government affairs. Instead of tending to the creative and intellectual output of their institutions, directors are like university presidents, spending their work hours in the endless search for more funds. Museums find themselves committed to ever more costly exhibitions and programs, supported by ever more costly advertising, while investing ever more money in the fundraising infrastructure necessary to secure these funds.

In all ways, museums, like the corporations described earlier, have become increasingly compartmentalized. Consider the range of specialists: curators (of many different subjects); educators (of school and general audiences); marketing and advertising departments; development and membership; exhibition designers and preparators; retail operations; food service; facilities and grounds; audience research; community outreach specialists; and guest services. How many of these museum professionals are actually in touch with the audiences they serve? How many of them are even in touch with one another? Except for occasional cross-departmental teams and large all-staff meetings, today's museum staff often exists in isolation from the core visitor experience.

Unfortunately, at the bottom of the employee pecking-order are the floor staff, whether volunteer or paid. These individuals, who generally receive the least pay and the least training in the organization, are actually the ones we count upon to support the public experience. Their transactions with the public are the ones that so often influence whether a parent, group leader, school child, or couple walks away feeling like they've invested their leisure or field trip time wisely or not. Yet, as is inherent in the hierarchical Industrial Age model, these key employees normally have little say in visitor policies, virtually no voice in what should or should not be exhibited, and no real influence on how the organization is run. That's because in the Industrial Age model the public, the museum's visitors and users, are outside of the business model; they are the recipients of what the museum does, they are not part of what the museum does.

Still enmeshed in its Industrial Age business model, the museum community finds itself locked into a way of doing business with significant flaws. Even if museums could stay on this current merry-go-round without falling off, the future would not look bright. The merry-go-round we're on is itself becoming an anachronism. The fundamental nature of society is changing in ways that support some of the things museums currently do. The great trends in society today, however, are moving in ways that significantly undermine the very nature of the museum business model as currently configured. Let's examine these new Knowledge Age trends, the accommodations museums are beginning to make, and the future they must accept as "now."

DISCUSSION QUESTIONS

- Do remnants of the Industrial Age remain within your organization? Are these productive parts of your organization, or just artefacts of your history?
- What percentage of your organization's expense budget is spent on exhibitions? What percentage of your organization's income budget is driven by attendance? How have these percentages changed in the last ten years?
- What percentage of your organization's expense budget is spent on marketing? How has this percentage changed in the last ten years? What evidence do you have that your current marketing strategy is delivering the results you desire?

NOTES

Epigraph: D. McCullough, address at Wesleyan University, June 3, 1984.

1. J. Trescott, Exhibiting a new enthusiasm: Across U.S., museum construction, attendance are on the rise, *The Washington Post*, June 21, 1998, A1; J. Lusaka and J. Strand, The Boom—and what to do about it, *Museum News* 77, no. 6 (1998): 54–60; G. D. Lowry, The state of the art museum, ever changing, *New York Times*, January 10, 1999, Arts and Leisure, 1; C. McGuigan and P. Plagens, State of the art, *Newsweek*, March 26, 2001.

2. Hilary Barnes, personal communication, April 12, 2004.

3. J. Bradford DeLong, *Cornucopia: The Pace of Economic Growth in the Twentieth Century*, Working Paper no. 7602 (Washington, DC: National Bureau of Economic Research, 2000), 11–12.

4. Ibid., 21.

5. Neil McKendrick, The consumer revolution of eighteenth-century England, in *The Birth of a Consumer Society: The Commercialization of Eighteenth-Century England*, ed. Neil McKendrick, John Brewer, and J. H. Plumb (Bloomington: Indiana University Press, 1982).

6. Donald Finlay Davis, *Conspicuous Production: Automobiles and Elites in Detroit, 1899–1933* (Philadelphia: Temple University Press, 1988).

7. Vincent Packard, *The People Shapers* (Bucks: Futura, 1978), 128.

8. Neil Harris, The divided house of the American museum, *Daedalus* 128, no. 3 (1999): 42.

9. R. Kubey and M. Csikszentmihalyi, Television addiction is no mere metaphor, *Scientific American* 284, no. 2 (2002): 76–83.

10. Lusaka and Strand, The Boom—and what to do about it.

11. A. Mintz, That's edutainment! *Museum News* 73, no. 6 (1994): 33–36.

4

The Brave New World of the Knowledge Age

The past few years have seen the rise and rapid growth in economic importance of a group of consumers whose attitudes, aspirations and purchasing patterns are unlike any before them.
—D. Lewis and D. Bridger

One of the classic museum descriptions from the world of fiction is found in J. D. Salinger's *The Catcher in the Rye*. On a quest to find his younger sister, the story's main character, Holden Caulfield, considers the possibility that Phoebe has gone to the natural history museum. For a moment, he pauses to reminisce about his own experiences. "The best thing in that museum," he tells us, "was that everything always stayed right where it was. Nobody'd move. You could go there a hundred thousand times, and that Eskimo would still be just finished catching those two fish, the birds would still be on their way south, the deers would still be drinking out of that water hole, with their pretty antlers and their pretty skinny legs, and that squaw with the naked bosom would still be weaving that same blanket. Nobody'd be different. The only thing that would be different would be you."[1]

As he raced through the park toward the museum, Holden Caulfield drew comfort from the idea that he would find it unchanged, reassured that it was one place where everything stood still. Yet, when he finally got there, he tells us, "a funny thing happened . . . all of a sudden I wouldn't have gone inside for a million bucks."

The museum Holden first described would resonate with many of us. Perhaps Holden's first encounter with a museum, like many of ours, was as part of a school group. Our sensory memories may be similar—the clattering of a marble dropped on the hard stone floor, holding the sweaty hand of a class-mate in line, peering into glass cases, sensing the smells of a rainy day. We might remember exotic exhibits, offering glimpses into worlds far away in time and place. We might also think of the museum as a place where every-thing seemed to hold still, not just for the moment but for years at a time. If that were so, just imagine the widening gap between the changes in our lives today and the museum of old.

Though it was Holden Caufield's personal crisis that kept him from enter-ing the museum, it is the museum community's professional crisis that mil-lions of Americans are also staying away. The long, leisurely days of wandering through a museum looking in awe at strange and wonderful things has become increasingly rare. If it happens at all, the visit is likely to be sandwiched between a soccer game and music lessons. The immersive magical quality of a leisurely visit has been traded for a check mark on a long list of "to dos." A quick purchase at the museum gift shop suffices for the luxury of lingering. A group planning a social outing discards the idea of a museum visit. "Been there, done that," they say and move on to the next newest thing.

It should be no surprise that Holden's favorite museum and many of those we remember from childhood seem anachronistic in today's rapidly paced society. Likewise, the changing patterns of visitation and changing expecta-tions of today's public are indications of the breadth of change in American society. They are part of the upheaval that accompanies the shift from one great era to another. In the previous chapter we described how the Industrial Revolution profoundly shaped the social and economic patterns of the twen-tieth century. With that history as background, we now explore the dramatic upheaval underway today that is initiating a new age, sometimes described as the Information Age, or, as we prefer, the Knowledge Age.

Just as the transition from the Agrarian Age to the Industrial Age disoriented the known world of the nineteenth century, the yielding of the Industrial Era to the Knowledge Age is racing breakneck through our lives, disrupting our famil-iar patterns and predictable expectations. As in the nineteenth century, change is filled with both promise and trepidation, but nothing will stop its movement. Our mandate for today must be to build the capacity of our institutions to change with the times and reestablish our critical purpose in society that we enjoyed previously. As we ask, "Why do museums exist? What is our purpose in this new world?" we need to see ourselves as institutions embedded in a world that is rapidly changing before our eyes.

As described previously, a museum's business model must respond to many realities, none more vital than the ecosystem in which the museum operates. The transition from an Industrial Age to a Knowledge Age has resulted in tremendous changes in virtually every facet of our lives. Daily we are told of new trends that we must accommodate to; some of these are lasting, many are short-lived. Sorting out what is important to attend to from what is not is difficult, but with no guidelines for judging the differences, making decisions about what to do is even more challenging.

We would propose that there are several major trends that museums need to attend to. These major trends can be grouped into three, broad, nonexclusive contexts: the Economic Context, the Social Context, and the Political Context. The profound changes occurring within each are fundamentally and permanently altering the ecosystem in which museums operate.

The Economic Context refers to the business environment in which museums operate. Of particular note are the profound changes in consumption patterns and competition. The Social Context represents the changing realities of what it means to be a person living in the early years of the twenty-first century, focusing on three major areas—the changing demographics of the developing world, the growing gap between the "haves" and "have-nots," and the growing sense of personal isolation felt in the developed world. Finally, all institutions and organizations operate within a Political Context, the legal and ethical realities of the larger society, and, without a doubt, the legal and ethical standards and requirements within our society are changing.

THE ECONOMIC CONTEXT: THE GROWTH OF THE INDIVIDUAL-CENTERED ECONOMY

The man having a snack in the café area of Sutton Place Gourmet in Bethesda [Maryland] had been eavesdropping on our conversation for nearly 30 minutes. Dressed in a fleece vest and jeans, with a cell phone hanging from one pocket, he had been leaning closer and closer, listening as Mark Ordan, the new CEO of the Sutton Place Group, talked exuberantly about his plans to improve the specialty food chain, including lowering prices, adding new products and, starting this week, changing the store's name to Balducci's.

Finally, the man couldn't stand it any longer.

"Are you a manager of this store?" he asked. Before Ordan could answer, the man continued. "I come to Sutton for my steak and my Godiva chocolate. I expect to pay more here. I don't want to see signs that say prices have been cut. It makes me worry that there's less quality now."

. . . The customer, contractor Tom Evers of Bethesda, [continued], "I can go across the street to Giant to buy milk if I want cheap. I know, coming through the door here that I'll pay more, but the quality will be worth it."

Behind Ordan, another voice chimed in. Jim Gracyalny, a retired government worker, told Ordan he shops at Sutton for fresh fish "even though my wife doesn't always like it because the prices are higher." At the big chain supermarkets, he added, "you never know how old the fish is."[2]

Imagine that, customers who *want* to pay more! Well, not exactly, but these are customers who are *willing* to pay more in order to get the quality and service they desire. Despite being bombarded by advertisements telling us that we need not pay retail anymore and news stories about budget-conscious shoppers, today there are many consumers like Tom and Jim whose quality expectations are more important than finding a bargain. Though this is not a new phenomenon, the nature of this sentiment among a growing number of consumers is new.

There have always been consumers willing to pay a premium price for coveted items. Historically, though, only a few had sufficient discretionary income to pay premium prices for such daily commodities as food. Not so today! The number of consumers capable of buying products of all kinds, particularly costlier items, has exploded. So too have the number of items for sale and the number of vendors selling them. The origin of this phenomenon is directly tied to the success of the Industrial Age, which, as we have seen, unleashed unprecedented capacity to produce goods and services inexpensively and, as envisioned by Henry Ford, also created unprecedented affluence among workers.

The Industrial Age business model set in motion a remarkable cycle. It created ever growing numbers of workers ready and able to buy goods and services, which, in turn, spurred demand for more goods and services, which, in turn, created more well-paying jobs to satisfy that demand, which, in turn, led to even more demand by these new workers, and so on. As a consequence, today's marketplace is glutted—with suppliers, goods and services, and consumers. Although there have been ups and downs in this economic cycle, the overall trend has been steadily up. The globalization of markets will only accelerate this trend; imagine what the addition of 3 billion affluent consumers (and producers) in Asia is going to do to competition for access to goods and services! Ironically, one of the main changes is that the marketplace has become less hospitable to the way of doing business that created this abundance in the first place—the marketplace of the Industrial Age. Developing in its place is a new marketplace, the marketplace of the Knowledge Age, a new entity whose outlines are only now becoming clear.

The marketplace of the twenty-first century is dramatically different than the marketplace of fifty, thirty, or even twenty years ago, and it continues to change rapidly. Three major changes have become dominant: consumer behavior, product customization, and relentless competition. Not surprisingly, all three of these differences ultimately have to do with information and knowledge.

Consumer Behavior

The buying habits and behaviors of the public are undergoing radical transformation, directly related to the superabundance of goods and services. Buying decisions today are quite different from those of our parents or grandparents. In affluent developed countries, far more of the population has discretionary money than in the past. Their primary decision as consumers is not whether or not there will be food on the table, but what type of cuisine to eat. Their issue is less whether there's a roof over their heads, but what style the roof is. Their question is not whether or not to expand one's horizons, but how to accomplish personal growth and in what ways.

The goods and services of real value and interest to these new consumers are ones that possess some value-added extra that makes them rise above the crowded field. Rather than selecting products merely on their utility, today's consumers make decisions on a product's ability to satisfy personal desires and lifestyles.

Product Customization

A crowded marketplace and customer demand are forcing major changes. Yesterday's mass production, marketing, and advertising approaches are becoming less and less successful as more companies are realizing that one size no longer fits all. At the dawn of the Knowledge Age, it is becoming increasingly apparent that success accrues to those who can produce not a *single* solution for the masses, but *multiple* solutions, each personally tailored to the specific needs and desires of individuals.

Accomplishing this transition is proving challenging. A number of organizations have begun to use technologies that permit a modicum of uniqueness for each consumer; however, these initial efforts are unlikely to yield a long-term solution. Such success will more likely be linked to building reciprocal relationships with consumers. Still, one thing is increasingly apparent: yesterday's ways of doing business will not capture the hearts and minds, time, and attention, and, most important, the dollars of tomorrow's knowledge consumer. Although businesses today are struggling with delivering on personalization, there's no shortage of rhetoric about personalization. During one commercial break on network television, the following four ads were run:

- A bank: "We deliver individual answers"
- A credit card company: "Everywhere that you want to go"
- A software company: "Your potential, our passion"
- A car company: "Because no two drivers are exactly alike"

Relentless Competition

These changes lead to our final point: it is no longer sufficient just to produce a quality good or service. With so many goods and services available, even the good ones will fail unless they somehow grab the consumer's attention. Today's marketing competition is fierce, and it has become increasingly sophisticated and relentless. In the Knowledge Age, rapid communications and shifts in information make competitive advantage ephemeral; an advantage today is no guarantee of an advantage tomorrow. Staying in the public eye will be one of the never-ending challenges of doing business in the twenty-first century.

The New Consumers

During the early years of the Industrial Age a significant driving force behind the consumption patterns of most people was a desire to improve one's social class—a desire to escape the poverty of the working classes and rise to the relative affluence of the middle classes. Tangible evidence for this transition was manifest in the goods and services one purchased. New cars, clothes, appliances, or even homes signified membership in the middle class and rising affluence.

As prosperity grew during the middle years of the twentieth century, more and more individuals achieved this goal. Data from the U.S. Census Bureau documents the rise in disposable income during the last four decades—an increase from $9,210 in 1960 to $24,479 in 2002 (using 1996 dollars as a standard). By the end of the twentieth century, millions of individuals living in America had become bona fide members of the middle class, both in income and in the pattern of goods and services consumed. So complete was this transformation that today a majority of consumers in this country have largely exhausted the things they *need* to purchase; instead they now focus on what they *want* to purchase.[3]

The goals of consumerism have also changed. The issue is no longer merely to identify one's social class, but, more important, to identify one's niche within that social class. The goods and services of today claim to meet more than basic needs. Today's goods and services claim that they will make the consumer happier, richer, more attractive, sexier, and more fulfilled. In fact, hundreds and thousands of products make this claim!

Consider the amazing panoply of choices within any category of consumer product. A stroll through the local shopping mall reveals not one, but dozens upon dozens of stores selling clothes. There are stores catering to women and stores for men. There are stores that focus on babies and toddlers, stores for children, and lots of stores specializing in clothing and accessories for teens. There are stores for larger individuals and others for the petite; there are even stores that specialize in clothing for pregnant women. There are clothing stores for the hip, punk, Goth, conservative, and suave, clothing stores for the economy-minded and clothing stores targeted to the wealthy. And those are just the stores in the mall. If you don't find what you're looking for there, there are more choices—other malls, other shops, catalogues, and now the Internet. Wherever you go in America, the consumer has choices—choices that focus as much, if not more, on presentation and image than on substance, quality, or endurance.

The Industrial Revolution of the past century created a new world of unprecedented material abundance. As described in the previous chapter, economist J. Bradford DeLong estimated that the economic buying power of the average American family increased sixteenfold over the course of the twentieth century.[4] Think about that! Imagine having sixteen times your family income and what you could buy! Can this kind of increase continue, or was the twentieth century just an aberration? There are quite a few economists who not only think this trend will continue, but suggest that the pace of increased affluence is quickening.[5] They predict the majority of that increase will come from decreasing costs.

The costs of personal computers offer an interesting example of such decreases. When they were first available in the 1980s, personal computers cost roughly $5,000 (about 15 percent of an average family's annual income). Twenty years later, vastly more powerful personal computers can be purchased for under $1,000 (less than 2 percent of an average family's annual income). One of the reasons IBM has transitioned from a computer hardware manufacturer to a service and consulting company is that it projects this trend to continue. IBM believes that the cost of new computers will decline to the point where they are as inexpensive as today's pocket calculators (and thus represent an insignificant percentage of an average family's annual expenses).

When the cost of goods and services shrinks so precipitously, consumers can exercise a vastly different buying strategy. Goods and services become truly consumable, and thus viewed as short-term, ephemeral decisions. If you are going to spend 15 percent of your annual income on something, you want it to be just right and to last a long time. If you are using pocket change for a purchase, on the other hand, you are less concerned about its longevity. You can afford to take a risk and to make purchases based upon short-term whims and desires. Thus, satisfaction in today's world means something quite different than it did a century ago.

Today, thanks to both increased affluence and to mass communications, all kinds of goods and services are available. Less than half of the average person's annual income is spent on basic life necessities. There are other changes too: more and more of society is participating in some form of higher education and exploring spiritual meanings as well. A century ago, only a very few individuals worried about "self-fulfillment." (Even if they knew what it was, who had the time and resources to pursue it?) Today, self-fulfillment is a driving goal. Freed from the tyranny of poverty and want, living a happy, fulfilled life is now a *primary* goal of living. Self-actualization in one form or another is driving an ever-growing number of individuals.

A few years back, Joe Pine and Jim Gilmore wrote *The Experience Economy*, in which they prophesied a growing change in consumer desires from goods and services to experiences, particularly transformative ones.[6] A year later,

David Lewis and Don Bridger suggested a similar idea in their book *The Soul of the New Consumer*.[7] All were addressing the phenomenon of contemporary society shifting its consumer expectations from basic needs to fulfillment of deeper needs. However, the approach all four authors came up with was essentially marketing driven—let's "make commerce theater." If there's no substance behind the solution, this will at best only be a short-term solution. We believe that longer-term solutions will require creating experiences that actually drive consumers closer to their desire for self-actualization.

Today's nonstop advertising tries to convince people that this or that product is what stands between them and self-fulfillment: consume your way to satisfaction! Ironically, the empty promise only creates more desire. Some of us have become addicted to seeking ever-escalating thrills from our consumption—the quicker the buzz the better. At the same time, increasing numbers of consumers feel manipulated and exploited by the business world and their unrelenting self-promotion. Most of us are increasingly skeptical. We may not be quite sure about how to revolt against such promises, but we recognize that our quest for high-quality, personalized experiences and purchasable goods and services that are fulfilling is difficult to achieve. An ever-growing number of us want something more out of our lives, and since we live in a world of commerce, something more out of our purchases. We want quality, value, and a sense of personal connectedness. In many ways we want what we lost a hundred years ago: personally meaningful experience—not mass production.

The Business Response

Businesses of all kinds have begun searching for ways to provide better service to their consumers while still maximizing profits. Sadly, most create an illusion of service rather than reality. Classic examples include the new "membership" programs of the mega-grocery stores and the increasingly common store greeter. Both are superficial measures, ones that serve the business far more effectively than the customer. For some, these practices increase the feeling of being one of just so many sheep—no true personal recognition, simply another sign of anonymity.

Training up-front employees to develop truly personal and sound customer relationships would have far more effective impact than reducing expenditures on the front lines or even replacing these vital "connectors" with more and more technology. Typically, the president of the airline doesn't take tickets at the airport and the director of the museum doesn't meet and greet visitors on weekends. Too often, in both the for-profit and the nonprofit worlds, the consuming public is often treated as the distant end of a chain, rather than an integral part of the circle.[8]

As if these insults were not enough, many businesses today actually penalize their best and most loyal customers. How could such a counterintuitive circumstance actually happen? It's just another case where the logic of the Industrial model runs full tilt against the sensibilities of the Knowledge Age.

A classic example is the pricing of airline tickets. The ready availability of highly sophisticated computer programs in the 1990s allowed airlines to create pricing structures that fluctuated daily, based upon algorithms of supply and demand. As a consequence, the price of the very same seat on a typical flight could vary by a factor of 10. Thus, a once-a-year traveler who purchased an airline ticket months in advance could pay a fraction of what it costs a frequently flying business person forced to purchase his or her ticket close to the date of departure. This makes perfect business sense if the goal is to maximize return on the product. This pricing policy makes absolutely no sense if the goal is to maintain a customer base and reward the best customers. Is it any wonder that low-cost airlines like Southwest with fixed pricing pushed so many big airlines into bankruptcy? Each time an organization dehumanizes its customers, diminishes the individual's control over the process, places quantity and short-term benefit over quality and longevity, that organization diminishes its chances for long-term survival and prosperity in the twenty-first century.

In Search of Individualized and Personalized Solutions

One of the dominant trends since World War II has been the increasing segmentation of markets and the push to create products and services designed to meet the needs of each particular segment. This trend first appeared in the magazine industry and has since been reflected in a wide range of areas. For example, the ubiquitous mid-twentieth-century rooftop TV antennas were replaced by cable TV because cable could provide scores of options to consumers. Cable TV is now locked in a war with the emerging satellite TV industry, which can offer even more options. Many are the organizations that espouse the importance of individualized and personalized service; few are the organizations that actually deliver this service.

The current best solution to individualizing service is what is called mass customization. It is a technology-driven approach that allows consumers to select from a myriad of choices and opt for those that meet their specific needs, wants, and desires, on their own time scale. The device known as TiVo is a prime example, allowing television viewers control over what they wish to watch and when they wish to watch it. With TiVo you can even "pause" a real time show while you make a sandwich or pit stop; that's "on demand"! According to Don Bouge, co-founder and CEO of Command Audio Corporation, "new technology is altering the listening [and viewing] experience from one in which [the consumers] have little control to one in which they have broad choice and complete control."[9]

Interactive websites are offering some manufacturers similar customer-driven controls. It is now possible for someone wanting to purchase a Nike shoe to go on-line and not only pick out a shoe style, size, and color, but also to customize the type of materials used and even the design that will appear on the shoe. Adidas has come out with a new shoe, complete with a microprocessor and miniature motor, which it claims continually adjusts the shoe to fit each individual's exact size and contours. A wide range of experts now agree that customization is increasingly the future. Individuals from many industries predict that everything from your alarm clock to your facial products will be customized in the near future. We believe in order to mitigate the dehumanizing process of consumerism, businesses will still need to work harder to involve the consumer in the process of producing goods and services and designing the concept of choice.

Consumers get involved in making a purchase for three reasons: (1) to save time; (2) to gain personal advantage; and (3) to increase their enjoyment.[10] Convenience stores, special coupons, buyers' clubs, and reward programs address some of these needs, but not the most important one. Far and away the main reason consumers get involved with a product or service is because of the enjoyment they derive in the process. Take, for example, the overwhelming success of e-Bay. The adventure of scouring the site for buys, stumbling upon great items, bidding wars—all feed into the fun of the process. Yes, there is an opportunity to get a good buy, but more important is the one-to-one interaction and the individuality of the purchase. Flea markets and craft fairs enjoy the same satisfaction of a one-of-a-kind experience—a far cry from a trip to the mall.

Competition

According to a wide range of experts, at some point in the next few years the push to promote and advertise everything is going to push us all over the edge.[11] Every available moment of every day will be filled with advertising. Every available space on our clothing, on our buildings, on our media, and even on our bodies will be looked upon as advertising real estate. One advertising executive recently said, "Advertising is intrinsically inescapable. The French are putting ads under their café tables. There's no way out."[12]

The future of advertising lies not in the blanket, mass marketing approach of yesteryear, however. The same individual as above goes on to say that the key to advertising in the future is relevance. "If it is relevant to the individual they'll pay attention, if it's not they won't."[13] Who defines relevance? The customer, that's who! Increasingly, what is required is what marketers call "one-to-one marketing"—marketing the particular product that is right for a particular consumer, not just marketing any old product to any old person. This approach requires a close match between the consumer and the product—a match built on need, or more ideally, on lifestyle and self-image. From this perspective, what will grab the hungry person's attention is a type or style of restaurant that fulfills that person's unique eating preferences and habits.

Without a doubt there will be increasing competition for consumers, but the winners will not be the ones who get their message out to the *most* people, it will be the ones who get their message out to the *right* people. Advertising professionals continue to move away from mass advertising, since it no longer works. We have now gone from segmented marketing to niche marketing, narrowing the audience. This is an evolution from trying to convince all men to buy a product, to all college-educated men who live in a certain city, to all college-educated men who live in a certain neighborhood and who also buy *Men's Health* and own a treadmill. This latter approach involves creating complex combinations of demographic and psycho-graphic categories in order to classify people into a finite set of categories.

Computers are making it ever easier to take this approach. For example, the "smart" system on Amazon.com works to create a profile of every individual who makes a purchase. In that way they can say, "If you like this book, you also might like these titles since other people who bought this first book also bought these other titles." And indeed, this system brings us much closer to being able to custom-market to consumers. This approach, too, can only go so far. The problem with each of these niche marketing schemes is that they pretend to know you, but in fact they don't actually know you. Clearly, even an approximation of such knowledge is far superior to no knowledge at all, but it currently falls far short of the ideal.

In the future, advertisers will need to get more and more personal, and more and more targeted in order to cut through the clutter of advertising noise in the marketplace. Technology and necessity will fuel the drive to keep better and more pertinent customer records and to maintain more selective communication. More marketing time and dollars will be invested in creating and maintaining relationships with existing consumers rather than trying to attract new consumers through advertising. In order to attract new customers, we will all rely on the most ancient and effective marketing tool of all, word-of-mouth. In the twenty-first century, creating a sense of community will be the goal of all organizations. Those that succeed will be very, very successful.

THE SOCIAL CONTEXT: DEMOGRAPHIC SHIFTS, "HAVES" AND "HAVE-NOTS," SOCIETAL STRESS, AND THE SEARCH FOR SECURITY AND IDENTITY

The key to a business's success may very well hinge on appealing to two large population cohorts, the Baby Boom generation and the Echo Boom generation. The assimilation of the Baby Boom generation has been called "population peristalsis," comparing it to the process in which a python digests a pig. As it moves along the digestive tract, the pig makes a big bulge in the python. In fact, today the python that represents the peoples of the developed world has not one, but two big bulges moving through it. The first bulge is the Baby Boom bulge created by the huge numbers of children born during the roughly fifteen-year post–World War II period, 1946–1963. Less well known is the second "bulge" —the Echo Boom children of the Baby Boom generation. Collectively, these two populations represent nearly two-thirds of the population. Their unique values, interests, and needs will dominate the marketplace over the next half century.

Baby Boomers are the most populous and influential generation in American history. Boomers grew up in a time of unprecedented prosperity and economic growth. They experienced even more rapid technological advancement than their parents, from the national embrace of television to Neil Armstrong's moonwalk to the digital age. They were blessed with unprecedented employment and educational opportunities, and their ingrained sense of entitlement justifiably earned them the designation as the "Me Generation." Their values were shaped by the Great Society, the expansion of suburbia, Nixon, the Vietnam War, color TV, the pill and "sex, drugs, and rock'n'roll."

In 2006, the oldest members of the Baby Boom cohort will be 60 years old, the youngest 43. And over the first quarter of the twenty-first century all of these individuals will move into their retirement years. As a consequence, the number of seniors in our society will double between 2002 and 2030.[14] To put this in perspective, it is staggering to realize that 2 out of every 3 individuals in the history of humanity who ever attained the age of 65 years is currently alive.[15] The age structures of societies were traditionally triangle-shaped, a few folks 65 years and older and lots and lots of folks under the age of 15 years (that's still what most of the developing world looks like). But not so any longer in the developed world. Today, the shape of that demographic profile looks like a dumbbell sitting on a thimble—the two fat parts are the Baby Boomers and Echo Boomers.

It is estimated that by 2050, nearly a third of all individuals in the United States will be over sixty-five (in Japan and some parts of Europe that number will be close to 40 percent).[16] It will be like a nation of Central Floridians, old people everywhere. And not just any old people, but old people who are used to having the world revolve around their needs and desires. Although like any older person, old Boomers will suffer from certain physical limitations, these new old folks will be very unlike yesterday's old folks. This will not be a rocking chair and shuffleboard kind of crowd. Everything they've done before suggests that they are likely to be the healthiest, most adventurous, most self-exploring, and most affluent old folks in history. The first wave of Baby Boomers had a median annual income of $63,426 in 2002, 25 percent exceeded $95,000,[17] and they will have accumulated net assets on average of $380,000 per household by the time they are 62.[18] And with ever greater amounts of time on their hands, they promise to become the most active consumers of leisure experiences in human history. Members of the Boomer cohort are already major constituencies of the museum community and as they find themselves with ever greater time and discretionary income they are likely to become many a museum's new best friends.

They'll have a run for their money in the leisure consumption department, however. Hard on the Boomers' heels will be another huge cohort—their children. The largest generation of young people since the 1960s is beginning to come of age. They're called "Echo Boomers" because they are the genetic off-spring and demographic echo of their Baby Boomer parents. Born between 1982 and 1995, there are nearly 80 million of them, and they're already having a huge impact on entire segments of the economy. And as the population ages, they will become the next dominant generation of Americans. They already make up nearly one-third of the U.S. population, and already spend $170 billion a year of their own and their parents' money, almost all of it on leisure items.[19]

Echo Boomers are a reflection of the sweeping changes in American life over the past twenty years. They were the first to grow up with computers at home, in a 500-channel TV universe. They are multitaskers with cell phones, music downloads, iPods, and Instant Messaging. They think nothing of doing their homework with music playing, while talking on their cell phones and carrying on a conversation with their best friends; their best friends, mean-while, are also talking on cell phones (to someone else) and working on homework (for different classes) on-line. They are the totally plugged-in citizens of a worldwide community. In many ways, they are the opposite image of their 1960s era "hippie" parents. Echo Boomers are not radical, free-love, indi-vidual, libertarians; they are serious, group- and success-oriented traditional-ists. On a recent *60 Minutes* feature on Echo Boomers, two college seniors, Nick Summers of Columbia University and Andie Gissing of Middlebury College in Vermont, were quoted. "I would say that my generation tends to be very overachieving, over-managed," says Summers. "Very pressured." "I would agree with that," adds Gissing. "A lot of people work hard or want to do well, I guess."

The *60 Minutes* reporter concluded, "It's no wonder they feel that way. From when they were toddlers, they have been belted into car seats, and driven off to some form of organized group activity. After graduating from 'Gym-boree' and 'Mommy and Me,' they have been shuttled to play dates and soccer practice, with barely a day off, by parents who've felt their kids needed struc-ture, and a sense of mission." Experts agree that this generation has been pro-grammed, scheduled, and supervised by adults like no other before it. Mel Levine is a well respected pediatrician and student of this generation. He stated, "This is a generation that has long aimed to please. They've wanted to please their parents, their friends, their teachers, their college admissions offi-cers."[20] It's a generation in which rules seem to have replaced rebellion, con-vention is winning out over individualism, and values are very traditional.

Historian Neil Howe, along with co-author William Strauss, has made a career studying different generations. Howe says all the research on Echo Boomers always reflects the same thing: they are much different than their self-absorbed, egocentric Baby Boomer parents.[21] "Nothing could be more anti-boom than being a good team player, right? Fitting in, worrying less about leadership than follower-ship," says Howe. "If you go into a public school today, teamwork is stressed everywhere. Team teaching, team grading, collaborative sports, community service, service learning, student juries. I mean, the list goes on and on." Howe thinks they are more like their grandparents, the great World War II generation—more interested in building things up than tearing them down. According to the *60 Minutes* piece, you can already see some results. Violent crime among teenagers is down 60 to 70 percent. The use of tobacco and alcohol is at an all-time low. So is teen pregnancy. Five out of ten Echo Boomers say they trust the government, and virtually all of them trust Mom and Dad.

They are the most sophisticated generation ever when it comes to media; they are also plugged in an average of thirty-eight hours per week. They create their own websites, make their own CDs and DVDs, and are cynical of packaged messages. They take their cues from each other. More than most previous generations, word-of-mouth, "buzz," influences their attitudes and behaviors. Even as they move into adulthood, the Echo Boomers seem to be clinging to the kind of "mob" social behaviors most previous generations discarded some time after middle school. And because their cohort is so large and so affluent, Echo Boomers are a generation used to being catered to.

How and to what degree this generation will find museums satisfying places to hang out remains an open question. Perhaps they will find museums just the "retro" kind of environments that they crave. Predictably, the leisure needs and wants of the Boomer generation will run full bore up against the needs and wants of the Echo Boomer generation. Museums and other free-choice learning institutions will need to delicately walk the fence between these two demanding groups. In the meantime, the challenges of meeting the diverging needs of Boomers' desire for individualized, long-term, quiet contemplative experiences will directly compete with the Echo Boomers' desire for group-appropriate, visually and aurally exciting, instant gratification experiences. There's also likely to be the challenge of differing financial capabilities. There is a growing disparity between the "haves" and "have-nots." For the first time in American history, parents expect their children to have incomes below what they have.[22]

"Haves" and "Have-Nots"

The dawning of the Knowledge Age has spawned unprecedented wealth and prosperity, but the wealth and prosperity are not equally distributed. Despite overall improvements in the standard of living, some individuals and families are falling behind in either absolute or relative terms. Although there have always been rich and the poor, one of the major achievements of the Industrial Revolution was the narrowing of that gap. Over the past ten or fifteen years that gap has not narrowed, it has widened.[23] In the United States, the top 10 percent of all households have average incomes sixteen times as high as those of the bottom 20 percent, but their wealth is 106 times as high. In the Industrial Age, the narrowing of the gap between rich and poor was through the creation of a large and stable middle class. In the Knowledge Age, at least so far, the distribution of wealth has taken a different course. The relative economic distance between the middle and lower classes has stayed roughly comparable; what has widened is the distance between them and the rich![24] The rich are getting richer; everybody else is stagnating. Median family income in the United States is essentially the same as it was in 1973.[25] And the disparities within the United States are small as compared with the disparities that are growing between the United States and other developed countries, and particularly stark is the growing gap between the most developed and the least developed countries.[26]

In a Knowledge Age, what is truly alarming is not merely the widening economic gap, but equally the widening knowledge gap. The world is dramatically changing and the United States and other developing countries are being rapidly transformed into Learning Societies, but not all citizens are being equally "transformed." Not everyone in the society is actively seeking and receiving educational experiences, particularly the all-important free-choice learning experiences that promise to bring individuals increased personal freedom and financial betterment. In short, there is a growing rift between the learning "haves" and "have-nots," a rift that ultimately affects all, including the museum community.

Speaking directly to these points, British museum educator David Anderson states in a recent museum policy book, *A Common Wealth: Museums in the Learning Age:*

> In 1944, Beveridge identified five great evils—the giants of want, idleness, ignorance, squalor and disease—that society must overcome. Today we might add a

sixth, cultural exclusion, which existed fifty years ago, and which continues to deprive many people of the opportunity to participate actively and creatively in their communities. Our society, while generally more affluent, has also become more atomised and more sharply divided. The last two decades have seen the emergence of a "second nation," a substantial minority which includes a disproportionate number of young people and adults whose lives are blighted by recurrent unemployment, poor housing, poor health and drug-related crime. One in three children now lives in poverty and in consequence suffers a significant educational disadvantage from birth. These divisions are reflected in museum audiences.[27]

Anderson goes on to say that fifty years ago cultural exclusion may not have been perceived by policy makers as problematic, but today it is a serious ill of society. The rift between the learning/cultural haves and have-nots appears to be growing daily and rapidly. The causes of this schism are self-perpetuating and fed by a positive feedback loop—well-informed and knowledgeable individuals actively seek out more information and resources and become even more well-informed and knowledgeable, while the less well-informed and knowledgeable individuals opt not to inform themselves and fall farther behind. The time to reverse this trend is now. Museums are among many types of organizations that are trying to work proactively on the problem. But efforts to focus on the "have-nots" are challenging and time-consuming, draining resources from efforts to attract and maintain current "have" audience levels. The needs and strategies to compete for these two groups grow increasingly disparate, and the museum's time and resources grow increasingly fragmented. There is no easy way out of this bind; both groups are essential to the long-term survival of the museum community, each requires and deserves ever more attention and commitment. For museum professionals, this will represent just one more stress in what is already a very stressful world.

Living in a Stressful World

We live in a world of rapid change, one perceived by many as increasingly dangerous and unreliable. Layered on top of this anxiety is the uprooted quality of today's society. Families and friends are widely scattered. As a consequence, there is a profound society-wide search for meaning and stability; people are seeking some kind of "center" and some kind of sense of security and serenity.

The results of this search are being played out in many ways, but the most frequent is through a search for identity, within either a group or a place.

Many people today seem to be increasingly uneasy about the future. News of terrorism, war, and random violence daily parades across our television screens and contributes to a mood of public anxiety and fear. It is no coincidence that the central issue of the 2004 American presidential election was security. People today are convinced we live in a very, very dangerous world—a reality tragically demonstrated on September 11, 2001, and reinforced by bombings in Bali, Madrid, London, and other parts of the world. Ironically, just as our society is making each of us more socially and physically isolated, our mass communications are making us ever-more networked. The footage of dozens of people blown up by suicide bombers in Tel Aviv, Israel, or Istanbul, Turkey, are presented on the evening news side by side with the footage of the robbery at the local convenience store.

America's mobility has also increased our sense of unease. The U.S. Census reports that in the one-year period, March 1998–March 1999, 43 million Americans, 16 percent of the population, moved.[28] At the beginning of the twentieth century, most individuals spent their entire lives within fifty miles of their birthplace and the majority of the population still lived in rural communities.[29] By mid-century Americans for the first time were more likely to live in an urban area than in a rural area, and by the end of the century, more Americans lived in suburbs than in cities, with only 3 percent living on farms.[30] With greater mobility, people moved to find work rather than looking for work wherever they lived. It is now estimated that on average, every American will move at least once every five years. This is good economically, but bad socially. Because of all of this mobility and translocation, Americans find themselves increasingly separated from their families, childhood friends, and familiar neighborhoods.

Over the course of the twentieth century, the separation and distances between families and friends grew greater. Once upon a time, not only did you know all of your neighbors, but most were related to you. The people you worked with as adults were the same people you played with as children. People knew their aunts and uncles and cousins because they lived next door. But this is no longer true. Today, most people are lucky if they know a few of their neighbors and many rarely see any of their relatives on a regular basis. People today live amazingly isolated lives—isolation precipitated by mobility, and, according to sociologist Ray Oldenburg, exacerbated by architecture.

This architectural isolation is due to what Oldenburg calls the demise of "third places" in our cities.[31] Oldenburg's third places are the gathering places in our community, the places beyond the "first" and "second" places of home and work. It is in the third places where we meet members of our community on neutral ground, leaving possible divisions such as class or industrial rank at the door in the spirit of inclusion rather than exclusivity. Oldenburg describes these third places as "the core settings of informal public life."[32] As the pub, church, and other free or inexpensive local third places have disappeared, so too have the feelings of community. Third places, according to Oldenburg, are necessary for community to arise and thrive. They are places where members of a community interact with others and come to know the ties they have in common.[33]

Oldenburg notes that cities of the Western world have seen a steady decline of such third places. This is especially true in America, where most of the population now lives in suburbs, out of walking distance from the informal places that bring people together. In the words of Oldenburg, "Houses alone do not a community make, and the typical subdivision proved hostile to the emergence of any structure or space utilization beyond the uniform houses and streets that characterized it."[34] Or, as Richard Goodwin complained, in the suburbs "there are no places where neighbors can anticipate unplanned meetings—no pub or corner store or park."[35] In fact, observation would suggest that most late twentieth-century architectural design discourages free association among members of the community.

During a recent interview Oldenburg observed that his ideas were influenced by, or more correctly created, in reaction to the ideas of Sigmund Freud. "Freud held that emotional well-being depends upon having someone to love and work to do. He made his mental health list one item too short. Besides a mate and a job, we need a dependable place of refuge where, for a few minutes a day, we can escape the demands of family and bosses."[36] In fact, Oldenburg is convinced that many problems of contemporary society, including alienation in the workplace and soaring divorce rates, directly link to the disappearance of third places. Some have argued that museums could fill this void, could successfully become community third places.[37] While the museum community debates whether museums are truly equipped to fill this role, the public is moving on. For many in the public the answer to how to feel more secure is to become part of a group.

In Search of Group Identity

Group identity is a complex thing, meaning different things to different people. For some, the single most important group is family, for others the group is represented by culture and ethnicity or religion. Still others have sought group identity through association with sports teams, social clubs, or special interest groups like Trekkies or celebrity fan clubs.

Robert Putnam became famous for asserting in his book *Bowling Alone,* a persistent decline in Americans' participation in groups.[38] Many social scientists question Putnam's conclusions. They point out that the declines have been in the large twentieth-century, top-down kinds of groups Putnam studied, such as scouting and PTA, while there have actually been compensatory increases in smaller, more loosely organized, twenty-first-century groups like book groups and health clubs.[39]

For all individuals, the need to belong to something larger than the individual is strong. A generation or two ago, much of that need might have been supported by family. Prior to World War II, most people lived out their entire lives in one place, often surrounded by family—parents and siblings, grandparents, aunts, uncles, and oodles of cousins. Today, this is increasingly unlikely to be the case. Crisscrossing the country, families move from job to job, city to city, and with them go their itinerate children. As a consequence, is it any wonder that many adults find themselves consciously trying to relearn and reestablish family connections?

One manifestation of this search for family roots has been the explosion in genealogical research, the study and tracing of family histories. Genealogy has been claimed by some to be one of the most popular hobbies in America, second only to gardening.

Another aspect of seeking identity is through connection to one's ethnicity. Worldwide there is an upsurge in those whose primary identification is as part of an ethnic/cultural community as opposed to being first and foremost a member of a national community. Not only is this true in historically contentious areas like the Balkans and Afghanistan, but also in such places as Western Europe and the United States. Today, it is common to identify yourself with both your country and with the culture from which you sprang, regardless of how diverse. Hence, people say I'm an African American, Asian American, or Italian American.

Such practice makes headlines. For example, the North African Muslim community in Europe has grown from a few hundred thousand in the 1950s to more than an estimated 10 million today. While the first generation of North African Muslims—mainly laborers—suffered from problems of adjustment, their sons and daughters are now torn between belonging to the culture of their parents and that of Europe. A stark image of this occurred recently in France after the government banned the wearing of obvious religious symbols in public schools, particularly in response to growing anti-Muslim sentiments. As part of a protest of that law, North African Muslim girls went to school wearing Muslim headscarves and at the same time had their bodies wrapped in the French flag. This was a clear expression of their desire to be integrated into French society, but without losing their distinct cultural/religious identity. Such identity issues are likely to become increasingly common in our diverse society.

We are also witnessing a rise in the number of people participating in all kinds of religious and spiritual activities. Many organized religions have seen their numbers rebound after years of decline, as have all kinds of alternative types of spiritual organizations. Inherent in the desire for self-actualization is a desire to create an island of calm within the turbulence of the greater world, to create stability through purposefulness. According to theologian Wade Clark Roof, this trend has been spear-headed by the now middle-aged Baby Boom generation.[40]

Dubbed the "quest culture" by Roof, the Baby Boomers' desire for spirituality grows out of their yearning for a wholeness of body, mind, and spirit; the impact of the media; and globalization. Although some of these individuals have returned to churches and synagogues, most remain unaffiliated with religious institutions. A broad and eclectic group of suppliers has arisen to serve their needs and interests: self-help groups, retreat centers, spiritual seminars, New Age workshops, meditation cassettes and videos, and an unending stream of books about spirituality and the world's religions. And while the Boomers have primarily chosen the individualistic, alternative approach to spirituality, not surprisingly, their Echo Boomer children are opting for the more traditional organized religion approach.

A Quest for Learning
The quest for something larger, something fulfilling, will emerge as one of the dominant themes of this new century. Our society seeks this calm in multiple ways—through religion, through exercise and sports, and, befitting a Knowledge Age, increasingly through learning.

Writing a quarter century ago, anthropologist Nelson Graburn speculated that museum-going would be part of a larger societal trend, part of the changing landscape of leisure and work in a postindustrial society. In Graburn's view, "leisure is displacing work from the center of modern social arrangements."[41] Graburn was accurately anticipating the transformation of the developed world into a "Learning Society."[42] In the Knowledge Age the need to learn takes on ever greater importance, ever greater urgency.[43] Every citizen perceives a need to learn not just at school or at work, but in all aspects of life, including and especially leisure.

Learning, as we have broadly defined it, has become so pervasive that it now is rapidly becoming the single largest leisure activity. For the first time in history, learning is what most Americans choose to do for enjoyment! And like everything else in our changing economy, the public wants their leisure learning to be a personalized, non-mass-produced experience—an experience that meets the individual's own unique requirements, interests, and needs. This is not the type of learning we got in school, but it is the type of learning we now expect to receive during our leisure time.

Evidence for this shift is everywhere you look, but the most scientific evidence comes from research conducted in Canada that showed that, on average, Canadian adults spend about eighteen hours each week engaged in some type of learning activity.[44] This represents a 50 percent increase in time spent on such learning when compared with similar data collected in the 1970s. The vast majority of this learning time, nearly 95 percent, was not for work or in order to earn a degree; it was learning freely engaged in for leisure purposes. Adults in the survey spent their free time learning everything from how to use a computer to keep track of their personal finances to learning better strategies and techniques for home renovations. Virtually all of the learning adults participated in occurred outside of school. Learning today is much more than schooling. In the twenty-first century, the learning strategy of choice for most people, most of the time, will be free-choice learning.[45]

Free-choice learning, learning that is intrinsically motivated, is something humans have always done. In the new Knowledge Age, free-choice learning will consume more and more of our time and will be elevated to a higher status and importance. Museums are well placed to accommodate this desire for self-actualization through free-choice learning. In fact, what could be more self-actualizing than intellectual growth and development related to the world in which we live? Systematically helping visitors actually achieve such growth in unique and personal ways will definitely require new practices and intentional programming.

THE POLITICAL CONTEXT: DEMONSTRATING
HONESTY, SUCCESS, AND COMPASSION

Not only is the new Knowledge Age an age of self-fulfillment, it is also an age of accountability. At the beginning of the twenty-first century corruption and unethical business practices have been widespread. We have seen fraud everywhere: in major companies like Enron, WorldCom, and Global Crossings; in the mutual fund industry; in transactions between government agencies and private businesses; and even in large and prestigious national nonprofits such as the United Way and Nature Conservancy. Building upon what was already a shaky foundation of trust these scandals have helped fuel the highest level of public distrust in U.S. history.

In a recent poll, eight people in ten disagreed with the statement "Directors of large companies can be trusted to tell the truth." Nearly two-thirds of those in full-time employment (65 percent) say they do not believe that "companies can be trusted to honor their pension commitments to employees."[46] And if this weren't bad enough, the public trusts business more than it trusts the government! While roughly two-thirds of citizens distrust the business community, fully three-quarters question whether the government really acts in the public interest, and only one in five believe "the government is doing a good job."[47] In short, people distrust the corporations and institutions they do business with, and they distrust their government to enforce the laws intended to make corporations and institutions behave honestly.

In reaction to society-wide mistrust have come increasing demands for accountability—accountability for conduct and finances and accountability for delivering on the promises made about products and services. In the wake of the corporate scandals of 2001 and 2002, the U.S. Congress enacted one of the most far-reaching laws to curb business wrongdoing in the history of the nation. This legislation, known as the Sarbanes-Oxley Act (SOA), promises to change forever the way for-profits and nonprofits alike do business. Most observers would agree that the SOA is the single most important piece of legislation affecting corporate governance, financial disclosure, and the practice of public accounting since the U.S. securities laws of the early 1930s. It places increased responsibility for the ethical and legal actions of a business on the members of the board of trustees and company directors. The law requires stringent oversight of all company policies and procedures, along with new and comprehensive sets of financial internal controls and checks and balances, on both the staff and board sides of the ledger. And it will inevitably add considerably to the complexity, and cost, of running an organization.

These new regulations are leading to sweeping new nonprofit board accountability standards as well. Independent Sector, an association representing seven hundred large nonprofits, foundations, and corporate supporters, has proposed that nonprofit boards voluntarily adopt a set of provisions similar to the SOA.[48] Among the provisions are that boards should sign off on IRS 990 reporting forms, the creation of separate audit and finance committees, and a document retention and development policy.

Accountability, though, is not limited to the rules by which businesses govern themselves; it is also about how businesses demonstrate they are achieving their goals. This is particularly true for nonprofit businesses. In the for-profit world, the ultimate accounting is the bottom line, the amount of money earned. In nonprofit institutions, accountability is measured in the good accomplished. How do you reliably and credibly measure good accomplished? Most nonprofits have never actually done so, but in the twenty-first century, those that do not figure out how to do so will find themselves out of business. In an increasingly distrustful society, merely promising to do good no longer suffices.

Continued public and private funding for nonprofits will ultimately depend upon demonstrating evidence of public good accomplished. Society increasingly is demanding that institutions evaluate their performance and provide concrete, tangible evidence of success. Such demands became a legislative reality at the federal government level with the passage of the Government Performance and Results Act (GPRA) in 1993, which required every government agency to establish specific objective, quantifiable, and measurable performance goals for each of its programs and report its success annually to Congress.

The demand for accountability is increasingly widespread. Many state and local government agencies have followed the lead of Congress. Private foundations are including similar language in grant applications. From all sides, nonprofit organizations like museums are receiving a clear message: to compete successfully for public or private funds in an accountability-driven environment, they must develop evaluation practices that provide a compelling picture of the impact of their efforts. In the Knowledge Age, funders want evidence that something of quality actually happened as a consequence of the programs they support. Such outcomes-based assessments will require institutions to invest more money, more time, and more thought in the assessment process. To do less will not be an option.

Demonstrating Compassion

In addition to expectations for accountability, the public will also increasingly demand that institutions be held responsible for being accessible, socially concerned, and friendly to the planet—in short, being good community citizens. Ironically, despite the public distrust of institutions to do "good," expectations that institutions *should* do "good" is at an all-time high. We demand that companies produce quality products and services, that they not mislead, that they adhere to strict safety and public health standards, and that they do not discriminate. But society's expectations for their institutions, both public and private, do not stop there. In addition, society also expects institutions to be good citizens. Whether working to improve the social fabric of the community or the ecological balance of the environment, society expects public and private institutions to work toward helping to make the world a better place in which to live.

As part of an annual survey of Americans' attitudes toward business, the number of individuals who believe that businesses should be good corporate citizens has steadily increased. More than two-thirds of consumers (69 percent) say corporate citizenship is "important to their trust in business."[49] However, in the same study, roughly half of the 2,770 individuals surveyed felt that the U.S. business community's commitment to corporate citizenship is heading in the wrong direction. Less than a quarter felt it was improving. "In the past, corporate citizenship was seen as something unique, a differentiator for businesses and their brands," said Rob Anderson, executive vice-president of the public relations and marketing firm GolinHarris. "Increasingly, the public is viewing corporate citizenship as an expectation and companies are seeing it as an opportunity, demonstrating that 'doing good' is a smart, pragmatic business strategy for 'doing well.'"[50] In other words, just like honesty and accountability, doing "good" is increasingly more than a nicety; it is becoming a business necessity.

The public notices and supports businesses that design their new buildings as ecologically friendly "green" buildings. They notice and support businesses that give back to their communities through support of social services, and they respond to companies that bolster the conditions of the underserved and economically disadvantaged. More and more, institutions will be judged by the good they do, and those that are perceived to do more good than others will be more likely to be supported. If this is true, then perhaps "doing good" will need to be more explicitly a part of institutional mission. Thus, another hallmark of the Knowledge Age is the end of "either-or" thinking. The way out of the "either-or" conundrum for museums is to create a "both-and" mission of education and public good and financial vitality since, above all, the business of museums must begin with a clear understanding of why the museum exists.

MUSEUMS IN THE MIDDLE

The dramatic changes in the world are already challenging museums. Museums can be found at every point along the spectrum of change. Some remain certain that today's audience will rediscover the joy in old practices. Others believe that only radical change will refuel a connection to modern society. We know that for some museum visitors, there is a comfort in sameness—a nostalgia that beckons them back. But for many others, the old museum is an anachronism. Great dark halls of unmoving figures, minimal labels, and the invitation to "look" but not "touch" are a thing of the past. They have lost their relevance in our bewildering new age.

What is strikingly clear is that today's museum is not standing still. No museum director is standing, hands in pockets, waiting for a better day. Indeed, many of our institutions have been remarkably entrepreneurial in the face of declining attendance and fragile funding. Many recent transformations have been bold and imaginative, idealistic and passionate, despite the uncertainty ahead; others have been bold, but arguably misguided. Most museum leaders recognize that we are in the midst of a great period of transformation, reflecting the shifting paradigms of a new age. Despite their awareness, though, they are struggling with contradictory visions. The crystal balls available to us currently are clouded, as in the midst of dwindling resources, we are seeking answers to our growing professional crisis. This age of accelerating change and new realities is posing troubling questions for our institutions.

- What, in fact, should the mission of museums be in a climate of uncertainty?
- How do we compete with more and more institutions—some with far greater resources—that also define themselves as both entertaining and educational?

- How do we challenge the time spent on electronic games and technological wizardry?
- How much of our limited financial resources should be dedicated to building community relationships?
- Can we compete in the noisy marketplace of change?
- What do our visitors long for; what would entice them inside?
- Do the static dioramas and gilt-framed paintings of the past still have lessons for a nation in flux?
- Is there a new kind of voice we can give to once-silent collections?
- Is authenticity still our claim to fame?
- And, finally, how will the answers to these questions help us establish new business models to assure sustainability?

Meanwhile, a flood of museum books present multiple new expectations for museums—many of which echo the changes in the outside world that we have already described. For example, we have been encouraged to:

- Keep the word *education* in the heart of our missions, but also to be more active, meaningful players in civic life.
- Be at the table of our communities, to use our resources to address deep social ills.
- Measure, evaluate, and document our impact on everything from family learning to tourism to the economics of our cities.
- Provide a sense of place, a safe haven for our audiences, a neutral forum for civic debate.
- Become builders of learning networks—seeking partners to support free-choice learning at the same time as we restructure school partnerships dictated by increasingly narrow curriculum standards.
- Be audience experts, marketing wizards, and solid competitors as others challenge the leisure-time market.

And yes,

- Maintain exemplary standards for our once defining museum missions: to collect, to conserve, to study, to interpret, and to exhibit.

We are being asked to be at once partners, teachers, learners, leaders, scholars, protectors, collectors, listeners, creators, and healers. Whether the topics we communicate are science, art, history, nature, technology, animals, or plants, we are encouraged to put them to the use of the greater good, defining ourselves as among the few institutions whose central mission is to enhance the human experience through the best and broadest use of all we have.

The challenges facing museums in the twenty-first century are arriving at the same time that many are struggling with dwindling financial resources. Many are questioning how to become a public forum, an educational leader, a technology leader, or a community partner without additional funds. With revenues based on a traditional mix of attendance, endowment, foundation and government grants, membership, special events, and such ancillary businesses, as shops and cafes, just breaking even requires an exhausting effort and significant human resources. Stability can be fatally skewed by any one of many external circumstances, from falling consumer confidence to ever-escalating gasoline prices. And as in the past few years—when all factors are negatively influenced at once —the bottom can fall out. The recent pattern of declining attendance is the strongest possible signal that bold and daring change is needed. In the chapters that follow, we will begin the process of describing how to rethink the business models of museums—how to begin to build a Knowledge Age museum that can thrive in this new age.

DISCUSSION QUESTIONS

- What are the changes in the marketplace that appear to be most directly affecting your institution? Which changes are working in your favor and which appear to be working against you?
- How will changing demographics and economic disparities impact your organization? What steps can you take to accommodate these changes?
- How has your organization attempted to incorporate new accountability requirements? Where are you in compliance and where are you lacking?

NOTES

Epigraph: D. Lewis and D. Bridger, *The Soul of the New Consumer* (London: Nicholas Brealey Publishing, 2000), 5.

1. J. D. Salinger, *The Catcher in the Rye* (Boston: Little, Brown and Company, 1951), 120.

2. C. Sagon, Formerly known as Sutton Place, *The Washington Post*, April 7, 2004, F1.

3. Ibid.

4. Op. cit., 21.

5. Cf. S. Zuboff and D. Maxmin, *The Support Economy: Why Corporations Are Failing Individuals and the Next Episode of Capitalism* (New York: Viking Press, 2002).

6. B. J. Pine II and J. H. Gilmore, *The Experience Economy: Work is Theatre and Every Business a Stage* (Boston: Harvard Business School Press, 1999).

7. Lewis and Bridger, *Soul of the New Consumer*.

8. Zuboff and Maxmin, *Support Economy*.

9. R. Laermer, *Trend Spotting* (New York: Perigee, 2002).

10. Lewis and Bridger, *Soul of the New Consumer*, 114.

11. Laermer, *Trend Spotting*, 103.

12. Ibid., 104.

13. Ibid.

14. M. Goldstein, *The Global Age Wave*, presentation developed for Voka-Vlaams (www.vola.be), 2004.

15. Ibid.

16. Ibid.

17. Robert Prisuta, Enhancing volunteerism among Baby Boomers, *AARP*, 2003.

18. J. Lach, Boomers breaking through, *American Demographics* 25, no. 8 (1998): 37–42.

19. S. Kroft (October 3, 2004), CBS, *60 Minutes*.

20. M. Levine (October 3, 2004), CBS, *60 Minutes*.

21. N. Howe (October 3, 2004), CBS, *60 Minutes*.

22. L. Thurow, *Fortune Favors the Bold: What We Must Do to Build a New and Lasting Global Prosperity* (New York: Harper Business, 2003), 116.

23. Ibid., 94.

24. Ibid., 95.

25. Council of Economic Advisors, *Economic Report of the President* (Washington, DC: U.S. Government Printing Office, 1999), 366.

26. Thurow, *Fortune Favors the Bold,* 35.

27. D. Anderson, *A Common Wealth: Museums in the Learning Age* (London: Department for Culture, Media and Sport, 1999), 13.

28. C. S. Faber, *U.S. Census Bureau Current Population Report: Geographical Mobility, March 1998 to March 1999* (Washington, DC: U.S. Government Printing Office, 2002).

29. T. Caplow, L. Hicks, and B. Wattenberg, *The First Measured Century: An Illustrated Guide to Trends in America, 1900–2000* (Washington, DC: The AEI Press, 2001), 232.

30. Ibid., 234.

31. R. Oldenburg, *The Great Good Place: Cafes, Coffee Shops, Bookstores, Bars, Hair Salons, and Other Hangouts* (New York: Marlowe & Co., 1989).

32. Ibid., 16.

33. Ibid., xxiii and 72.

34. Ibid., 4.

35. Richard N. Goodwin, The American condition, *The New Yorker,* January 28, 1974, 38.

36. Ibid.

37. E. H. Gurian, Function follows form: How mixed-use spaces in museums build community, *Curator* 44, no. 1 (2001): 87–113; R. Archibald, *New Town Square: Museums and Communities in Transition* (Walnut Creek, CA: AltaMira Press, 2004).

38. R. Putnam, *Bowling Alone: America's Declining Social Capital* (New York: Simon & Schuster, 2000).

39. M. W. Foley and B. Edwards, The paradox of civil society, *Journal of Democracy* 7, no. 3 (1996): 38–52; R. Samuelson, The 'bowling alone' phenomenon is bunk, *Detroit News* editorial, April 11, 1996.

40. W. Roof, *Spiritual Marketplace: Baby Boomers and the Remaking of American Religion* (Princeton: Princeton University Press, 2004).

41. N. H. Graburn, The museum and the visitor experience, in *The Visitor and the Museum*, 5–32; prepared for the 72nd annual conference of the American Association of Museums, Seattle, WA, 1977.

42. J. H. Falk and L. D. Dierking, *Lessons without Limit: How Free-Choice Learning is Transforming Education* (Walnut Creek, CA: AltaMira Press, 2002).

43. Ibid.

44. J. Lewington, More Canadians pursuing informal learning, survey reveals, *The Globe and Mail*, November 11, 1998, A13.

45. Falk and Dierking, *Lessons without Limit*.

46. Mori, www.mori.com, June 28, 2003.

47. Ibid.

48. Independent Sector, *Sarbanes-Oxley and Implications for Non-Profits*, Washington, October 10, 2003.

49. GolinHarris, www.golinharris.com. June 14, 2005.

50. Ibid.

Building a Knowledge Age Business Model

5

Experiences That Matter

No company can succeed today by trying to be all things to all people. It must instead find the unique value that it alone can deliver to a chosen market.
—M. Treacy and F. Wiersema

"There are lots of little things that the kids can get involved in, and we can do something different every time—being a member, it's nice [to be able to go back again and again] because one day it might be the dig, then the next time they're not interested in that because they've done it already, and they're more interested in the sights and sounds, putting on the costumes and protecting their eggs. There's just enough going on, we can always spend at least an hour there.

"When you go inside the big area where the weather changes constantly and there are the thunderstorms, there's someone actively perched in the middle to answer questions about different dinosaur skeletons. And in the working area, where you look behind the glass, someone is sitting right at the fossil area where you can pick up bones and learn about them. He was very helpful, as was the other man in the dig area. They were always communicating with the kids [while they were] camped out right in the middle of the pit. All of the staff were very positive, wonderful, very interested. I would say happy to answer questions, not at all put out, and very informative."[1]

Sylvia Freed,[2] mother of two elementary school-aged children, could not say enough good things about The Children's Museum, Indianapolis's newest permanent exhibition, *Dinosphere: Now You're in Their World*. Sylvia was just gushing with praise for the new exhibition, which includes one of the largest displays of real juvenile and family dinosaur fossils in the United States set within a repurposed large-format film theater in order to immerse visitors in the sights, sounds, and smells of the Cretaceous Period, "when dinosaurs ruled the earth." *Dinosphere* is more than exhibitory though; it also includes a full complement of interpretive programs such as a hands-on dig site, opportunities for visitors to interact with a mascot called Rex, listen to a first-person interpretative experience by Sherlock Bones, who describes how one looks at the skeletons of dinosaurs to pick up clues to their habits and lifestyles, talk to scientists working in a functioning Paleo Lab, and informal facilitation throughout the exhibition by costumed staff wearing polo shirts, safari vests, and hats. In addition to these activities within the gallery, there are a series of complementary programs developed for families to precede or extend their *Dinosphere* experience, including family-oriented overnights, day trips, a fossil dig out West, evening events, Playscape Preschool classes for children ages three through five, Playscape Graduates classes for children ages five and six, and one of the finest collections of dinosaur art in the nation where children and adults can both view and make dinosaur art.

Yet all this in our opinion is not what really makes *Dinosphere* special. *Dinosphere* is special because it is the embodiment of a new visitor-centered business model at The Children's Museum. When Dr. Jeffery Patchen took over as president and CEO of The Children's Museum in 2000, he understood that just because the museum was the largest and one of the most well-respected children's museums in the country was not going to be sufficient to ensure its survival in the twenty-first century. Despite its past successes, the museum's revenues and attendance had plateaued and newer attractions were threatening to further erode its once unchallenged dominance of the family leisure market in Indianapolis. In short, he felt that the museum needed to make a profound shift of focus, a shift toward what he felt was the real audience of children's museums—not children solely, but families. Over a five-year period he steadily, though not always easily, redirected the institution's mission from being child-centered to being family-centered. Like most children's museums, all of the museum's exhibitions and programs were designed with a child-centered perspective. The role of the family was acknowledged, but primarily in service to the child's learning. Patchen now wanted to focus all of the museum's energies on the "creation of extraordinary *family* learning experiences."

So, with support from the Institute for Learning Innovation, The Children's Museum initiated a multiyear systemic research and evaluation effort designed to better understand the perceived learning needs of families in the greater

Indianapolis area and the role the museum plays in facilitating those learning needs. Findings were fed into changes into all aspects of the museum's efforts—from visitor services to interpretive programming and exhibition design. One major example of this effort included incorporating family learning in an integral way within all aspects of *Dinosphere's* design and development, a project that was conceptualized and begun soon after Patchen arrived at the museum. From the beginning of planning and development, family research findings were integrated into every aspect of the *Dinosphere* exhibition and programmatic experience development process in order to create a visitor experience that fully and completely supported family collaboration and conversation, as well as appealed to both children and adults. As the following quotes collected from parents as part of the *Dinosphere* summative evaluation[3] five years later attest, the museum appears to be succeeding in being a place where adults and children learn together as a family:

> *[We also enjoyed] what's being done as far as dinosaur excavation and paleontology. It was interactive enough for a child to be interested, as well as an adult. (Father)*

> *[There is] something for everyone there; visually you did such a wonderful job, it was beautifully made, and we got to the point of feeling like we know a lot about dinosaurs. (Mother)*

> *I just thought that they had stuff to do for both adults and kids. It wasn't where parents only did it or kids only [did it], it was kind of a mixture—pertinent for both. (Mother)*

> *Because it was a very good mix of age-appropriate things for youngsters, there were some underlying challenging, interesting things for adults. For example, Dr. Bakker is a world-renowned paleontologist, which meant a lot more to me than my daughter; but having him draw a picture for her was great. She really liked that. (Father)*

> *Initially, it was enjoyable for both [adults and child]. We've been back several times since, and the more we go back the more it's for him and not the adults . . . He gets better at the games, he gets interested in things that he wasn't able to do before . . . that's not to say that we [the adults] don't find it enjoyable. [We really enjoyed] the dioramas, the skeletons and the fossils and the way they were reinterpreted. I enjoyed the gallery . . . where you could see the old interpretations, and how the skeletons have been relooked at because we have better science now; I liked to compare and contrast. I find that very interesting and engaging. Also, I like the computer game around on the backside where you have to design a dinosaur so that he*

won't fall on his face; we found that really helpful to explain levers and fulcrums to our son, for science. (Mother)

I learned where dinosaurs were in the world, I probably knew at one time but forgot. I learned about the origin of dinosaurs. [My grandson] learned the same things—we talked about the origin of the dinosaurs. It was fun and educational. (Grandmother)

For too long, museums have tried too hard to be all things to all people. As Michael Treacy and Fred Wiersema state in their best-selling book *The Discipline of Market Leaders,* trying to be all things to all people is a strategy that just won't fly in today's complex and highly competitive marketplace.[4] As we've tried to describe in the previous chapters, the world has and continues to change rapidly. Gone are the simple "truths" of previous times. No longer can a museum survive merely by collecting excellent objects and presenting them with commendable scholarship in an orderly fashion.

Here are some questions about your museum business and the publics you serve:

- Do you really know why your visitors come and what they hope to get out of their experience?
- Do you know what your visitors actually do in your museum and why they do these things?
- Do you really know why some visitors stay as long or as short a time as they do?
- What is the one thing you are not providing your various publics today that they are secretly longing for?
- Do you know what percentage of your public considers you an irreplaceable resource?
- Do you know how a new, or existing, competitor could take away your audience?
- What are two things about your institution that you cannot, under any circumstances, change?

If you already know the answers to these questions, then you don't need to read this chapter. But if you are like most museum professionals, you probably have only a general sense of how to answer these questions, a sense that may or may not be accurate. This, then, is the goal of this chapter, to begin to clarify some answers to these questions and to do so within the context of recent research on museum audiences.

As previously outlined, museums must increasingly position themselves first and foremost as educational businesses, organizations that provide high-quality free-choice learning experiences to a learning-hungry population. Museums must operate within a community filled with other institutions also trying to serve the public's free-choice learning needs, institutions that have the potential to be fierce competitors, or loyal collaborators, or both. Museums operate within a marketplace where the rules are rapidly changing. Consumers are actively seeking value from each and every transaction. They are seeking safety and comfort, and at the same time are increasingly cynical and distrustful of institutions. And more than anything, consumers today are seeking greater personalization; they want to be treated as unique, as individuals. We live in an age where the one-size-fits-all approach of the twentieth century no longer works. So, who is visiting our museums and what are they seeking? How can we meet the public's needs if we don't know what those needs are?

THE MUSEUM PUBLIC

Mary and Molly are friends, and together they are visiting their local history museum. Throughout the visit, Mary busily chats with her friend Molly, talking about her preparations for Thanksgiving dinner and occasionally using the historical objects on display as verbal props in her conversation. Meanwhile, Molly spends her time nodding at Mary while intently gazing at objects and intermittently reading the labels. How can we understand what is going on here and what this visit means to these two people? How satisfied will each person be with her museum experience and what are the likely long-term impacts of the visit? What insights might we have gleaned about these impacts had we known something about the reasons these two women visited the museum this particular day? And, perhaps most important, how could we have increased the success of this visitor experience for both woman had we not only known their reasons for coming, but anticipated them and facilitated them?

John has been trying to answer these questions for the better part of his career. After thirty-odd years of research, John currently believes that the single most important thing to know about visitors like Molly and Mary is how frequently they visit museums and what the reasons are for visiting this particular museum today.

Considerable time and effort has been invested in understanding why people visit museums. Historically, and even today, much of the research on museum visit motivation has been driven by marketing concerns, and a disproportionate number of studies have treated demographic variables such as age, income, and education as the variables of greatest importance.[5] Although most museum people know that such marketing studies consistently indicate strong correlations between museum-going and higher levels of education and income, we should be wary of this finding. We should not confuse correlations with causation. Although demographics have been found to correlate with a lot of things, from going to museums to buying decisions for things like toothpaste and magazine subscriptions, they have been consistently shown to be poor predictors of why people come to museums and what they do once there.[6] Knowing that someone is a forty-year-old, male, white college graduate will not tell you whether or not he will visit your museum, or anything about what he will learn in your museum if he does visit! A more robust way to understand why people visit museums, and hence what they expect to get out of the experience, is to talk to visitors directly and ask them about their motivations for visiting. Many investigators have attempted this approach and the results include a wide range of answers, such as social and recreational reasons; educational/learning and self-fulfillment reasons; reasons related to culture, awe, reverence, and restoration; and reasons related to identity.[7] Taken together, this research suggests that there are some clear patterns related to visitor motivations, but little consensus among investigators as to what those patterns are.

Another conclusion one can reach from this research is how conceptually isolated it seems to be from the total museum experience. Although we have known for years that there is a strong relationship between a visitor's reasons for coming to a museum and the outcomes of the museum experience,[8] earlier studies rarely seem to connect these dots. Rather than viewing entry motivation, in-museum behaviors, visitor satisfaction, and long-term impact as separate, albeit correlated events, we need to think about visitor motivation, behavior, satisfaction, and impact as parts of a single, inextricable whole. Doing this requires a reinterpretation of how we think about and construct our entry motivation categories. It suggests that we should start with the idea that learning, broadly defined, is a major motivation for visiting the museum, a major aspect of what people do within the museum, a major contributor to visitor satisfaction, and a major outcome of the museum experience. As discussed earlier, by learning we are referring to a wide range of changes in the individual, not just the acquisition of facts and concepts, but also changes in how the visitor understands friends and family, knowledge of the community and its resources, and changes in appreciation and understanding of natural and human-made beauty.

Building on what we know about learning, we might then want to think of the reasons an individual opts to visit a museum—motivation—as actually being a complex psychological construct assembled from a myriad of sources, including the visitor's prior knowledge and experience with the setting, perceived social relationships and expectations, the social and cultural meaning she or he attributes to the institution, and the individual's personal interests and sense of identity. In this view motivation represents a psychological predisposition that directly relates to all aspects of the museum experience, including learning. In other words, the total visitor experience flows directly from entry motivations, and although it is influenced by the exhibitions and programs encountered in the museum, recent research suggests that this influence is surprisingly less than we had previously assumed.[9]

These ideas converge on a single idea, that learning is strongly influenced by motivation, and an individual's motivation relative to learning and behavior is closely aligned with that individual's sense of self and identity.[10] Every museum visitor is trying to satisfy a particular need on that day, a need with which she or he may or may not be fully conscious. We should not assume that this "search for identity" is some deep, spiritual quest. Although museums may be a setting for finding God or understanding how one's parents influenced one's values, they more typically satisfy more prosaic but equally important needs such as being a place where a parent can support his child's growth and development or a curious individual can indulge her desire to find out more about nature. It is also important to appreciate that although every visitor is truly using the museum experience in order to help satisfy some need, those needs can vary from day to day. In other words, today I can come to your museum to satisfy my interest in Matisse and tomorrow I can come in order to satisfy my need to be a good host for my visiting cousin from Dubuque. Even within the confines of a single visit an individual's identity needs can shift, depending upon what he or she sees or experiences, although our research indicates that for most people, most of the time, identity motivations tend to be stable across a visit.

What does all this mean for the business of museums? It means we can now begin to more deeply and accurately understand what museums actually mean to our public. Most museum professionals have traditionally thought of museums as places for the collection, study, and exhibition of objects and ideas; however, this is not how the public views these institutions. *From a visitor's perspective, museums are best thought of as settings for the expression of personal identity.* Although this is certainly not how visitors would articulate their view of museums, it is how our research and that of others suggests they actually experience it.

This insight is huge! This perspective allows us to deeply understand our visitors; to begin to understand in much more profound ways why a person would visit such an institution, what influences her or his actions inside the museum, and equally important, what she or he is likely to take away from the experience.

VISIT-MOTIVATION AS IDENTITY

With major funding from the U.S. National Science Foundation, John and his colleagues have been applying these ideas to understanding the visitor experience at a range of museums, initially science centers, zoos, and aquariums, but increasingly other types of museums as well. A key breakthrough came when a group of individuals were recontacted and interviewed roughly two years after their visit to one of the permanent exhibitions—*World of Life*—at the California Science Center in Los Angeles. This study was one of a continuing series of investigations at the Science Center as part of the ten years and counting LASER (Los Angeles Science Education Research) project.

Previously, a random sample of roughly two hundred science center visitors had been intensively investigated before, during, and after they visited the *World of Life* exhibition.[11] All of these individuals were asked during their post–*World of Life* visit interview (conducted between November 2000 and April 2001) if they would be willing to be recontacted at some, unspecified later date. Of the 191 visitors who were interviewed after leaving the exhibition, 9 out of 10 (n = 171) volunteered a phone number, an e-mail address, or both. In the summer of 2002 we attempted to recontact a random sample of these individuals with the goal of interviewing 50 individuals. Only 110 of the recontact numbers were still valid; still we ultimately were able to conduct face-to-face interviews with 45 individuals and telephone interviews with an additional 7 persons over the course of the summer/early fall of 2002. Our recontact interviews were conducted in a conversational style and lasted between 40 minutes and 2 hours—on average longer than the original visit to the *World of Life*. The interviews included a wide range of questions, most of which were open-ended. Incorporated into our protocol was an effort to understand, nearly two years after the initial visit, how these individuals made sense of their experience. We were interested in a wide range of possible variables that might help us understand long-term visitor outcomes, one of which was identity.

First, all fifty-two individuals told us that they found the experience very satisfying and beneficial. As we probed more deeply we discovered that these individuals' perceptions of satisfaction, benefit, and even learning could be directly tied to their purpose in attending the science center in the first place. The ways in which the individuals described their identity-related reasons for visiting the California Science Center seemed to fall within five broad categories of *self*, each category actually a cluster of seemingly closely related identities. We named the five identities that emerged *The Explorer, The Facilitator, The Professional/Hobbyist, The Experience Seeker,* and *The Spiritual Pilgrim*.[12]

The Explorer

These individuals said they visited because of curiosity or a general interest in discovering more about the topic/subject matter of the institution. In fact, a number of these visitors self-described themselves as curious people. Several individuals indicated that they visited places like the California Science Center because museums like this reinforced who they are, in essence, their self-image. Comments like, "If you don't try to revisit your knowledge in some way by reading or watching TV or [visiting] museums like this I think you forget a little bit on the educational part and these things are very important." And "The more you are exposed to [science], the more you are going to want to learn and you know hopefully want to strive for more." They either volunteered, or when specifically asked indicated that they did not really care about whether others enjoyed their visit; this visit was about them, first and foremost. As one visitor stated: "Oh sure I was here with my family, but they were on their own. I came because I wanted to see the Science Center, not because of my family." Another said, "I want to go and learn something new too. It's kind of a selfish thing." As with all of these categories, the Explorer group was not a single type but actually a cluster of several closely related types of "selves." For example, Explorers were individuals who identified themselves as science lovers or as learners/discoverers or individuals who said they were curious people.

The Facilitator

In stark contrast to those in the Explorer group, another group of individuals said they were visiting in order to satisfy the needs and desires of someone they cared about other than themselves, in particular, with this group, their children. When asked why they came they would say things like "Science is important for the children." This group included a large number of what we might describe as committed parents who said they liked the Science Center because of its focus on science and its interactivity, making it an enjoyable place for children and their learning. One mother said, "[I] wanted [my daughter] to pick a few things, not many things because she's so young, just focus on a couple of things that we could talk about later." Although they saw this as a valuable experience for their children, a number of these individuals were quick to add, "I wouldn't be here without children" or "I personally would rather go elsewhere." Although most of the people placed in this category self-described themselves as "parents," there were also a couple of individuals who indicated that their purpose in visiting the science center was to please a spouse or boyfriend/girlfriend, and in one case the individual was "hosting" a visiting relative and his family.

The Professional/Hobbyist

This group was related to the Explorer group, but these were not your typical Explorer types. These individuals said they possessed a strong knowledge and interest in the content of the institution and that their primary motivation was not general but specific. Some even said they were more interested in learning about how the information was conveyed rather than in the information per se. Examples of this latter situation were one individual who said, "I'm a science teacher and I always get ideas for how to convey tough concepts by visiting science centers" and another who said, "I'm in the medical field and [the Science Center] does an extremely good job in describing to nonmedical people how our body works and how we process food and turn it into energy [which I use when talking with others]." Another spoke of the desire to learn some specific nuance of the content: "We home school our children and we were studying human development at that time. We used the chick and frog hatching exhibit as part of our lesson for that day. . . . I explained to [the] kids about how the chicks hatched and which eggs would work and which did not." The Professional/Hobbyist individual was visiting with an eye toward enhancing his or her profession, avocation, or hobby.

The Experience Seeker

These individuals, often tourists, were motivated to visit primarily in order to "collect" an experience, so that they could say they've "been there, done that." When probed, many of these individuals indicated that they came in large part in order to fulfill the expectations of others ("My brother-in-law was on my case because I hadn't taken the kids here yet"), or driven by recommendations or opinions of others ("We were on vacation and looking for things to do and the guy at the hotel said, you should go to the California Science Center"). This category also included a variety of different types of selves; the person who said he or she was a tourist, and another who said he or she was the kind of person who likes "fun and exciting" things to do on the weekend. Also there was the individual who was satisfying his brother-in-law's directive and described himself as wanting to make sure he did "good" things on the weekend with his family. When probed further about "good things" he said, "like making sure we see the new movies when they come out, going to Disneyland at least once a year, maybe going to the ballgame, you know, things like that." It is not that people in this group don't remember and even learn things, but the experience is filtered through a recreational lens. For example, one individual said, "I remember things because they [children] thought that was pretty funny. The burping of the body and where it makes sounds as the food goes up and down and stuff like that, all the little gross sounds, they loved that."

The Spiritual Pilgrim

Although relatively scarce in our Science Center visitor population, there were individuals who visited in order to reflect, rejuvenate, or generally just bask in the wonder of the place. (*Note:* This group is likely more abundant in other types of museums, for example, art museums and aquariums.) In the case of the Science Center, these were individuals who expressed an awe or reverence for the subject matter or setting: "The Science Center is a place for introspection, a place for 'science.'" Only one individual in our sample fell specifically in this category; he felt that going to the Science Center enabled him to satisfy a need to be "surrounded by science"; for him, he was enacting a reverential self.

When we analyzed our data, we found that these categories were actually predictive of various kinds of learning. We were able to take these fifty-two individuals and place them into one of these five categories, or some combination of the categories. Within this particular group of individuals, virtually all fell into one of three categories—they visited the Science Center primarily because of their desire to satisfy their *Explorer* self; they visited based upon their desire to satisfy their *Facilitator* self (primarily in the role of parent); or they visited for some combination of these two. As indicated above, a few individuals fell into the remaining three categories, or combinations of these, but given the small sample size we were dealing with we excluded these individuals from further analysis. We then compared the changes in each of these group's understanding and knowledge of life science concepts over time (preexhibition, immediately postexhibition, and eighteen to twenty-three months later). Figure 5.1 shows that individual's knowledge of life science in the three groups—*Explorer, Facilitator,* or the combination of *Explorer* and *Facilitator*—changed over time in different ways. As can be seen, there was little if any difference between these three populations either prior to the visit or immediately following the visit, but after nearly two years had elapsed, significant differences emerged in the three populations' knowledge of the life sciences. Although some of the positive learning effects of the visit persisted among the visitors who were largely motivated to visit in order to provide a quality experience for someone in their family (e.g., their children, spouse, or close friend), these individuals showed significant decline in their life science knowledge over time. By contrast, those individuals who visited primarily, or at least in part, for the purpose of satisfying their own personal learning needs and curiosity maintained the life science knowledge they gained over the long term. This data strongly supports the idea that visitors' motivations for visiting and their perception of self influence how and what visitors learn from museums, particularly in the long term.

But this wasn't the only learning that was influenced by an individual's identity-related entry motivation. Early in the interview each individual was asked to respond to a range of questions about the social dynamics of his or

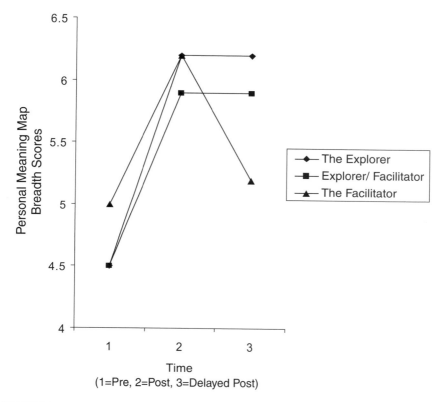

FIGURE 5.1
Change in biology understanding (as measured by changes in Personal Meaning Mapping "Breadth" scores) by self and time.

her experience. By contrast with the above results, when asked to recall details of their visit, the individuals we categorized as falling within the Facilitator or combination *Explorer/Facilitator* categories were noticeably better at providing such details than were *Explorer* individuals. In fact, many of those in the *Explorer* group found it extremely difficult to talk about the social companions with whom they had visited. By contrast, the socially motivated individuals could not only accurately recall who they were with, but spontaneously described the benefits of the visit almost totally from the perspective of the other individuals, both at the time of the visit and subsequently. In other words,

Facilitator and *Explorer/Facilitator* individuals exhibited markedly superior social learning as compared with *Explorer* individuals. These findings represent just two of several similar relationships we were able to discover using self as a construct.[13]

Around the same time as these findings were emerging from the California Science Center study we were also finding similar relationships between an individual's entry motivations and exiting learning in a study we conducted at two museums in Australia—Powerhouse Museum, Sydney, and Scitech Science Centre, Perth.[14] In the Australian study, a hundred visitors to each of these two institutions were randomly interviewed as they entered the museum, and at the end of their visit; a subset of visitors were interviewed again four to eight months later. The focus of the study was on investigating the short- and long-term impacts of exhibit interactives on visitor learning. As we analyzed the data we consistently found that visitors' specific expectations for what they would learn/do in the museum or science center tended to relate directly and predictably to the outcomes they self-reported deriving from their experiences. The following examples of Powerhouse Museum visitors' pre- and immediate postvisit interviews illustrate this general trend:

> Previsit Interview: *This is a place to think about history and the future. People can learn [about] what has happened in the past and then can learn how to change the future. That's very important.*
>
> Postvisit Interview: *The [museum] provided information on the big issue, but no one ever told me what was going to happen, or when. I did learn, for example, that it takes thirty years for the effect of banning CFCs to take effect. Thus by 2010 . . .*
>
> Previsit Interview: *This is a place for education for the children, enjoyment, great fun.*
>
> Postvisit Interview: *My daughter tried doing it; it did not work. It was great fun, though. Lots of fun.*
>
> Previsit Interview: *It is a place to get information. Learning about concepts you don't really know about.*
>
> Postvisit Interview: *One of [the] things I learned was that I had a misconception about physics.*

We also discovered that visitors' self-reported understandings of their experience shifted over time (immediate postexperience interviews compared with follow-up telephone interviews), but they still remained consistent with their initial expectations. After several months' delay, visitors tended to forget the specific things they had "learned" during their visit, replacing those memories with a more conceptual and "big picture" recollection—what we called "perspective and awareness." Individuals who had said they expected their experience to be primarily social, however, months later reflected on the social nature of their experience; people who had expected their experience to be primarily about discovering new things, now reflected on the new things they had discovered.

Encouraged by these results we next attempted to determine whether this typology of identity types could be used to describe the motivations of visitors utilizing other types of museums. Again with support from the National Science Foundation, in the spring and summer of 2004 we collected data from 3,115 individuals at ten aquariums and zoos from across the United States. The results indicated that visitors to aquariums and zoos can indeed be validly and reliably categorized as being motivated to visit based on one or more of these same five categories of self. With a sufficiently large sample of visitors, all five categories of self were not only present but well represented.[15] Equally important, these five categories were able to capture the full range of reasons visitors gave for visiting. As was found with California Science Center visitors, it was common for zoo and aquarium visitors to fall within more than a single category, in other words, to have multiple motivations for visiting. The vast majority of visitors, roughly 90 percent, were characterized as having some combination of these five motivations, but typically one or two dominated. We also saw indications that these dominant motivations created a lens through which the entire museum visit was experienced. Thus, based on this data, fifteen identity categories—the five main categories and ten combinations of primary and secondary motivations—appear to describe the identity needs of most museum visitors. Although other variables in addition to self were also explored, none seemed to equally predict both entry motivation and self-reported exit learning.[16]

We are currently using this construct to investigate intensively the behavior and learning of close to a thousand additional individuals visiting four different U.S. zoos and aquariums and have plans to extend this research to both history and art museums. It is our belief that this way of categorizing visitors will significantly improve our understanding of how visitors behave and learn. The long-term payoff is not just academic research. As suggested earlier, this line of research allows us to rethink what we offer our public and what it will take to satisfy them.

MEETING THE NEEDS OF OUR PUBLIC

So going back to the series of questions posed at the beginning of this chapter, this new way of thinking about museum visitors provides some very concrete ways to approach and answer these fundamental questions:

- Why do your visitors come and what do they hope to get out of their experience?
- What makes your visitors do the things they do?
- Why do some visitors stay as long or as short a time as they do?
- What is the one thing you are not providing your various publics today that they are secretly longing for?
- What percentage of your public considers you an irreplaceable resource?
- How could a new, or existing, competitor take away your audience?
- What are two things about your institution that you cannot, under any circumstances, change?

The ideas presented above suggest that all people visit museums with predetermined motivations for visiting the museum, motivations of which they may be only weakly conscious. These motivations strongly influence how they experience the museum, how they behave, their satisfaction with the experience, and the long-term memories and understandings they derive from their visit. This is true whether the visitor enters as an Explorer, Facilitator, Professionals/Hobbyist, Experience Seeker, Spiritual Pilgrim, or some combination of one or more of these. Each of these types will experience the museum very differently, each will have different needs and expectations for the visit, and each will leave with different memories and outcomes. The museum can support and facilitate these experiences or it can ignore or hinder them. From a business point of view, which of these types of visitors does your museum primarily attract? Is this the identity type you can best serve or most want to serve? How do you facilitate/hinder the satisfaction of these motivation types?

For example, if you are an institution that attracts a large percentage of teachers with school groups or families with children, as do most science centers, natural history museums, zoos, aquariums, and children's museums, you are likely to have a disproportionate number of Facilitators among your adult visitors. What does it take to make a Facilitator happy? Obviously, providing great experiences for children seems important, but is that enough? Actually, no, a great experience for children is only one part of what brought the parent/grandparent/chaperone to the museum, but it is not what is totally satisfying. Remember, we're talking about identity here. What will make Facilitators happy is the affirmation that they have been successful in their role as a facilitator. In other words, they need to get feedback that the experience was truly a special and beneficial one for their children, and ideally they want to get recognition for this. Although teachers and parents are expected to be altruistic toward their children, most teachers and certainly most parents appreciate receiving recognition for their altruism. Occasionally, but not often, that recognition comes from the children. But shouldn't the museum itself provide that recognition? The answer is an emphatic *yes*, but rarely does this happen at most museums. How many museums *explicitly* thank people for coming, for fulfilling their identity needs? For example, every museum that serves a large number of Facilitators should go out of their way to thank Facilitators as they are leaving for being such good Facilitators. In the case of teacher and parent Facilitators, the museum should be thanking them for being such good teachers/parents today, telling them that their children not only had a good time but learned a lot. Do you think that will encourage the teacher/parent to come back again? You bet it will!

As Jeff Patchen at The Children's Museum understood, however, many parents who come to places like museums are equally coming for themselves. It is really about child *and* adult learning. Therefore, the experience needs to not merely be "good for children" but needs to be good for adults too. In other words, it needs to satisfy the adult's desire to be both a Facilitator and an Explorer. As the quotes at the beginning of this chapter so powerfully show, parents found it satisfying that they, too, could learn from the experience. This kind of satisfaction is fundamental for sustaining repeat visits. Remember that even at such family-centered institutions as zoos and aquariums, only a very small percentage of visitors (12 percent) were coming only for a single moti-vation, for example, to be good parents. The vast majority of adults were there for several reasons, most commonly because they both enjoyed animals/fish and because they wanted to be good parents.

Every museum likely possesses a unique profile of visitor identities—a sub-set of the fifteen combinations that predominates. Although the profile may vary somewhat from season to season, and perhaps even from year to year, there is likely an underlying stability. A museum whose visitors are almost exclusively Facilitators and Explorers, for example, would want to design the look and feel of their museum's experiences quite differently from a museum whose visitor profile was made up of mostly Spiritual Pilgrims and Experience Seekers. Understanding your museum's visitor profile should allow you to cus-tomize your visitor experiences to meet your visitors' needs, but only if you can successfully match each visitor's specific experience with her or his specific personal motivational identity-needs. To suggest this is a nontrivial task is not an understatement. The Children's Museum example represents a step in the right direction. The hypothetical Alabaster Natural History Museum example provided at the beginning of this book represents a bigger step in this direc-tion. Suffice it to say, at the present our abilities to truly customize experiences for our visitors is still in its infancy.

REACHING AUDIENCES NEW AND OLD

Some combination of the five identity-related motivations described in this chapter represents the visiting motivations and needs of virtually all members of the museum-going public and probably most other free-choice learning organizations as well. These are the needs of people who currently visit muse-ums and they are arguably the needs of people who currently do not visit museums. The fact that some people do not go to museums does not mean they do not have these same needs or that they would not derive great satis-faction from going if they knew that the museum could satisfy those needs. Non-museum-going results from a mismatch in either expectations, delivery, or both. We believe that historically far too much emphasis has been placed on the "delivery" side of the equation rather than on the "expectation" side.

Most museums are committed to broadening their audiences, reaching out to traditionally underserved groups. Although in part this desire stems from altruism, most museum professionals understand this is not really just a nicety, but actually essential to the long-term survival of museums. Given the demo-graphic shifts described in the previous chapter, fewer and fewer people will fall within the traditional target audience of museums; more and more will fall within the category of "traditionally underserved." As emphasized at the be-ginning of this chapter, however, these historical demographic correlations were and will become increasingly useless in predicting who will or will not come to museums. More important will be two factors: (1) historical patterns of visita-tion, which work against museums since individuals from historically underrep-resented groups grow up without a museum-going tradition;[17] and (2) the ability of museums to communicate to new audiences that they can meet their needs.

We strongly believe that it is in this latter area that both the greatest oppor-tunities and the greatest challenges for broadening audiences reside. Whether rich or poor, black, brown, white, or yellow, long-time resident or recent immi-grant, all people possess similar needs. All people are curious about the world, all have loved ones they care about, all seek new experiences, all have interests and avocations, all desire escape from the stresses of the everyday world. Not all people, however, view museums as places that can satisfy those needs, and arguably, museums do not represent the best place for all people to in fact sat-isfy those needs. But certainly, there are many more people who could find museums satisfying to their identity-needs than currently avail themselves of museums. And certainly, there are many more things museums could be doing to ensure that the exhibitions and programs they offer afford experiences that would support the needs of audiences not traditionally visiting.

Museums cannot be all things to all people and should not try to be. But museums can be more things to more people than they currently are. We believe that it should be possible to significantly expand museum audiences by focusing on the key clusters of identities the museum wishes to support and then figuring out how to communicate specifically to segments of the traditionally under-served community that the museum can and will help them satisfy those iden-tity needs. It may require different language, different strategies for commun-icating and staying in touch with audiences, perhaps even variations in how exhibitions and programs are presented, but the underlying needs that the museum experience satisfies should not be different with different audiences. Successful outreach programs around the country have found this to be true. For example, when the Virginia Museum of Fine Arts sought to reach out to the African American community of Richmond, they found that love of art was not just a "white" thing. They discovered that Richmond's large African American population was interested in all kinds of art, not just African art. They also found out that blacks did not typically think of the Virginia Museum of Fine Arts as the place where they and, most important, their children could go to see and experience art. Among the key factors that helped to break down the long-standing barriers to increased African American use of the Virginia Museum of Fine Arts was reaching out to parents and families by creating opportunities and experiences that supported their children's learning about art; parents came to see their children perform and to support their children's art education experiences. Over time, more and more African American families came to see the museum as a good place to visit as a family and a good place to view interesting art. Over time, more and more African American adults came to see the museum as a place where they could satisfy both their Facilitator and their Explorer identities.[18] Over time, African Americans in Richmond came to see the Virginia Museum of Fine Arts as a place that could make a difference in their lives.

Making a Difference

The museum business model of tomorrow must begin by considering the good it wishes to create for some reasonable segment of the public. As one of the most astute observers of museums, the late Stephen Weil, said, "the establishment and operation of a museum is not an end in itself but is only justifiable by the museum's dedication to one or more public purposes. . . . Museums matter only to the extent that they are perceived to provide the communities they serve with something of value beyond their own mere existence."[19]

This view was also succinctly summarized by Harold Skramstad when he noted that the old museum mission of collecting, preserving, and exhibiting has yielded to a new, more concise question, "so what?"

> My point is to suggest that the mission statement of most museums, which often states, "Our mission is to collect, preserve and interpret fill-in-the-blank," will no longer do. Such mission statements do not answer the vital question "So what?" Increasingly, the mission statement of a museum, its essential statement of "value added," is going to have to contain not only a concise and clear statement of what the museum does, but a description of the outcome of its actions and a sense of the value that this outcome has in the larger work of the community.[20]

Successful museums will create business models that are designed to provide a specific public with something of worth that they desire and are willing to support financially. There are many ways to generate revenues, but all must ultimately fulfill the real needs of real people, and often the multiple needs of multiple sets of people. In sum, the key to being able to really meet the needs of your public is to understand deeply and specifically who your visitors are and why they are seeking out your museum. This speaks again to the need for greater personalization and customization. Satisfied visitors stay longer, come more frequently, and tell others that they, too, should visit. The more tightly aligned the experience is with individuals' own fundamental needs, the more profoundly and intensely satisfied they will be. This is not just marketing rhetoric. Our research would suggest that any movement toward customization based upon motivation and identity will help ensure that the experiences your public has lead to a significantly enhanced perception of value. The better you understand your visitors the more likely it will be that you will know why people come to you, why they do what they do in your museum, why they stay, what you are currently not providing people who visit your museum, and, most important, why those that come value you. As vitally important as it is to understand the needs and desires of your publics, however, answering these questions alone will not suffice to create a successful business model. After all, it takes two to tango—your business is a relationship, an intricate dance between your institution and your publics.

It is just as important that you also know something about your own organization; you need to deeply understand why you are unique. In other words, what is special and irreplaceable about your museum? How are you similar to, as well as different from, the other organizations in your community? What can you do better than anyone else? Answering these latter questions is not more important than understanding your audience, but it certainly is not less important either. Creating a successful business model, one that specifically works for your institution, requires knowing your audience and knowing yourself. Each museum possesses a unique set of assets, and these assets are what attracts and ultimately forms the foundation of public satisfaction.

DISCUSSION QUESTIONS

- Who currently uses your institution and why? Who does not and why not?
- What is the single greatest resource you provide your public? Who else in your community offers the same or a similar resource?
- What percentage of your current users consider you an irreplaceable resource? What would it take to double that percentage?

NOTES

Epigraph: M. Treacy and F. Wiersema, *The Discipline of Market Leaders.* (New York: Basic Books, 1995), 1.

1. L. Dierking, V. Kaul, and J. Stein, *DINOSPHERE: Now You're In Their World,* summative evaluation report (Annapolis, MD: Institute for Learning Innovation, 2005).

2. Pseudonym.

3. Dierking, Kaul, and Stein, *DINOSPHERE.*

4. Treacy and Wiersema, *Discipline of Market Leaders.*

5. See review by J. H. Falk, Visitors: Who does, who doesn't, and why, *Museum News* 77, no. 2 (1998): 38–43.

6. J. H. Falk, Factors influencing African American leisure time utilization of museums, *Journal of Leisure Research Learning* 27, no. 1 (1995): 41–60; J. H. Falk and L. M. Adelman, Investigating the impact of prior knowledge, experience and interest on aquarium visitor learning, *Journal of Research in Science Teaching* 40, no. 2 (2003): 163–176; J. H. Falk and M. Storksdieck, Using the *Contextual Model of Learning* to understand visitor learning from a science center exhibition, *Science Education* 89 (2005): 744–778.

7. For example, Falk, Visitors; J. H. Falk and L. D. Dierking, *The Museum Experience* (Washington, DC: Whalesback Books, 1992); L. Gore, M. Mahnken, J. Norstrom, and D. Walls, *A profile of the visitors: The Dallas Museum of Natural History,* unpublished manuscript, University of Dallas, Irving, TX, 1980; N. H. Graburn, The museum and the visitor experience, in *The visitor and the museum,* 5–32, prepared for the 72nd annual conference of the American Association of Museums, Seattle, WA, 1977; M. Hood, Staying away: Why people choose not to visit museums, *Museum News* 61, no. 4 (1983): 50–57; N. Merriman, *Beyond the Glass Case* (Leicester, UK: Leicester University Press, 1991); R. S. Miles, Museum audiences, *The International Journal of Museum Management and Curatorship* 5 (1986): 73–80; T. Moussouri, *Family agendas and family learning in hands-on museums* (unpublished doctoral dissertation, University of Leicester, 1997); J. Packer and R. Ballantyne, Motivational factors and the visitor experience: A comparison of three sites, *Curator* 45 (2002): 183–198; S. G. Paris and M. Mercer, Finding self in objects: Identity exploration in museums, in *Learning Conversations in Museums,* ed. G. Leinhardt, K. Crowley, and K. Knutson, 401–423 (Mahwah, NJ: Lawrence Erlbaum & Associates, 2002); A. J. Pekarik, Z. D. Doering, and D. A. Karns, Exploring satisfying experiences in museums, *Curator* 42 (1999): 152–173;

R. Prentice, A. Davies, and A. Beeho, Seeking generic motivations for visiting and not visiting museums and like cultural attractions, *Museum Management and Curatorship* 6, no. 1 (1997): 45–70; S. Rosenfeld, *Informal education in zoos: Naturalistic studies of family groups* (unpublished doctoral dissertation, University of California, Berkeley, 1980); M. Wells and R. J. Loomis, A taxonomy of museum opportunities—adapting a model from natural resource management, *Curator* 41 (1998): 254–264.

8. Cf. Falk and Dierking, *The Museum Experience*; also J. H. Falk, Assessing the impact of museums, *Curator* 43, no. 1 (2000): 5–7; J. H. Falk, T. Moussouri, and D. Coulson, The effect of visitors' agendas on museum learning, *Curator* 41, no. 2 (1998): 106–120.

9. Falk and Storksdieck, Using the *Contextual Model of Learning*.

10. J. Falk, The impact of visit motivation on learning: Using identity as a construct to understand the visitor experience. *Curator* 49, no. 2 (2006): 151–166.

11. Falk and Storksdieck, Using the *Contextual Model of Learning*.

12. Falk, An identity-centered approach to understanding museum learning.

13. M. Storksdieck and J. H. Falk, An investigation of the long-term impact of a science center visit experience, *Science Education* (in prep).

14. J. H. Falk, C. Scott, L. D. Dierking, L. J. Rennie, and M. Cohen Jones, Interactives and visitor learning, *Curator* 47, no. 2 (2004): 171–198.

15. J. Heimlich, J. Falk, K. Bronnenkant, and J. Baralge, *Segmenting Visitors to Zoos and Aquariums by Self*, technical report (Annapolis, MD: Institute for Learning Innovation, 2005).

16. Ibid.

17. For example, Falk, Factors influencing African American leisure time utilization of museums.

18. L. D. Dierking and M. Adams, *Spirit of the Motherland Exhibition: Summative Evaluation* (Annapolis, MD: Science Learning, Inc., 1996).

19. S. E. Weil, *Making Museums Matter* (Washington, DC: Smithsonian Institution Press, 2002), 4–5.

20. Harold K. Skramstad, Changing public expectations of museums, in *Museums for the New Millennium*, ed. S. E. Weil (Washington, DC: Smithsonian Institution Press, 1998), 38.

6

Understanding What's Important

The most visible differences between the corporation of the future and its present day counterpart will not be the products they make or the equipment they use—but who will be working, how they will be working, why they will be working, and what work will mean to them.
—Robert D. Haas

One of the largest outdoor history museums in the country, Old Sturbridge Village (OSV), knows that it cannot continue to deliver the same living history experience that has distinguished it for more than fifty years. Like other institutions of its kind, the Village has documented declining attendance for more than fifteen years. In fact, a graph of attendance patterns, laid on top of that of another New England living history attraction, reveals an almost identical pattern, a clear sign that the once-popular model is no longer attracting a twenty-first century audience. In business terms, the product, living history, appears to have reached the end of its life cycle. The Village's business model has relied heavily on earned income, all of which is related to attendance. A decline in visitors means lower shop sales, food sales, and lodging, accelerating the downward financial spiral. The Village was facing a serious financial crisis when Beverly Sheppard arrived as the new president and CEO in 2002. The situation worsened in the following months as New England struggled with a lingering recession, the ongoing dearth in tourism following September 11, and a year of brutal weather—always an issue for outdoor attractions.

Despite the attendance decline and its resulting financial impact, OSV continues as a much-revered place in the minds of many of its members and long-time visitors; its leadership in formal education has been a hallmark of its work. The Village still serves as many as a hundred thousand school students a year and is known for the excellence of its teacher workshops. A recent series of jokes, spread through e-mail, includes the line: "You know you are from Massachusetts if you visited Old Sturbridge Village in the fifth grade." The Village is not only part of the lore of the region, it is also vital to the economic development of the town of Sturbridge, a cornerstone of Massachusetts tourism, and a site of enormous beauty, authenticity, scholarship, and expertise. The time period it interprets, 1790–1840, has particular resonance for today's world, if presented in new ways. Forging a fresh direction for Old Sturbridge Village, along with building a solid business model was essential to OSV and its community, plus it would benefit the larger community of living history sites nationwide.

Village leadership responded with a two-part approach—a series of quick changes, referred to internally as "triage," and a comprehensive study to guide long-term change. The lessons Beverly and her staff are learning from both can translate into useful guidelines for undertaking massive institutional change. Two core sets of questions have grounded the initial process:

- Who are OSV's core audiences today, why do they continue to come, and how can they become partners in a search for new answers?
- What are the inviolable assets and strengths that define Old Sturbridge Village? In particular, how can the institution realign its key assets—human and financial—to strengthen its current position?

Triage

In a time of crisis, finding quick answers to such important questions may seem impossible, but even the "triage" phase needed to be based on reality. A thorough analysis of attendance data, studied through many different lenses, identified two distinct and different trends for OSV: (1) a growing audience of families with young children; and (2) a growing audience of visitors living within an immediate twenty-mile radius. This information alone provided a starting point for some quick additions—all designed to encourage repeat visitation of these emerging audiences and attract others like them. An audit of

OSV's "family friendliness" identified some deficiencies that could be relatively easily remedied. Within weeks, by the all-important summer months, numerous low-tech, hands-on activities were added to the Village experience, greatly augmenting opportunities for children's free play. The Village animals were repositioned to afford up-close encounters. Old-fashioned baseball games were organized on the Common for visitor participation and an ice skating rink was established for wintertime fun. Longstanding holiday celebrations, like the Fourth of July, were embellished with more family activities, adding picnic lunches, a host of participatory games, and activities inviting visitor reflections on the meaning of the day, today and in the early nineteenth century. As simple as these additions seem, they conveyed an immediate feeling of new liveliness and a welcoming atmosphere—images that could be easily marketed within the neighboring towns.

As the inevitable staff layoffs and cutbacks took place, "triage" took on new meaning. Without a doubt, the hardest work in this early stage was critically reexamining the institution's core assets—its staff, collections, property, and intellectual property—to see what needed to stay, what needed to go, and what needed to be redefined or repurposed. Old Sturbridge Village had relied exclusively on live interpreters as the source of visitor information about the Village period. Now, with fewer interpreters than ever, it became necessary to offer a wider array of learning resources—from signage to hands-on activities to a judicious introduction of technology. Not only was the change necessary to solve staffing reductions, it also was vital to address the limitations of a "one size fits all" approach to interpretation. Once again, need produced many learning opportunities. Each addition became a "test case"—using staff observations and visitor interviews to gauge reactions. The placement and presentation of signage has been gradually undertaken to offer more visitor information. Hands-on additions, such as a second potter's wheel (for supervised visitor use) in the Village pottery, invite more direct visitor engagement. Technology as a teaching medium in the historic Village is being carefully tested. The results are encouraging. Few visitors find the signage intrusive. A video placed in an unused household buttery has led to suggestions for more videos of that kind, and hands-on activities are clearly welcome. These small steps are creating a sense of "things happening" and are also testing the efficacy of new directions.

Long-Range Strategic Planning

The big ideas for the Village's future, however, are emerging through concurrent long-range strategic planning. The process has invited many voices—from member surveys to community focus groups. Every staff member (there are over 340) has been invited to participate and a special board/staff/overseer steering committee has met for more than a year. Each board member serves on at least one planning committee, undertaking intensive study of topics ranging from the supporting businesses within OSV to its broad campus needs.

From the outset, it was agreed that strategic planning would be built on these four inviolable Village assets:

Subject Expertise: OSV is probably the world's expert on early nineteenth-century rural New England history—an expertise reflected in its remarkably recreated Village setting, the depth and variety of its collections (archives and artifacts), and the extensive scholarly research that supports it all.

Educational Excellence: OSV enjoys a long history of educational excellence focused on schools—highly regarded for its early leadership in school/museum partnerships, the quality of its teacher education, and the deep penetration into schools throughout the region.

Family Appeal: OSV's audience patterns favor family audiences, demonstrating growth and expertise in supporting intergenerational learning and offering facilities appropriate for all ages.

Existing Campus: OSV's campus offers many assets: a range of buildings that can be repurposed in their use; ideal location at the juncture of two of Massachusetts's busiest highways; and a natural setting that presents a variety of landscape features.

A new institutional mission and vision were essential to begin the planning process. If today's visitors do not find the Village story relevant to their lives, then a continued focus on the content of early nineteenth-century history no longer makes sense. The staff wrestled with questions of relevance. How can the lens of New England rural history connect visitors to a deeper interest in history? How can it become meaningful in their lives? How can it be made appealing and inviting to an intergenerational audience?

Matching the Village assets with these needs and with a broader under-standing of today's world has led to a bold new vision for the institution and a reconfiguration of its assets. The Village is now moving toward a comprehen-sive new concept. It will become the Sturbridge Village History Experience, incorporating several different components, one of which is "Old Sturbridge Village." Without losing its long established identity as an outdoor living his-tory site, the Village will now become a complex of "museums" and learning facilities, each offering a different pathway to historic understanding across the lifespan. Each can be visited alone or in combination with any of the others, offering many different ways to match price with experience. Three will be completely "weatherproof," expanding the opportunities for site visits year round. The themes and content of each will be interrelated, providing the potential for many different thematic tours that link across all five components.

As envisioned, the Sturbridge Village History Experience will take a num-ber of years to complete in its entirety. Its financial success is still an unknown, but with careful evaluation of each phase and continued close conversations with the public, the Village staff and board believe they are moving in a strong direction. Focusing OSV's future around a center for lifelong learning is the institution's best bet for keeping the Village vibrant in the years ahead.

KNOWLEDGE AGE ASSETS

Every museum in the land is blessed with assets that define the institution and make it unique. Historically, museums have considered their primary assets to be the Industrial Age triumvirate of land, capital, and labor. In museum "speak" we could equate "land" with a museum's building, land, and, most important, its collections. The museum's "capital" was assembled through a few primary channels—endowment (assuming it was fortunate enough to have one), generous gifts from patrons, or governmental support. Labor, the least important of these resources in the old museum model, was of course represented by staff; a staff member's value was predicated on how central she or he was to the care and maintenance of the collection. In the Knowledge Age, these priorities have become totally reversed. The greatest asset any museum possesses in the twenty-first century is its human resources—staff, volunteers, trustees—and the knowledge these humans possess. Collections today are still valuable, but only because of the intellectual content they represent, the stories they can tell. Without knowledgeable staff capable of revealing those stories, most collections are only partially optimized. Finally, an additional internal asset has emerged in recent years that also is fundamental to the success of a museum, the very abstract factor called institutional identity, or brand.

As recently as 1982, a Brookings Institute study determined that tangible assets (e.g., buildings, machinery, capital) represented 62 percent of the market value of the average company. Ten years later, those same assets represented only 38 percent of market value, and by century's end they amounted to only about 15 percent of the average company's market value.[1] Human resources, intellectual resources, and brand are the new asset "triumvirate" of the Knowledge Age. These assets formed the foundation of Old Sturbridge Village's turnaround; these were the assets that could and needed to be most critically realigned in service to OSV's new business model. As we'll see in the following chapters, other assets are also important, but these three represent the foundation of any successful twenty-first-century business model.

HUMAN RESOURCES

Recently, a cross-section of staff at a well-known institution met to begin shaping a new interpretive plan. They were curators, educators, researchers, visitor services staff, the director of development, and the director. They opened the conversation by sharing stories of memorable museum experiences in their own lives. From childhood memories came stunning descriptions of place, feeling, and wonder. The stories quickly moved to moments of revelation, conversations recalled, and the sparks that lit lifelong interests. For a brief time, they set aside their different museum roles to share in a common passion—a deep love for the institutions they serve.

One researcher talked about the wonder of seeing the enormous airplanes hung from the ceiling of Chicago's Museum of Science and Industry, connecting them to his uncles' stories of World War II. Another described a visit to an unfurnished historic house where a talented guide helped her "see" the house through the remnants of its past. Many noted how their visits were brought to life through the skills of staff or volunteer facilitators.

They composed lists of words that flowed through their memories—*awe* was a consistent one, *discovery* another. They agreed that their personal excitement grew from the recognition that museums are not passive storehouses of objects, but places where personal experiences and insights are created. The exercise was an important reminder that, whatever else their jobs entailed, staff, too, are museum visitors.

In museums, we often talk about our stakeholders—usually quite abstractly, as if they are the "others." We think in terms of the parents and children, the researchers and scholars, the teachers and classrooms, all who come through our doors. In fact, our stakeholders include an even more familiar group. They are all of us as well—staff, volunteers, and board members. We are all part of the dramatically changing world that is building our new museum paradigm. Our ability to find new ways to work together and shift into new models is critical to the future of museums. Successful change really must begin with us.

Staff

Most of us begin working in museums because we believe in the work, because something in museums moves us, because we can see them continuing to make a difference in the world. We translate this conviction into a myriad of roles, defining ourselves by our individual set of functions—curator, registrar, administrator, educator, marketer, and fundraiser, among others. We quickly divide into areas of special interests, skills, and frameworks. Each has its own expertise—and traditionally an unspoken hierarchy—and we've been known to protect our professional turf quite fiercely. The battlegrounds between curators and educators are legendary; each has been quite eloquent in defending divergent perspectives. Curators have been called the high priests of museum culture, and educators have been accused of "dumbing down" the scholar's work. Marketing specialists are treated with ambivalence by both, accused of violating the sanctity of museums by bringing the "sordid" trappings of a consumer society inside our walls. Yet, it would seem that all begin their work with a strong belief in the mission of museums.

A museum staff is an assembly of talents and responsibilities. Its composition and structure has changed as the museum's mission has turned outward and the business of running a museum has grown exponentially more complex. Finding staff with experience and talents that transcend the classical museum roles of curator, registrar, conservator, and even educator is challenging. With a growing emphasis on building connections to the outside world, museums require people with whole new sets of skills, both individually and collectively. Like most parts of our Knowledge Age society, the business of museums has become increasingly complex, resulting in a greater emphasis on the work of teams rather than individuals.

Today's museums need individuals with expertise in research and visitor studies, community facilitation, tourism, group tours, volunteer coordination, and any number of fundraising roles. The growth of such auxiliary audience amenities (and revenue producers) as museum shops, food service facilities, and rental properties require retail and sales expertise in businesses that are very different from classic museum work, but also different than ordinary retail and food service. Also needed are a variety of information technology experts, some to develop and manage various database systems, others to design websites and media-based learning experiences, and still others to support the digitization of collections and the management of digital files. Finally, many museums are now hiring outreach staff, work that requires special talents for mentoring, translating, facilitating, and building trust. It means going where the people are, at the times convenient to them, which may mean places other than the museum. All of these represent major shifts away from the academically centered training that leads most people into this business, and these shifts will only be effective to the extent that the whole institution is committed to the process. Bringing new voices into the museum means accepting multiple kinds of authenticity and affirming and acknowledging the community's sense of self and expertise. This is a fundamental shift in museum thinking.

Many directors have found such staff in unexpected places, often within their partnering community organizations. For example, community outreach specialists require a very special set of experiences and aptitudes. They must have attitudes of openness and sensitivity and a talent for organization and facilitation. Although existing museum staff members are often sensitive and understanding of cultural differences—qualities necessary in this work—the creation of trust may require someone from outside the museum, someone who comes from the community itself. In one instance, a museum sought to develop learning experiences for the children of migrant workers. A wide range of social services had been established to support these workers, offering potential partners. Since most of the migrant families spoke Spanish, the museum looked toward its bilingual staff to help organize the project. When the museum educator noted that she was quite fluent in Spanish and felt comfortable working with the organizations and the family members, she was soundly contradicted by a member of the community. "It is not just language," the community member said. "It's the gestures, the emphasis, the idioms, the slang, the inside jokes, the relationships among the people"—none of which the museum staffer could possible know from her academic training. "No," the community told the museum, "the project requires someone of the people themselves."

The most likely place to find "someone of the people" in today's museum is on the front lines—receptionists, guards, cloak room clerks, sales staff, volunteer docents, gallery teachers, shop and food service staff. These are the individuals most directly dealing with the museum's visitor experience; they are also likely to be the lowest paid and least trained. In the bottom-up, customer-first world of the twenty-first century, this historic practice will need to be seriously rethought. Front-line staff need to be thoroughly trained in customer service, they also need to be well versed in the goals and content of exhibits, the time and place of activities, and the museum's mission. Front-line staff should not just be the beneficiaries of such "training" but they too should be placed in the role of trainers. They are often the most astute at understanding and predicting visitor needs and should, therefore be integral, contributing to all project teams. A warm greeting, a thoughtful answer, helpful advice, all can set the tone for an individual's visit success. The following example illustrates just how important quality front-line staff can be.

Alice, a woman in her eighties who frequently walked the museum gardens, arrived at the site with her granddaughter. She looked forward to the friendly greeting from the museum staff that always made her feel at home. That day, a new staff member, Jan, was at the desk. When she asked to see Alice's membership card, Alice was deeply offended. Fortunately, Jan was not only well-trained in customer service, she was also committed to the museum's goal of making each visitor feel welcome. She quickly apologized and then kept an eye out for Alice's return. When she saw Alice preparing to leave, Jan stepped from behind the desk, introduced herself, and spent a few moments learning about Alice and her family. She was on hand for the next visit as well, with a warm and personal greeting. Imagine what a difference Jan's attentiveness made to Alice and her family and their attitude toward the museum.

Understanding good customer service is not necessarily a given. Some people come by it naturally as a part of their outlook on life. But everyone can learn to be more attentive and training like this should be a part of the professional development of *all* staff. Teaching customer service is also a practical and direct way to demonstrate good team learning. Everyone in the process is focused on a single goal, that of making each visitor's experience as thoroughly positive as possible. A warm welcome can be genuinely offered and individually delivered. Knowing how to speak to children or anticipate the needs of older visitors is part of the package. Planning for efficient processes, whether issuing tickets or taking food orders, is a sign of caring. It does not take that much extra effort to train staff to be able to identify the characteristics of groups so that they can tailor an orientation to the specific nature and needs of each group that visits, whether it involves young children or adult members. Tailoring the directions and information to meet individual needs yields tremendous benefits far beyond the extra intellectual investment that it requires.

Similarly, caring for the cleanliness and convenience of facilities, the clarity of wayfinding aids, and the logistics of programming make huge differences in the way an institution is perceived by the public. Such small details are direct statements about the institution's attitude toward its visitors; all dramatically influence the likelihood that a visitor will leave feeling positively about the museum, and will choose to return and encourage others to also visit.

There are also ways to build such details into museum operations. For example, some customer service training programs urge that all staff be empowered to offer a preselected set of "consolations" to unhappy guests without going through the cumbersome or tedious process of seeking out a manager and getting permission. In this way, a front desk clerk can quickly refund money to a disgruntled visitor or a waitress can offer a free dessert, all along with an apology and sincere interest in the customer's welfare. Too many museums simply make available a formal comment card (or suggest a letter to the director), resulting in a slow response, if there is one at all. The unspoken message is that only someone on high can address visitor dissatisfaction. If the staff is working as a community itself, sharing in common goals, any one of them should be able to step into an unhappy situation and make an effort to correct it on the spot. With good training and a shared commitment, each individual speaks confidently for the whole.

Trustees

Traditional wisdom tells us that all things are connected. In other words, you can never change just one thing. The internal changes required of the twenty-first-century museum clearly extend not just to the bottom of the hierarchy but to the top as well. The organizational role of boards and trustees also needs to be critically reappraised in light of this century's new realities. Historically, the role of the board of trustees was defined by the admonition, "Give, get, or get off," a not so subtle way of underscoring the financial expectations of a board. Identifying and cultivating the wealthiest members of a community and rewarding them with the position of trustee has been accepted practice in the nonprofit community for decades. Most trustees have understood these financial expectations and have graciously accepted them as a civic responsibility, accompanying their prominence and leadership within the community. Most also serve thoughtfully and conscientiously, volunteering their time and energies to secure and manage critical funding, setting policies for effective governance and overseeing financial responsibility. America's museums have relied upon the generosity of trustees and donors and owe their growth and success in many ways to the willingness of such volunteer leadership to combine financial support with institutional governance.

In today's world, the downside of treating boards as if their primary responsibility was to reach into their own deep pockets—and encourage others to do so as well—is that this practice has created an image of museums as private clubs where social standing creates an elite cultural class. Gala fundraisers, accompanied by newspaper social coverage, spotlight for the community the well-known benefactors enjoying lavish events. Even when museums reach out to the public with free days, popularized exhibits, and a well-meaning attitude, the image of wealth and privilege remains. For much of our public, the museum requires unspoken credentials, from social status to intellectual superiority, building an enormous barrier to our audience-related goals. We take on split personalities when our trustees and our intended audiences are consistently of two different worlds.

By legal definition, trustees and boards hold their museums' collections and other assets in public trust, assuring their stability into the future. This role creates boards whose responsibilities are primarily fiduciary in character. They are essentially managing the property of others (the public) with the same qualities of prudence and honesty as they would their own assets. They perform these responsibilities in many ways: ensuring the diligent management of the museum, reviewing and approving policies that support institutional integrity, accepting and monitoring institutional budgets, and acting as advocates for the museum among many kinds of constituents. The changes precipitated by the passing of the Sarbanes-Oxley law only make these responsibilities more challenging and more important than ever. In recent years an additional requirement has steadily risen in priority on the list of institutional expectations. Museum boards are now expected to ensure that the museum is accessible to as wide a public as possible. This latter role is raising considerable discussion and debate about the composition of the "new" board of the twenty-first century.

The new museum, seeking to both represent and connect with its diverse constituents, will be successful at this complex task only if it maintains a close interaction with its intended audiences and establishes a strong bond of trust. We would contend that such trust is only superficial if our boards and staffs do not represent our changing constituencies. In short, both should reflect the diversity of our intended audiences. This importance of transitioning to a more fully representative board greatly exceeds some kind of nod to "tokenism." It is bound up in the sincerity of the museum to entertain many kinds of language, perspective, practice, and culture as integral forces in its organization.

Consider, for example, the role of boards as conduits to their communities, as advocates for the institution, ensuring that the museum serves as wide a public as possible. How is that possible if the board has no genuine ties to the variety of publics that are the museum's targets of impact? What, indeed, is the public response when it sees no representation within? How sincere are the museum's efforts to broaden access and representation if voice is separated from vote?

Ron L. Kagan, director of the Detroit Zoological Institute and Society, writes:

> We need to look not just for more diverse voices but more diverse voting. It is not just about race, religion, gender and age. It's about having the entire community's hearts and minds represented in the most critical decision-making forum—the board of a museum . . . This is not to suggest that political and affluent civic leaders aren't wonderful. But there naturally tends to be greater allegiance to users than to nonusers, and the only way you get people to be users is if they feel that the museum is relevant and a part of their community experience. Museums can't be self-reinforcing, closed environments.[2]

Being of the community also makes it more likely that partnerships will reflect a coming together of both the subtleties of language and the frameworks of reference that impede open communication. The work of the board itself is enriched when discussions and debates provide new opportunities for shared points of view, where the work ahead for the museum is actually taking place in board-related decision making. Another aspect of this change is in the board's ability to communicate with the museum's donor base, expanding and diversifying it as well as bringing the institutional vision to its supporters. Though finding ways to identify and cultivate new leadership is often awkward and discouraging at first, it is a critical step in transforming museums into more authentic civic enterprises. A diverse governing body enables museums to move from the periphery (or off the hill) into the heart of their communities.

Volunteers

Diversity in the new museum must permeate all parts of the organization—board, staff, and volunteers. Volunteers are the parents, the teachers, the neighbors, the friends of our potential audiences, and are thus very influential. They also reflect the institution's culture—hopefully, one of respect, openness, and inclusion. Volunteers at all levels are often the lifeblood of museums. From their roles in governance, such as on the board, to their services as "unpaid" staff, volunteers play multiple roles. They are extra hands and talents, voices within the community, advocates for museum missions, and welcome faces during difficult times. Their work has real and significant financial impact on the institution and offers museums a range of talents that cannot be fully achieved through paid staff. Though not technically "in the loop," they are often privy to many internal decisions and tensions and are required to be discrete and sensitive to such issues. As much as any other component of the organization, volunteers must share in the institution's vision and its value-driven operations. Like our front-line staff they are often the interface with the public. Also like front-line staff, volunteers are often the last to learn about what the museum is doing, what it stands for, and where it is going. If we expect such collaboration, we must build a climate for collaboration. As ambassadors and supporters of our work, our volunteers need to be part of our extended team and receive the same quality of internal respect, information, training, and care as our paid staff. We also need to put as much effort into diversifying our volunteers as we do our staff and boards.

The Museum as Both an External and Internal Learning Organization

The goal of the twenty-first century manager is optimizing the mix of talents of the staff; it's difficult to find good staff. So difficult that ever greater time and energy needs to be devoted to retaining, rather than recruiting, good staff. Every effort should be made to support and encourage staff's intellectual curiosity and desire to stay fresh and engaged. Most staff members choose to work in museums because of their desire to learn; it is important to feed that desire. A key aspect of retaining good staff is investing in continuing education for staff. We hasten to add, however, that museums should not fall into the rut of thinking "continuing education" means just taking classes; remember, we're supposed to be experts in free-choice learning. And as has been recently discovered, most people learn best through free-choice learning, not just for hobbies but also in the workplace.[3]

A useful framework for thinking about how to support museum staff learning is provided by the writings of Malcolm Knowles, considered the "father" of adult education. According to Knowles, "the main reason why adult education has not achieved the impact on our civilization of which it is capable is that most teachers of adults have only known how to teach adults as if they were children."[4] Knowles's principles for adult learning, which have been added to and refined by him and others since the 1970s, provide a good starting place for any museum attempting to support staff continuing education:

1. Adults *want* and *need* to learn.
2. For adult learning to be meaningful, learners need to have a major role in defining their own learning goals, based on individual needs, interests, and values, at their own pace and in their own way.
3. Adults require learning environments/situations in which their own knowledge and experience is valued and utilized—one-way transmission of information by an "expert" or "teacher" is of less value than a two-way dialogue, in which adults can share and actively use their own knowledge and experience.

We need to build financial resources into our budgets that allow every staff member the time to pursue their own learning needs. We also need to empower and train our managers so that they can expertly guide each staff member in wisely and efficiently using their learning time so as to benefit maximally both themselves and the museum. If we do this, the whole will be considerably more than the sum of the parts. For example, a key component of the Family Learning Initiative at The Children's Museum, Indianapolis, described in the previous chapter was a multiyear commitment to training staff leaders from every museum department in family learning—essentially a graduate program run within the confines of the museum, complete with lectures, discussions, reading assignments, and applied projects. The result is that today The Children's Museum has significantly increased its internal capacity and expertise and now its own staff, rather than merely outside consultants, are nationally recognized as family learning experts. Building internal capacity takes time, but it pays huge dividends down the road. At the end of the day, a functional staff is a knowledgeable, listened-to staff.

Fostering Creativity and Innovation

Management by walking around is how David Packard, one of the co-founders of Hewlett-Packard, described his management philosophy. Susan Wageman of The Tech Museum of Innovation, San Jose, notes that

> [Packard's] philosophy was that managers should get out into the business and talk to people at all levels, so they will really know what is going on—and pick up on ideas that supervisors or middle managers may not recognize as valuable. In our first museum, many of the offices were laid out so that we had to regularly travel through the public areas of the museum. This helped all staff stay in touch with our visitors. Today, some staff rarely leave the museum, the shop is off site, and the rest of us work in cubicles in another building. Many museums require employees who do not regularly work with the public to take a turn working on the front lines so they become more connected to the organization's mission. Mangers are encouraged to walk around and talk to staff both within and beyond their domain of responsibility. Even before I became a manager, I realized that this practice was a great opportunity for me to communicate my ideas to the leadership when they were actively listening. I am always prepared with questions or ideas to discuss when members of the leadership stop by on their rounds.[5]

"Innovation does not just happen," says Wageman, based upon insights gained from her recently completed master's degree research on organizational change and grounded in experiences garnered over the past ten years of working at The Tech during a time when the museum underwent major change and expansion.[6] Quite the contrary, as Peter Drucker points out, innovation requires conscious and purposeful effort.[7] For example, technology firms like General Electric, Hewlett-Packard, and ABB have systematic processes for soliciting and identifying new ideas from their staff. According to Wageman, for this practice to be effective it is essential that the possibility for adoption be obvious and that decisions not to follow up on ideas be followed swiftly by honest feedback clearly justifying why no action was taken. She gives an example from The Tech. "One forum that The Tech has created to seek out ideas and innovations is the Food for Thought luncheon. The President invites a diverse group of staff from different departments to an informal lunch (hosted by a generous Board member) to discuss whatever they wish. Some of these conversations have resulted in immediate changes to practices that had not been recognized by the leadership as needs." Wageman goes on to say,

> My research showed that innovative organizations tended to be defined by decentralized decision-making, lateral communication, and few hierarchical distinctions. Information flow was open and pervasive and the organizational structure relatively flat. Organizations which were structured to be reflective about their practice, trying to learn from their mistakes (and successes!), seemed to have an advantage because they were more capable of considering different points of view, enabling innovation to flourish. Rigid formal structures did not recognize nor implement innovative ideas. Although my research suggested these approaches led to innovation, they had to be adapted to each unique circumstance, because the solution for one particular institution did not always fully meet the needs of another.[8]

According to Wageman, informal social situations are an important key to innovation. "The informal systems of an organization—lunch gatherings, water cooler conversations, unofficial collaborations between people, and such—are ... an integral part of every organization, but not always recognized as critical to the entire system. Formal systems include the organizational structure, rules, job descriptions, defined processes, meetings, etc., but informal systems are created by staff as ways to socialize and get work done." Both informal and formal structures are important conduits for innovation. But most organizations have traditionally only valued one of these structures—the formal ones. In the *Joy of Work*, corporate executive and educator Dennis Bakke writes that the conventional employer assumes that 95 percent of all important decisions in an organization are made by executives, managers, and board members. In a "joy of work" environment nearly all important decisions are made by nonleaders.[9] His assumptions are supported by organizational researchers who discovered that in order for organizations to foster effective innovation, they need to ensure that formal systems do not squelch the informal systems. Formal structures, even when pledged to support innovation, if not sensitive to the needs of these informal systems can tend to institutionalize existing behaviors and ways of doing business, stifling rather than encouraging new ideas. Enabling innovation requires trusting employees and their ideas.[10] Again Bakke: "We should also remember that the key to a great workplace is the freedom to make important decisions and take responsibility for the results. Other elements of the workplace contribute to the joy of work, but none . . . compares with being treated as an important and trusted decision maker."[11] When museums overstructure their management and feedback systems they "constrain the best source of creativity available to them—the distributed knowledge of their workforce"[12] As Wageman says, "A system that encourages interactions between and among staff and that allows for open and pervasive communication provides the best opportunities for innovation."[13]

Well-known creativity researcher Dr. Teresa Amabile of Harvard Business School has discovered what some of the most common creativity killers are for children. We've adapted her findings into a short list of some of the most common creativity killers in the museum workplace:

- Micro-Management—if everything an employee does is judged and second-guessed, then the individual will focus on minimizing mistakes rather than figuring how to maximize success.
- Rewards—excessive use of prizes, such as gold stars, money, or "toys," deprive an employee of the intrinsic motivation for success; everything becomes externally motivated.
- Competition—putting employees in a constant win-lose situation, where one person will get singled out as successful and others held back, puts a damper on creativity.
- Restricting Choice—telling employees which activities they can pursue or making decisions for employees rather than encouraging them to forge their own solutions severely limits experimentation and novel ideas from developing.
- Pressure—although all jobs involve pressure, adding to these pressures by setting unrealistic time, satisfaction, or financial pressures almost always leads to reduced productivity and diminished creativity.

Building Community and Collaboration within Your Organization

Fostering creativity and innovation is arguably the primary job of today's director. To accomplish this, the director must not only work with individuals but with all members of the museum community; she or he must be able to engage with all parts of the museum's constantly evolving ensemble of staff, trustees, and volunteers. In an essay in *The New Paradigm in Business* Kazimierz Gozdz refers to such an ensemble as an organization acting as a "community."

> An organization acting as a community is a collective lifelong learner, responsive to change, receptive to challenge, and conscious of an increasingly complex array of alternatives. As leaders work to maintain community within organizations, a new kind of leadership, involving virtually everyone in the organization emerges.[14]

Because of the increasing complexity of museum work, the trend toward departmental specialization, and even subspecialties, has continued to grow. Take the development department, for example. Today it may have a major gifts division, an annual campaign staff, a membership team, a division for fundraising events, a corporate giving specialist, and others, all requiring specific expertise in separate aspects of fundraising. Although they share the common goal of supporting the museum, their work can quickly become divided and fragmented. The fragmentation increases when other departments that are also communicating with the public, such as education, marketing, and publications, are located in another corridor and focused in their own direction. Each undertakes a separate piece of the work without synchronizing their messages or their goals. The issue of internal communications is a common one and museum staff can get quite creative at times in addressing it. Managers put together all kinds of structures to keep communication flowing, from endless departmental meetings to top-down management teams to a growing use of cross-departmental teams. The coordination process alone can be daunting and the meeting time exhausting.

Many in the museum have become increasingly aware that working in silos contributes to internal strife and, worse yet, little cohesive service to our publics. If museum staffs are divided internally, they inevitably communicate their power struggles through mixed messages to their publics. Faced with reinventing museum work, most museums have acknowledged that such divisions of labor and attitude can only hold them back. They keep them from addressing common goals and set up artificial barriers. As one director commented in an interview with researcher Sherene Suchy, "Professional relationships are about human relations, not professional ghettos."[15]

The ability to achieve and sustain the dynamic of community is extraordinarily difficult. It begins with a strong and shared common purpose, a strength that should be inherent in our nonprofit identity, but one that is not often activated in our operational structure. The practices of a learning organization are as applicable to museums as they are to businesses. They require choice, practice, and commitment. Leadership becomes a shared responsibility, deriving its strength from a core set of values, shared vision and commitment on everyone's part to serve as stewards of that vision. The transformation of the museum into a cohesive learning organization aligns it with the new paradigm of business practices, bringing the museum into the community of change that has become the energy of this new century.

Peter Senge writes in *The Fifth Discipline* that not just team work, but "team learning" is an essential skill toward transforming our institutions.

> The discipline of team learning starts with "dialogue," the capacity of members of a team to suspend assumptions and enter into a genuine "thinking together." To the Greeks *dia-logos* meant a free-flowing of meaning through the group, allowing the group to discover insights not attainable individually. . . . Team learning is vital because teams, not individuals, are the fundamental learning unit in modern organizations.[16]

What is painfully obvious is that "teams" don't just happen by putting people in the same room. Working collaboratively and flattening museum hierarchies requires new skills, the skills of project management that are more common perhaps in the changing workplace than in museum studies programs. That said, there are innovative museum studies programs like Cooperstown, New York, and University of Texas, Austin, that are trying to address these issues by focusing on leadership and change skills. Building better teamwork is a multistep process. Before the work begins, each team member must be candid about his or her expectations. Then jointly the group must identify and challenge one another's assumptions, arriving at a set of common goals. Commitment to the discipline of team learning involves techniques that must be studied and mastered before they are integrated into one's business practices. In the case of the museum team, the success of its cooperative work demands that *responsibility for the audience* is the clear, inviolable rule; all members of the team must be equally committed to and responsible for this goal. The museum of the twenty-first century must use its vital human resources first and foremost as a tool for managing change.

In his book, *Managing in a Time of Great Change*, Peter Drucker writes about this era as one of sharp transformation, noting basic shifts in worldview, values, social and political structures, arts, and the key institutions of our society. Drucker believes we are now in a society of organizations that are seeking to integrate knowledge toward a common task, a process that places a new emphasis on alliance, teamwork, and partnership. Our work within museums shares that goal, and Drucker further reminds us that in order to succeed, the theory and the goals of a business must be known and understood throughout its organization.[17]

All parts of the museum's human resource ensemble are keys to institutional success. A sound business model must assess these key assets, understanding possibilities and limitations, strengths and weaknesses. The business model should be built upon those strengths. The business model also must either minimize the liabilities created by human resource limitations or include a strategy for turning liabilities into strengths. For example, at Old Sturbridge Village it was financially necessary to reduce the number of paid staff used as live costumed interpreters, clearly one of the key aspects of the OSV visitor experience. Historically, the Village prided itself in not using volunteers on the grounds because they felt that it would reduce quality (read here expertise in nineteenth-century life, not necessarily the quality of the visitor experience). Based upon an idea that actually came from one of its members, the Village is now actively investigating ways to augment its paid interpreters with a cadre of committed, well-trained volunteers. Training will include not only lessons in nineteenth-century history and crafts, but also lessons in interpretation and customer satisfaction and service. A key strategy that is emerging involves recruiting from the ranks of OSV members. One of the benefits of being an OSV member is the opportunity to have (and pay for) the privilege of receiving special, intensive training in early nineteenth-century skills and public interpretation. The ultimate reward is being able to wear a costume and be part of the interpretive team at the Village. Early indications are that both members and the public are finding this experiment a great success. This is one of those innovations that feels like turning lemons into lemonade.

INTELLECTUAL ASSETS

In a recent "open letter" to the public, Wildlife Conservation Society President and Chief Executive Officer Steven E. Sanderson states:

> In the pages that follow, I will set forth some ideas and guideposts that mark the path of the Wildlife Conservation Society as it begins its Second Century. In 2002, we navigate great currents of change in the world of conservation, non-profit organizations, and the life of New York City. Our challenge is to build on a great heritage while we learn and change as an organization and create a vibrant new program of action. Our quest is unique and compelling, our mission fresh and powerful. We uniquely combine a great living wildlife collection and zoo complex with a worldwide conservation mission. The intellectual capital represented in our staff rivals that of many major scientific research facilities. Our goal is the conservation of wildlife and wild lands for future generations, essential in its own right and a reaffirmation of the best of the human spirit.
>
> Throughout our first century, science and exploration undertaken by the Wildlife Conservation Society have served conservation around the world. WCS is made up of scientists, educators and curators generating new conservation knowledge . . . Our future strategies will revolve around two of WCS' most precious assets, the Bronx Zoo and the International Conservation program. We will devise strategies for a Bronx Zoo Renaissance and the conservation of wild landscapes, forever.[18]

Like the majority of zoos and aquariums in the twenty-first century, the Wildlife Conservation Society has placed increasing emphasis on its role as not only a repository of interesting animals, but as a fundamental player in world conservation efforts. The keeping of animals in captivity can, in fact, must, be used for both educational and conservation-related ends. The value the Bronx Zoo and other similar institutions bring to society is not just that they are popular educational leisure settings but equally that they represent significant intellectual capital about animal behavior and conservation. When we ask, "Who are we?" it is important to begin with the human resources that comprise the museum, but without question we also possess great intellectual resources including our collections, writings, and, in some cases because of their uniqueness or historical value, even our buildings and land count as intellectual assets.

The Institute of Museum and Library Services refers to collections in two categories, living and nonliving, a choice of words that only begins to hint at the vast and indescribably varied collections in this nation's museums. The value of these collections cannot begin to be calculated. Few institutions could ever begin the vast challenge of assigning monetary value to their collections in any meaningful way. They range from irreplaceable ancient sculpture to common rough-hewn tools, from rare vestiges of long-lost cultures to modern pieces of propaganda. Their sources are equally varied—representing eccentric and discerning collectors, church and royalty, cellars and attics, artists and creators, looters and gravediggers, hoarders and prophets, or the earth and sea itself. They may be specially built, as in the large collections of hands-on materials that are the laboratories of science museums, or the reproductions that are commonly used in teaching collections. They are the flora and fauna of the earth, the minerals and gems, animals, insects, fish, and birds that make up our known environments. They draw out our curiosity, questions, admiration, and wonder. They are the power of museums in so many ways, offering us rare encounters with aspects of our natural and man-made environments that we are unlikely to meet in our daily lives. They require care and repair, feeding and tending. Their housing needs are intricate and complex, whether they must be maintained in surroundings of carefully controlled temperatures and humidity or in environments that simulate the natural places from which they came. Our responsibility to our collections is enormous, and as we consider our business planning, it must also be with this hallowed stewardship in mind.

In this new Knowledge Age we have entered, our collections bring value to the museum in direct proportion to the "knowledge" they provide. The objects do *not* "speak for themselves." The intellectual value of a museum's collections is directly tied to the use of those objects to provide answers to questions society finds valuable. Sometimes that value is straightforward and directly understood by all. Everyone today seems to appreciate that paintings by Impressionist masters such as Renoir and Monet, an original Guttenberg Bible, or even popular culture items such as Dorothy's ruby slipper from the *Wizard of Oz* are valuable cultural legacies and worthy of preservation and display—their intellectual content is assumed. The value of other collections is more obscure and it is incumbent upon the museum to establish their importance. For example, the late nineteenth- and early twentieth-century natural history museum legacy of rooms and rooms filled with dead creatures seemed to be of limited and dubious value as we approached the end of the twentieth century. Natural history museum curatorial staff were being fired, or more accurately retired, for even if someone thought it worth maintaining these collections, there were few new taxonomists coming along to take their place. Then someone realized that these collections were priceless and irreplaceable resources for our understanding of biodiversity and global change; these collections represented a time capsule, a window into a world largely destroyed by development. All of a sudden, natural history museum curators were in huge demand, and universities started encouraging graduate students to once again think about working with collections. Still, all those beetles on pins are worthless unless we make the effort to understand and communicate the secrets they possess.

·Many institutions are trying to figure out ways to make their knowledge more accessible—to scholars and the general public alike. In particular, digital technologies are revolutionizing such information sharing. More and more institutions are digitizing their collections and putting them on-line where anyone and everyone can access them. To date, though, like many new technologies, the costs of digitization often seem to outweigh the benefits. Still, the promise is so compelling many have become deeply invested in the effort. One of the most successful efforts has been the Colorado Digitization Project (CDP), a collaboration of Colorado's "information-rich institutions"—archives, historical societies, libraries, and museums. As the project itself states, "Access to information is a critical component to everyday life in Colorado. Information supports all aspects of daily life, business, education, and recreation. Today's technology offers many options for accessing an ever increasing amount of information." Over the past decade, the CDP has used web technologies to deliver full text, graphic, audio, and video information to information seekers wherever they live, whenever they desire it.

As business writer Lester Thurow notes, "The private ownership of productive assets and the ability to own the output that flows from those assets lies at the heart of capitalism. Property rights are what allow businesses to buy and sell their goods and services. Without them a market economy cannot exist."[19] In the Knowledge Age, ideas too become assets and thus capable of being bought and sold. In fact, intellectual property is at the heart of the new knowledge-based economy. Again according to Thurow, "Knowledge does not come free. Investments must be made to extract it. Intellectual property rights are becoming more important as other sources of competitive advantage become less important."[20]

Appropriately, then, not all museums are eager to just give away their intellectual capital. More and more museums are entering into business arrangements with commercial interests wishing to turn the museum's intellectual property into dollars. Licensing a Van Gogh image for use on a coffee mug or a photograph of a nineteenth-century cowgirl for use on a tee-shirt can be very lucrative for a museum; besides, the products can also be sold in the gift shop, which leads to more revenues. But museums need to be wary of giving away long-term assets in exchange for short-term gains. The true value of many of these intellectual properties has yet to be determined. In the Knowledge Age, museums need to be mindful of the fact that while information is cheap, knowledge, particularly authentic and authoritative knowledge, is rare and valuable. Understanding how to manage and exploit intellectual assets, be they tangible assets like collections or buildings or intangible assets such as the ideas and theories that derive from museum scholarship or expertise, should be important parts of any museum's business model. For example, when plotting the turnaround of Old Sturbridge Village Beverly Sheppard began with the Village's subject matter expertise in late eighteenth-/early nineteenth-century New England rural life, plus its educational expertise and of course the historic artifacts embodied in the Village itself; collectively these assets, along with their reputation for being a great place for families, formed the foundation of their new business model. The first three were fundamental, but so too was the latter; being widely known as a great place for families and for learning about life in old New England was a highly valuable asset. This was part of Old Sturbridge Village's brand!

BRAND

The following story recently appeared in the *Philadelphia Business Journal*:[21]

Long name replaced with "Penn Museum"

With a name like University of Pennsylvania Museum of Archaeology and Anthropology, it's not hard to understand the need for a catchier, less formal title. After a failed attempt at branding the museum "UPM," Penn has started using "Penn Museum" in hopes of grabbing visitors that might otherwise be scared away.

"We're field-testing the name," said Pam Kosta, assistant director of public information at the Penn Museum. It was actually her boss, museum director

Jeremy A. Sabloff, who came up with the idea. As a whole, Penn has made similar changes—for example, adopting a sleeker logo.

The shorter, Penn Museum moniker is making its debut in outdoor advertising touting "Royal Tombs of Ur," a traveling exhibit of ancient treasures from Iraq. The advertising is being featured on 200 SEPTA buses, as well as billboards on I-95 and at Broad and Pine streets. It's also featured on banners on the front of the museum and some 50,000 promotional bookmarks.

The museum is filled with treasures from Egypt, Mesopotamia, the Greco-Roman world, the Americas, Asia and Africa. It is well known in academic circles, but Penn wants it better known in Philadelphia. "We're not changing the museum's [official] name," Kosta is quick to add. "The name is accurate. But many people call us 'the University Museum,' and there are university museums across the country."

A lot of museums are attempting to figure out how to brand themselves these days; in fact, many are spending big bucks on consultants to help figure out how best to do this. Over the last decade branding, or in some cases re-branding, the museum has become a commonplace prescription for whatever ails the institution. What in the world is this all about? Is this just another business-wanna-be fad or is it really important?

In 1985, Albert and Whetten wrote a seminal essay entitled "Organizational Identity."[22] They were inspired to write their paper when budget cutbacks in 1979 at the University of Illinois created great unrest and an "identity" crisis as to the nature of the university. Competing metaphors such as "church" versus "business" suggest some of the tension that ensued. Thinking out from this experience, the authors speculated that at their core, organizations (like people) have identities that are based on what is central, distinctive, and enduring about them. One of the greatest assets a museum has in the Knowledge Age is this identity, which if properly managed can bring great benefit to the organization, and if improperly understood and managed can bring great harm. We suggest that the issue of identity, which includes both internal matters of vision and values and issues of how the institution presents itself to the outside world such as its mission, its products, and its services, are of fundamental importance to a museum. In the business world, this idea of identity has come to be referred to as an institution's brand. Your brand is what you stand for. It is how you communicate that core essence to the rest of the world. Defining your identity is at the heart of branding, and it is a fundamental Knowledge Age asset. Taking our cue from corporate America, it behooves each museum to deal with the changing competitive structures of the world by more effectively managing this key asset; but the emphasis is on *effectively managing*. If done with depth and integrity, branding can add great value to your museum. If not done well, it can cost you money, or, even worse, undermine the kind of public value you hoped to gain.

Brand is a slippery concept that is often confused and misused. A brand is the definition of your institution that exists in the mind of the customer, says Chris Pulleyn, chief executive officer of Buck & Pulleyn, a Rochester, New York–based agency specializing in brand strategy.[23] Your museum's brand is the space you've captured in the minds of customers—it's all the things that come to mind, all the expectations they have, when they hear the word *XYZ museum*.

Captured in your brand is all of your content—your rich collections, primary experiences, and deep knowledge of both—it is what defines you as an institution. But this identity only becomes meaningful within the context of how it is presented and perceived by the public, how it builds points of connection with individuals and organizations, and how it provides catalysts for individuals, organizations, and whole communities to come together and develop meaningful transactions. Your brand is the promise you make about your work—a guarantee of quality. As with any promise, it implies a relationship, this one between you and all your potential audiences. It tells them what to expect from your products and services. A brand tells them how you are relevant to their lives, and how you are different from other museums. In short, a brand suggests to the world how to perceive your work before they've even experienced it for themselves and, ideally, prompts them to want to experience it themselves if they haven't already.

A museum's brand is not a thing, it is an idea, a concept, something that only exists in the minds of people. Managing such an abstract entity is not easy. An entire discipline of brand management has sprung up in order to provide guidance in this challenging task of shaping those elusive mental images and leveraging them to gain a competitive edge.

Good brand management is fundamental to a good business model because it helps to drive the strategies, products, services, and value you provide your publics. It begins with understanding what your institution currently means to your publics (brand identity) and what you want it to mean (brand aspiration). While plenty of organizations know how they want to be viewed, what mental space they want to capture, staying true to the brand aspiration in every aspect of the customer experience—from graphics to public service announcements to fundraising—is what separates those institutions that succeed from those that are merely ambitious.

Brand aspiration is the benchmark against which all outreach efforts of your museum should be measured. If you are brand-driven, your museum's mission statement puts into words how your brand aspiration will be delivered. It makes what Pulleyn calls a "brand promise" to the customer.[24] Exhibitions, web presence, programming, policies, services, and expectations of staff are the ways in which the promise is either kept or broken.

Clearly the success of museums in the Knowledge Age can only be realized through an appreciation for and wise use of all of an institution's internal assets—the human resources of staff, trustees, and volunteers; the intellectual resources of collections, the knowledge they contain, and staff expertise required to unlock that knowledge; and organizational identity, the museum's brand. However, these assets provide only a partial description of what an institution is in this new world of the twenty-first century. In the Industrial Age, institutions were always defined from the inside-out, but in the Knowledge Age institutions are equally defined from the outside-in. An enumeration of a museum's assets cannot and should not be limited to those that exist inside the institution. A museum's assets and its business model must equally include a clearly articulated understanding of how it is situated within the community in which it resides. Who we are includes who we are in relation to our many stakeholders, both inside and outside of our institutional walls.

DISCUSSION QUESTIONS

- Is your organization a learning organization? What strategies are you using to support and build the capacity of each and every individual?
- How is your organization fostering creativity and innovation? How are both the informal and formal structures of the organization being utilized in support of creativity and innovation?
- How is your organization managing its intellectual capital? What strategies are you using to ensure long-term payoff from these assets?

NOTES

Epigraph: Robert D. Haas, *The Corporation Without Boundaries: The New Paradigm in Business* (New York: Jeremy P. Tarcher/Putnam, 1993), 101.

1. R. S. Kaplan and D. P. Norton, *The Strategy-Focused Organization* (Boston: Harvard Business School Press, 2001).

2. Ron Kagan, *Civic Engagement Starts With the Board,* in Mastering Civic Engagement: A Challenge to Museums, ed. American Association of Museums (Washington, DC: American Association of Museums, 2002), 69.

3. Cf. S. Wageman, *How to Foster Innovation Within Your Science-Technology Center: Observations from Under the Seat Cushion. Handbook for Small Science Centers* (Lanham, MD: AltaMira Press, in press).

4. M. S. Knowles, *The Modern Practice of Adult Education* (New York: Association Press, 1970).

5. Wageman, How to Foster Innovation.

6. Ibid.

7. P. F. Drucker, *The Discipline of Innovation* (Boston: Harvard Business Review, 2000).

8. Wageman, How to Foster Innovation.

9. D. Bakke, *Joy at Work: A Revolutionary Approach to Fun on the Job* (Seattle: PVG, 2005).

10. H. J. Sherman and R. Schultz, *Open Boundaries: Creating Business Innovation through Complexity* (Reading, MA: Perseus Books, 1998).

11. Bakke, *Joy at Work,* 196.

12. Sherman and Schultz, *Open Boundaries,* 8.

13. Wageman, *How to Foster Innovation.*

14. Gozdz Kazimierz, *Building Community as a Leadership Discipline: The New Paradigm in Business* (New York: Jeremy P. Tarcher/Putnam, 1993), 108.

15. Kent Lydecker, interview with Sherene Suchy, in *Leading With Passion: Change Management in the 21st Century* (Walnut Creek, CA: AltaMira Press, 1996), 75.

16. Peter M. Senge, *The Fifth Discipline* (New York: Doubleday, 1990), 10.

17. Peter F. Drucker, *Managing in a Time of Great Change* (New York: Truman Talley Books/Plume, 1995), 31.

18. Wildlife Conservation Society, The Second Century. http://www.wcs.org/media/file/secondcentury, 2002, accessed July 5, 2005.

19. L. Thurow, *Fortune Favors the Bold: What We Must Do to Build a New and Lasting Global Prosperity* (New York: Harper Business, 2003), 169.

20. Ibid., 170.

21. P. Van Allan, Long name replaced with "Penn Museum," *Philadelphia Business Journal*, April 9, 2004.

22. S. Albert and D. Whetten, Organizational identity, in *Research in Organizational Behavior*, vol. 6, ed. L. L. Cummings and B. M. Straw (Greenwich, CT: JAI, 1985).

23. Beth Dempsey, The Library Journal, Reed Business Information, www.libraryjournal.com, 2004, accessed July 5, 2005.

24. Ibid.

7

Being Community

An interesting shift is taking place in museums across the country. The traditional, internally focused conversations about "audience building" and "outreach" are giving way to discussions about how the museum can build and sustain community relationships and place itself at the heart of its community.
—Daniel Kertzner

Most museums would argue that they exist to serve their community, that they are there to support civic engagement and build social capital, but how many of these museums have made the effort to actually go out into the community and ask their community what it is *they* really need, and then deliver? This is exactly what the Boston Children's Museum is doing. After talking with a range of community leaders, including school superintendents, principals and teachers, newspaper publishers, foundation chairs, Chamber of Commerce members, local and state economic development agencies, directors of cultural institutions, corporate executives, and political leaders, including the mayor, the museum heard that a common theme was the need to provide an antidote to the continuing, mostly negative changes occurring in Boston—if the museum was willing, they could play a role in improving both the social and physical qualities of this very urban, increasingly ethnically, racially, and culturally diverse community.

Inside-Out

In the mid-1990s the Boston Children's Museum decided to address what it called its "urban mission." As the museum's director, Lou Casagrande, recently related to John in an interview, "Demographic shifts are changing the way we need to think about the learning experiences we offer, the staff and leadership of our museums, and the services we offer our communities. The rich mix of cultures in any major city is an opportunity to explore multiple perspectives and gateways to learning. Positioning the museum as a common meeting ground to bridge cultures requires diverse programming, staff, and partnerships." Over the past several years the museum seriously rethought its mission, its staff, the partnerships it entered into, and, not only what, but where it did business. In short, it seriously rethought and revamped its entire business model around the goal of being one of, if not the most, important social service providing organizations in the city of Boston—a social service organization whose focus was children and families and whose service was supporting a community's need for quality education and support in the area of diversity and intellectual health.

In the process of making this shift the Boston Children's Museum has made a long-term commitment to serving urban Boston children and families by "being an innovative multicultural center that builds communities and bridges neighborhoods." The museum believes that despite the increased diversity in Boston and other parts of the United States, children are actually growing up in greater isolation from other ethnic, racial, and cultural groups than they were a generation ago. Responding to concerns within their community, the museum has resolved to do something about this. Through a variety of cultural offerings—exhibitions, festivals, performances, and arts programs— the museum is striving to make cultures visible and accessible, encouraging multisensory, interdisciplinary, object-based immersion. The museum seeks actively to introduce children and families to real people through authentic activities. In fact, the museum believes that diversity issues should not just be implicit in what it does, but explicit. Again, according to Casagrande, "We believe that it is good and important to talk about culture, race, country of origin, and ethnicity to develop a sense of culture. [Boston Children's Museum's] vision is to be a meeting ground where diverse groups come together to learn about each other."

Casagrande describes the important transformations the museum has had to make in order to be this new kind of institution. "We needed to reposition ourselves to our external stakeholders and reinterpret ourselves internally around this new mission. To grow and be successful, we needed to get rid of the old model of internally driven brilliance; we needed to turn ourselves inside-out." Making this transformation took time and was at times painful, particularly for many of the institution's staff, who believed that what they had always done should be what they should always do, especially since the institution under the leadership of former director Michael Spock had helped to invent the modern "children's museum" genre. Thus a major part of the transformation was in the staff. Casagrande notes, "We have hired only people committed to our urban mission. For seven years I hired no 'museum' people; I only hired people who had bought into the premise of the urban mission." Major transformation also needed to happen at the level of the board. "Board buy-in took several years. I began running joint board meetings with community leaders. Eventually, the board not only understood, but embodied our urban mission." And, finally, the transformation required changing how the institution did its business, as Casagrande explained: "Museums are people magnets and therefore attractive to neighborhood developers. Further, museums are neutral parties who can bring together commercial organizations, city planning agencies, funding sources, and others behind an urban redevelopment project." Today, all of the museum's activities reflect this perspective.

Casagrande's goal was to transform the business strategy of this major children's museum, long known internationally for the innovative quality of its exhibitions and programs, essentially a product-dominant position, into an experience-dominant position. Instead of being the toast of the museum professional crowd, the Boston Children's Museum wanted to be the toast of Boston, known to *all* members of the Boston public as a place for great family and child experiences centered around issues of cultural diversity. A key focus of this strategy has been community partnerships.

Community Leadership
Responding to the widespread public concern over the loss of "third places" outlined in Chapter 4, the Boston Children's Museum is working to create a network of community places that can serve as safe, neutral, and friendly spaces for communities to meet, talk, and play. Working in collaboration with the owners of several adjacent office building complexes, the museum developed a nearby open space area as a community space and in the process met both the needs of the building's owners, who had to comply with open space requirements, and the needs of the local community, who longed for more quality open spaces. This is not the activity of a typical children's museum, but

it is the business of an organization committed to meeting the needs of its community partners.

In keeping with their strategic decision to do business primarily through collaborations, the museum has actively sought out and brokered meaningful collaborations with a wide range of agencies and organizations in the Boston area. One example of this has been the museum's participation in the Mellon CityACCESS: An Investment In Youth project. CityACCESS is funded by the Arthur F. Blanchard Trust and is a collaboration of six community-based organizations: Artists for Humanity, Boston Nature Center, Boston Children's Museum, The Food Project, Malden YMCA, and MetroLacrosse. The project was created to influence the future of Boston's diverse population of young people positively by providing enriching out-of-school opportunities through a diversity of venues and experiences.

The museum's approach to the CityACCESS project has been to focus on offering both job and life skill opportunities for inner-city youth. The museum sponsors thirty-six inner-city young people each year (known as Teen Ambassadors), empowering them to discover their potential through unique work apprenticeships. In addition, the five teens from this program who best demonstrate a commitment to their work and future are awarded a $5,000 scholarship for higher education upon completing the program. Teen Ambassadors at the Boston Children's Museum serve as museum staff. They get involved in a wide range of programs, including acting as hosts to the neighborhood "City Celebrations" at the museum as well as staffing museum experiences at community fairs and festivals. The Teen Ambassadors develop both personally and professionally while working with diverse communities throughout the Boston area.

The City Celebration project provides one more example of how the museum has transformed itself into a community service vehicle. Through City Celebrations the museum provides city residents with a permanent, low-cost venue that community organizations from throughout the city can use as a place to come together and share. For example, a key feature of City Celebrations are the Friday Night Lights programs, when a neighborhood can have access to the museum's professional-quality theater for youth (or, for that matter, adult) performances. In this way neighborhoods—families, seniors, school and community group teachers, and leaders—can highlight the talents of their communities with an audience of youth and adults from other communities—

all at virtually no cost to the neighborhood (other than the $1 per person admission charge).

Programs like these require substantial grant funding, but in the long run the museum has defined itself as not only a part of the community, but as a fundamental catalyst for change in the community. By listening to and addressing the needs of its community it has established itself as a keystone member of the community, one deserving of significant funding by public, private, and corporate donors. Casagrande estimates that before this transformation the museum's success rate with grants was comparable to industry-wide averages of about 25 percent. Now he asserts that the museum's success rate is close to 95 percent. By becoming what Boston's mayor was recently quoted as saying, "the most important arts and cultural institution in Boston for children," the museum has experienced record increases in visitor-generated income, grant-funded income, ancillary income, and contributions, all while becoming more representative of the diverse population of urban Boston. Despite significant challenges early on, including declining revenues and serious concerns raised by some staff and board, the museum is now thriving programmatically and financially. By building strong collaborations with other organizations in the city, strengthening its staff and board, and strengthening and improving its city-wide brand, the museum has positioned itself for years of future success.

Indicative of this change in brand and business strategy, the museum has rethought one of its major financial assets, its real estate on the Boston wharf. It has expanded and renamed the site, calling it "Children's Wharf." Although the museum represents the major presence at the site, it is not the only facility there. The museum has leased space to a range of other child- and family-focused businesses. In the process they've created a children's campus that includes pre- and after-school programs for children and an independent revenue stream of approximately $1 million a year for the museum through the rents charged to other tenants. Again, the goal is not to dominate as a product provider, but as a place for child- and family-centered experiences.

Will the museum's current programs and projects suffice to keep it strong over the coming years? Of course not! Like any business, the museum will need to adapt its programs and efforts continually to accommodate the shifting needs and funding opportunities in the community, but its business model will continue to provide guidance for those changes. The Boston Children's Museum has redefined its priorities from being primarily an institution whose function is to help the community learn about those issues it internally decided were important to one whose primary institutional function is to be a meeting place and supporter of what the community has said it needs; collaboration is at the core of everything the museum now does.

As the Boston Children's Museum example demonstrates, an institution's assets need not be restricted to the traditional boundaries of the institution. Through partnerships and collaborations an institution can transcend the limitations of staff, collections, buildings, and even budgets. The key is not only in talking the talk about the museum being part of a larger community, but in actually walking the walk. For too long, museums have thought and behaved as if they were isolated jewels, set amid the rabble of the rest of the world. Museums are increasingly coming to appreciate that they are fundamental parts of the community, in fact, not just one community but a series of intersecting communities—communities of geography (e.g., national, state, and local), purpose (e.g., education, social service, culture, entertainment), interest (e.g., art, history, science), and commerce (e.g., tourism, education). Opportunities for collaboration exist within and between each of these communities. Historically the most prevalent museum partnerships involved the schools.

NEW ROLES AND RELATIONSHIPS WITH SCHOOLS

Like many institutions, the Japanese American National Museum (JANM) had long offered the conventional docent-led school tours. Over time, however, they began to appreciate that this model was no longer meeting their needs or the needs of the students and teachers they served. The major exhibition being used for school programs was *Common Ground: The Heart of Community,* which "presents an overview of Japanese American history from early immigration to the present day through artifacts, photographs, artwork, and media installations." The exhibition design team did not anticipate or build into the exhibition the capacity for large school group experiences. The exhibition consists of a series of small galleries that cannot accommodate groups larger than forty; however, schools typically brought sixty to 120 students at a time. If this was not problem enough, as word of mouth spread around Los Angeles about the exhibition, the museum was being visited by multiple schools on the same day.

As JANM educator Lisa Sasaki said in a recent article, "Without the ability to redesign *Common Ground,* we faced the same dilemma that many other museums encountered: should we continue to make slight changes to our existing exhibition and program to accommodate larger and/or self-guided groups or were we stuck with the same type of school field trip experience forever? This question led to a whole host of other questions: How do we engage students in the galleries and create an environment that encourages learning while discouraging inappropriate behavior? Could students learn in the exhibition without docent facilitation? Within our typical school group visits, were students receiving and retaining the exhibition's message? And most importantly, were the school tour programs providing students with "long-term and meaningful learning"?[1]

The museum's conclusion was that students were not in fact achieving the outcomes it hoped for. It was faced with the painful choice of just continuing with what it was doing and accepting the limitations, trying to retrofit existing exhibitions and programs, or starting fresh. The museum decided it was time to "accept the limitations of the old paradigm of tour-based museum field trips and try to build and embrace a new model instead of merely attempting to fix an old system."

Again, according to Sasaki,

> While the Japanese American National Museum hosts over 23,000 students per year through its school visit program, it is ultimately teachers who decide whether or not students come to the National Museum. In general, museum programs focus on the learning process of students during their time on-site; yet it should be impossible to look at students without also contemplating the needs of teachers. While we might bemoan the lack of preparation students receive before their visit, we sometimes forget that classroom teachers face their own pressures and concerns. In an age where student achievement is gauged by proficiency in content standards and evaluated by standardized testing, educators—strapped for both class time and money—are forced to look more carefully at the field trips that they take and the time in the classroom that they dedicate to preparation and follow-up.
>
> As teachers search for the most educational return on their investment of time and resources, the old method of "walking lectures" or "walk and read" tours that fail to engage students degenerates a school program into simply a way to fill students' time. What then do educators need? What can museums provide teachers that they cannot receive from another source? Instead of assuming the answers to these questions—which may change year to year, grade to grade, or school district to school district—the National Museum decided to convene educator advisory groups for various educational projects, allowing them to share their years of experience and knowledge with museum staff so that their needs and expectations could be incorporated into the program's

development. . . . Museums cannot answer all of these questions while the students are on-site. It is only by working in collaboration with classroom educators that we can create a plan of action that ensures that all school visits have purpose, inside of the classroom and out.[2]

The result is a series of programs that dramatically shifted the emphasis from being museum-focused to ones that were student-focused. Given the freedom to become actively involved in determining both the content and experience of their visit, students are taking greater ownership of their work. Museum staff are now observing how much more engaged and insightful students seem to be. And teachers are commenting on how inspired they are by the experience and how they have begun to adopt these same techniques in their own classroom efforts.

Sasaki concludes her article by quoting from the teacher who had her high school students create murals while interned in a World War II concentration camp in Arkansas; these murals form the foundation of the temporary exhibition in which this new school approach has been piloted. "Miss Jamison, . . . [who] over 50 years ago practiced self-directed learning when she allowed her students to decide what subjects they wanted to depict in their murals, once said: 'A good painting is a thing of lasting beauty. Long after the poster paint has peeled off the beaver boards, these murals, painted by these eight high school students, will be remembered.'[3] Our hope at the Japanese American National Museum is that we too can create a thing of lasting beauty. With an engaging and meaningful school program, long after students leave the museum behind, we hope that the lessons learned within its walls will be remembered."

The desire of museums to become forces for social good in the neighborhoods they serve is not limited to Boston and Los Angeles. Museums across the country are adding their voices and values in an effort to build more livable communities. In the early decades of the twentieth century, John Cotton Dana at the Newark Museum was creating services for his museum "to be of immediate, practical aid to all of the community that supports it."[4] He was a pioneer in developing the partnership role of museums with schools, putting museum collections and knowledge to the service of formal education.

Museum and school partnerships remain central to museum services, resulting in large formal educational departments that work closely to relate the museum's expertise to the curriculum needs of those they serve. Field trips, classroom outreach, traveling exhibits and teaching kits, and teacher workshops are classic museum education services in communities of all sizes. In this new age, museums are also finding themselves renegotiating their historic school partnerships. As schools undergo the great turmoil launched by new standards of accountability, many are restructuring the pace and focus of classroom learning. Schools are increasingly anxious about testing, and administrators are demanding that students spend less time away from the classroom. Much like the Japanese American National Museum, these changes in long-established field trip patterns are forcing museums to reconsider their on-site offerings and explore the effectiveness of outreach programs, distance learning, web-based field trips, and other new formats. Many museums are finding such shifts enormously frustrating, not only because they are eliminating a major revenue stream, but also because museum educators rightly believe that students are losing out on a highly significant learning experience.

The teaching expertise of museums is clearly recognized by many longtime school partners, so much so that museums are increasingly called upon to fill in the gaps where formal education leaves off. Across the country, numerous art museums, with both studio and art history expertise, are supplying the faculty and art-based experiences for students whose schools no longer support art education as a core part of their curriculum. Where such arrangements are being made, museums have to negotiate carefully the financial support for their services, as they are taking on considerable new responsibility. Similar arrangements are being made within other disciplines as well, as science and history museums are finding themselves filling in educational gaps or being asked to find new ways to participate in interdisciplinary lessons.

Museums are likely to find the formal educational programming of their institutions increasingly disrupted. They may find themselves stepping into a larger leadership role in formal education as educational reforms increasingly run up against the Industrial Age models still predominant in most schools, rather than the Knowledge Age models of learning that museums are advocating. As schools and government experiment with issues of testing and accountability, trying to assure that schools work for all students, many educational reformers are talking about working in very different directions. Many see the need for a redesign rather than reform. Some reformers are experimenting with concepts of "learning communities," believing that redefining how communities support education is as essential as transforming practice in the classroom. Finding ways to build new ties between young people and adults that give students greater opportunities to direct their own learning are common calls from many new thinkers. They also cite the transformation of education now possible through technology, a transformation that breaks down the traditional teacher-moderated model of learning with more independent, self-directed learning. The essence of integrated, universal, multimedia digital networks is one of discovery, one of the most powerful motivators in the learning process.

The new goal of formal education may be to give each student the core skills and confidence to set forth on his or her own pathway of lifelong learning. Such a process will require a generous provision of learning resources and knowledge navigators willing to assist in the learning journey. For museums committed to school partnerships, the types of services and resources may change. Museums can be leaders in designing new learning models and testing their effectiveness, but change needs to be conducted in collaboration with school partners. As in the JANM example presented above, increasingly the guided field trip should give way to experiences in which students themselves are engaged in setting their own learning goals and constructing meaning from and with one another. Students themselves should add content to the institutional website, participate as guides for others, post their own discoveries, and participate in finding the most effective ways to use the resources around them in their own communities.

Students must also be better prepared for a changing workplace that now requires workers to understand how to access information and synthesize it into meaningful knowledge. They must be able to think with the technology and be flexible, creative, and comfortable with change. In a fascinating essay, Marvin Bailey and Ruth Blankenbaker imagine learning in the future to be taking place in "learning environments," not in classrooms isolated from their communities. No longer studying separate and distinct subjects, they are learning and practicing thinking within Domains of Knowledge. "Rather than being force fed bite sized chunks of information within distinct disciplines of study, learners are guided to learn how to feed themselves."[5] The new environment is holistic and mutually engaged in problem solving and discovery, sharing knowledge and building ideas collectively. In many ways, museums already offer such environments and could step into a major role as formal educators in the future.

Some museum professionals are advocating that museums should take the role of supporting the learning outcomes neglected by schools. As schools become increasingly focused on standards-based testing driven by legislation such as No Child Left Behind, whole areas of the curriculum are being eliminated.[6] Not only are the academic areas of arts, cultural history, and science being neglected, but key process domains such as group learning, critical thinking, and problem solving have become victims of a teach-to-the-test approach. Beyond these areas, a whole range of nonacademic life skills ranging from the practical such as paying bills and showing up on time for a job to fundamentals such as civic engagement and responsibility have fallen off the school's radar screen.[7] These changes in the nature of museum-school relationships are just the proverbial tip of the iceberg as the dawning of the Knowledge Age forces a rethinking of all aspects of the museum's role in supporting a Learning Society.

BUILDING COLLABORATIONS TO SUPPORT LIFELONG LEARNING

Evidence of these shifts in attitude toward collaboration and personalized, lifelong learning began to appear at the national level around the turn of the century. In 1999, the Institute of Museum and Library Services (IMLS) issued a white paper as a call to action for museums and libraries to construct a bold, new learning network. Stating that "learning across a lifetime, supported throughout our communities, is increasingly essential to a healthy and productive society,"[8] the IMLS publication urged museums and libraries to address the challenge of collaboration in order to provide wider access to their collections and awareness of their roles in a learning society. The white paper was followed by a series of think tanks and meetings to define realistic possibilities for working together and creating a daring new vision.

Around the same time, the rapid changes in technology that moved Thomas Friedman to declare that "The World is Flat"[9] were causing individuals from all parts of the public education sector to appreciate that they needed to *really* begin talking with each other. In the fall of 2002 nearly a hundred leaders representing libraries, museums, public broadcasting, all levels of education, public policy, and technology came together to move the conversation to a new level, followed by a set of action steps. Hosted by Pennsylvania State University on the fiftieth anniversary of public broadcasting, the conference concluded with the following statement, agreed upon by all in attendance:

As knowledge-based institutions and public service media, we believe it is our job to assist citizens with their lifelong learning, preparing them to live in this new world of the twenty-first century. Given the promise that digital technology holds for creating learning opportunities, we are specifically committed to uniting in common cause to share, to learn, and to support the fullest application of these technologies for all.[10]

At the heart of these new conversations is a growing awareness that technology offers the promise of breaking down the silos of different formats—libraries, museums, archives, schools, and universities—and creating a seamless flow of available resources. Digital collections, integrated through technology, would not only reach new audiences, but also redefine the individual learning experience. As our boundaries become more porous, our learning institutions can no longer operate as separate, isolated entities. In each of these gatherings, participants have expressed a sense of urgency to move quickly so that the potential of creative work does not pass us by. As Richard J, Gowen, president of the South Dakota School of Mines and Technologies, observed:

Our technology provides us with the chance to do what this world has not seen before, and that is to work with each person, one at a time, in building a nation of learners that will enhance our country's economic growth, build the robust human networks that support democracy, and bridge the gaps between individuals and groups.[11]

Several highly innovative digital projects have been funded in recent years by such government agencies as the Foundations for the Arts and Humanities, the National Science Foundation, the Department of Commerce, and the Institute of Museum and Library Services, each of which has provided specific grant categories for new applications of technology. IMLS and the Corporation for Public Broadcasting are also co-funding a grant program encouraging fresh ideas for alliances between museums, libraries, and public broadcasting. Many of the funded projects include components that serve as models for others.

The projects vary in size and intention. One modest project that has resulted in a wonderful new set of materials for elementary-age students and teachers is the Brooklyn Expedition (www.brooklynexpedition.org). The website provides access to collections at the Brooklyn Public Library, the Brooklyn Children's Museum, and the Brooklyn Museum of Art. Its content is organized around themes supported by each of the institutions and presented for younger children and their teachers. As an interactive site, it also includes a teen web-development team who have posted essays and photographs of their Brooklyn neighborhoods on the website. Each of the three institutions involved in the project also offer computer resource centers where children who may have limited access to computers can explore the site on their own.

Many universities have established digital library collections as materials for wider support of their educational missions. In turn, many of these have attracted outside participants, such as museums and libraries, to link to and expand their core content and offer new opportunities for research and interpretation. One of the oldest such projects, which continues to add partners, is the Perseus Digital Library (www.perseus.tufts.edu). Established at Tufts University in 1987 as a digital collection of resources on the ancient Greek world, the Perseus project has expanded to include resources about ancient Rome and the Renaissance and has produced two CD ROMs drawn from its collections. Collaborators from around the world have joined the project and include such museums as the Boston Museum of Fine Arts, which has recently added links to its Egyptian excavations at the Pyramids of Giza.

The Valley of the Shadow (www.valley.vcdh.virginia.edu) illustrates the potential of digital collaboration in other ways. Historian Edward Ayers first planned the research project as a publication that would examine comparative stories of the North and South during the Civil War. Stories were drawn from two counties, Augusta County, Virginia, and Franklin County, Pennsylvania, in close proximity to one another but on opposite sides during the war. Quickly, the potential for a technology-based project was apparent, developing from primary sources located in multiple sources. The project also drew the attention of residents who held family collections that they were willing to make available for digitization. A computer terminal located at the Woodrow Wilson Birthplace, a historic site in Staunton, Virginia, shares the information and continues to draw public attention and collaboration in the project.

A third university model is the previously mentioned Colorado Digitization Project (www.cdpheritage.org) originally launched by the University of Denver to create access to the history and culture of Colorado, a state with widespread resources, many of which are located in rural areas. The project created mobile digitization services to include the collections of small and distant libraries and historical societies, building unprecedented access to their archives and artifacts. As a major service to the field, the staff of the Colorado Digitization Project documented their work and best practices. Their site today contains sections of guidelines and protocols. One supports the process of digitization and the other provides highly useful and replicable models for teacher workshops and curriculum development.

The job of creating broad on-line collections that document human culture is daunting from the perspectives of time, human resources, and cost. Each of the above examples is clear evidence of the value and promise of such efforts, however. Building new learning tools for the future requires vision, a willingness to collaborate, and a mindset toward experimentation. These are not tasks to be undertaken by single institutions, but ones that are best served by a coalition of educational and cultural resources. Ultimately, the goal is to create such virtual libraries as "open sources"—learning networks that are freely available to all. They also require that we think differently about how we are structured to participate in such new kinds of alliances. Although the potential and enormous public service of building such vast learning resources is seen by many as an essential step toward equitable access, the funding streams to support such work remain unclear. Finding new paradigms for collaborative funding is an essential step toward moving forward.

As the participants at the Penn State conference noted: "As we move from being primarily suppliers toward being enablers, we will find ourselves asking, 'What business are we really in? What business are we not in? We will need new business models as we consider the core competencies that are necessary to take advantage of all the opportunities before us." One speaker called the process "classic business process reengineering."[12]

BECOMING COMMUNITY ANCHORS

A Western Canadian economic development association recently issued the following press release:[13]

Campbell River

- The Daybreak Building Society will receive $322,250 towards the development of the Campbell River Maritime Heritage Centre and B.C. [British Columbia] Centre for Aquatic Health Sciences. The total project cost is $644,500.

- This Maritime Heritage Centre will create a museum and cultural tourism attraction for Campbell River. The goal of the Centre is to increase the length of stay by visitors to the community. The B.C. Centre for Aquatic Health Sciences will also contribute to the community's growing economic status as a cluster for aquaculture research and development, services and innovation.

In recent years, community service in museums has also taken on a much broader meaning, moving beyond just educational services. Increasingly, museums are making themselves much more central to the life of their communities, helping them to define their individuality and bringing them together in meaningful conversation. Some of their new value in community conversations comes from how they are linked to such issues as tourism and economic development, components of civic life that have been tied to museums for many years. The cultural life of a community is often touted as one of its main attractions by Chambers of Commerce, industries, and realtors, seeking to attract new residents and businesses to a region.

Perhaps most important in this connection is the role of museums in preserving and exhibiting a community's unique story, the heritage that sets it apart from other places. A traveler today could easily move from airport to airport, city to city and eat, shop, and stay in nearly identical commercial places. Malls across the country feature the same merchandise, the same stores, and even the same architectural features. Motel and hotel chains are ubiquitous in service and appearance, and well-known restaurant chains offer identical fare coast to coast. The traveler in search of what makes a city unique will often find its heritage best preserved in its museums and historical sites. Museums also are the places most likely to organize regional commemorations, ethnic festivals, and local history events that capture the flavor of place. They build community identity and bring residents together to celebrate what is special about their own experience. Often, their location is a significant factor in the revitalization of neighborhoods and as anchors for downtown cultural districts.

Museums have become gathering places as well, forums for the discussion and debate of local issues. When one community in Pennsylvania encountered accusations of racism in its redistricting, it turned to a local historical society for its records of similar tensions in the past and the lessons learned through the civil rights leadership of an earlier time. In St. Louis, the Missouri Historical Society has transformed itself into a recognized forum for the discussion

and resolution of neighborhood and community issues. The Society even re-
wrote its mission statement to reflect its commitment to the resolution of
community problems. The Association of Children's Museums includes in its
mission statement the concept of bringing children and their families together
"in a new kind of town square."

BUILDING COLLABORATION WITH VISITORS

The Ontario Science Centre, along with the Exploratorium, is credited with
helping to invent one of the most successful types of museum of the twentieth
century, the hands-on, interactive science center, a place for exploration, enjoyment, and open-ended learning. But now the Ontario Science Centre has
embarked on an ambitious effort to totally reinvent itself. Motivated by what
it perceived to be a growing national consensus that innovation is essential to
securing Canada's future in the new century, the Science Centre determined
that its new mission should be to cultivate creative citizens interested in science and technology. To this end they have embarked on a major institutional
transformation—one that involves a total reconfiguration and repurposing of
roughly a third of their considerable space by 2006. According to the Centre's
website, "these new spaces will be designed to directly address a changing
world and build on a prominent history." Although they will continue to seek
to appeal to all ages, the institution is placing considerable emphasis on developing the skills and attitudes that lead to innovation in children and youth. "A
sustainable culture of innovation in Ontario and Canada will depend on more
young people interested in and excited about futures in science and technology." The museum has dubbed this new initiative "Agents of Change."

As museum Director General and CEO Lesley Lewis explained to John when
he recently talked with her, "this was an intellectual capital campaign." In stark
contrast to the two other major museums in Toronto that also launched capital campaigns around the same time, the Royal Ontario Museum and the Art
Gallery of Ontario are raising money for bricks and mortar; both are attempting to build landmark architectural statements designed by world-class architects. The Science Centre's campaign is pitched at building minds, not edifices.

And it is not just corporations that have bought into the museum's vision,
so too has the Science Centre's public. The museum has actively sought and
received input from thousands of the visiting public. Primarily the museum
has asked visitors not for money but input into what it is trying to accomplish.

As Director Lewis said to John several times, "the key to succeeding in this new century is knowing your public and knowing what they're looking for." Visitors were asked to answer survey questions, they have helped with concept testing new computer programs and exhibit interactives, and their input was solicited regarding exhibit design issues. All of this while answering such important questions for visitors as, where did the Sport Hall go? The answer (on their website), "The Sport Hall has found its way to a new location. With all the construction going on around here, we needed to move this popular exhibit area to a new home. It's now located in an even bigger space on Level D."

Perhaps no partnership in the Knowledge Age will be more important than the one that is forged with your users. Given the Industrial Age concept of top-down management, it is not surprising that "partnerships" and "collaborations" have traditionally been thought of as relationships that happen between organizations. In the bottom-up world of the Knowledge Age, relationships between individuals and organizations will become increasingly common. If they are not already, more and more museums will soon find themselves actively and enthusiastically reaching out to their users, particularly their most frequent users, in order to build lasting and meaningful relationships.

Take members, for example; most museums currently treat these most important users more like distant cousins than as brothers and sisters. Though it is typical to fulfill the museum's obligations by inviting members to special events and openings and to keep them informed of all of the "doings," they are often satisfied to take their membership money and run. The biggest concern is making certain that requests for renewal are sent on time. Museums are extraordinarily shortsighted if they do not see members as far more than annual dues payers! They are the audience that has already selected you and voted with their feet and their wallets. They are your steadiest customers and they should be your partners in everything you do, particularly change.

When Old Sturbridge Village conducted an on-line members' survey, they hoped for a modest, but representative response. In fact, within one week, more than a third of their members had responded. What a remarkable statement about their personal interest in the Village! Many responses revealed a deep love for the institution, accompanied by concerns about changes over the years. They were forthright and articulate about their interests and often filled in the open-ended questions with personal anecdotes that testified to their loyalty and allegiance. The Village's first step in responding was its own quick action to restore some long abandoned benefits and to expand others. It used the survey as an opportunity to increase communication with members and to begin a conversation on many levels. It also recognized that members offered it a very important testing ground for new directions. When invited to participate, members enthusiastically responded. Today, Old Sturbridge Village members are the first to try new programs in the education center, to give feedback on exhibitions in development, and to join the Village in discussions about the future. The museum is also deepening its engagement with the Village through a host of member-only programs, many of which are fee-based. These members have told the Village that the exclusivity of these programs is highly valued and they are offering ideas for even further customization of the OSV museum experience. Increasingly Village staff know their names and interests and, for the first time in many years, members' visits to Old Sturbridge Village are climbing dramatically.

Membership is far more than a line on the revenue column of the budget. A museum's members can be the best museum advocates one could have. As member satisfaction increases, their willingness to tell your story, test your products, and engage more deeply with you grow as well. Creating energy and enthusiasm for new ideas and renewed goals among members has exponential benefits. When they learn, you learn from them as well. Your partnership with them is a powerful asset for the future.

The bottom line is we need to do more than just "serve" our audience. We need to talk with our audience and listen to what they have to say; we need to see their concerns and interests as our concerns and interests. As Edwin Schlossberg wrote in his book *Interactive Excellence: Defining and Developing New Standards for the Twenty-First Century*:

> The conversation that exists between members of an audience about what they are experiencing, and the conversation that exists through the audience as a whole, is the substance of our culture. Our culture exists in these conversations. Realizing not only that these conversations are occurring but that they should be consciously included in the consideration of a design or composition is central to (any) interest in creating environments.[14]

REACHING OUT TO ALL MEMBERS OF THE COMMUNITY

Museums play an important role in validating human experiences. The exclusion of whole groups of people from museum collections, research, and exhibitions has created heartache, bitterness, and distrust for many. In 1992, the American Association of Museums recognized this painful history and issued a call to action through its important publication *Excellence and Equity*.[15] It urged museums to become more inclusive places and to reflect society's pluralism in every aspect of their operations and programs. At the end of the twentieth century, *Excellence and Equity* states: "*Diversity—cultural, intellectual, environmental, social, economic, ethnic, national, educational and generational—is seeking full expression.*"[16]

Reaching new audiences and building trust often require collaboration—strategic alliances that forge connections. For example, the Jefferson Patterson Park and Museum, a Maryland-based museum, sought to bring more of its neighborhood's history into its collections, recognizing that the voices of African Americans in its surrounding towns were not represented in its collections. To redress this omission, the museum staff knew that partnership was a necessary strategy. First, they linked their own expertise in exhibit development with the nearby Banneker Museum's expertise in the regional African American experience. They then reached out to the community to listen to its stories and build working relationships. Through community advisory groups, visits into the communities at hand, and the respectful sharing of stories, a history long ignored gradually emerged. The audience then selected a topic for exhibition and programming, stating a need to talk about the days of school segregation and the gains and losses of integrating regional schools. Together the museums and their communities gathered oral histories and personal photographs to create a website and exhibition where students and the public alike could probe the impact of one of our country's great social changes.

If museums are to be successful in reaching out to diverse communities, two words become essential—*connecting* and *validating*. Connecting requires attention and work. It requires that the museum be attentive to its communities and the wider social contexts in which it operates, that it go where the people are, and that it forge closer ties with its communities. If the museum forms advisory boards, it must use their advice. Museums need to encourage new scholarship and new scholars, make their collections accessible, and pay attention to language and subtlety. When museums begin to talk across cultures, they need to appreciate that language can be tricky; words and meanings can be misunderstood. Validation means that each community has accepted one another's truths. Validation makes it clear that reaching out to diverse audiences is not a one-way gesture, but an exchange, an invitation to find and expand common ground.

The relinquishing and sharing of authority can be the most difficult step in reaching out, a difficult and threatening process. Museums have traditionally been tremendously authoritative institutions. Their claims to authority are based on a long and respected scholarly legacy. Handing over the interpretive process to others, whose interpretation may be more personal or rooted in tradition rather than scholarship, requires a willingness to accept that there are other criteria for knowing and understanding.

Many innovative museum projects have used shared authority and multiple voices in stunning combinations. The Latino Community History Project at the Oakland Museum, for example, teamed scholars in Latin American history with inner-city youth to collect, preserve, and exhibit the history of several Latino communities in Oakland. The scholars identified existing materials, developed a curriculum for the youth program, and modeled how to collect community stories. The young people served as the bridge to their communities, learning much about their own heritage while documenting it for others.

The rise of ethnically specific museums in the last several years is another testament to the role that museums can play in validating the experiences of whole groups of people who have not seen themselves included in established museum settings. These institutions are growing out of the continuum of community development, providing an important and authentic voice to diverse communities. Irene Y. Hirano, executive director and president of the Japanese American National Museum in Los Angeles, spoke about her museum and the trend toward similar institutions at the Smithsonian conference, *Museums for a New Millennium*, in 1996. She cited her own background in community organizations as central to her museum leadership, allowing her to build the museum from the perspective of the community it is designed to serve. Her closeness to the community was essential to its conceptual development, a history that was told from "personal perspectives, accurately, sensitively and in a meaningful way to a broad audience."[17] Irene further stated,

> After many years of silence, Japanese Americans realized that the interpretations of their history would be left to others to tell. This fueled an intense need to give their history a home. That was the motivation behind the creation of our institution, to ensure that not only future generations of Japanese Americans would have a home for their culture, but that their history would be viewed within the context of a broader American experience, and that visitors from around the country and around the world would come to learn that history.[18]

Ron Chew, director of the Wing Luke Asian Museum, echoes the need for drawing leadership in a community-based museum from nontraditional strengths and skills. To build long-lasting community linkages, he supports hiring practices that bring meaningful input from all ages to the process. He writes that "the whole process of creating a different kind of museum—a community-rooted museum—begins with the hiring of people with different kinds of skills."[19] Their fresh viewpoint and ties to those outside the museum encourage new practices and creativity in finding ways to be inclusive and dynamic. The exhibits at the Wing Luke Asian Museum are driven by community interest and experience, reflecting the current interests and issues of the people who are most invested in the museum as an expression of their specific needs and culture.

The Mashuntuckett Pequot Museum in Connecticut, seeking more honest, complete, accurate, and comprehensive interpretation of the Native American experience, decided to support the development of new content. It repeatedly found the images of Native Americans in children's stories distorted and caricatured. As it developed its own children's library, the museum established a budding scholars program where native children are taught how to research their own history. At the heart of this program are new books, written by an emerging group of native authors; these books strive to erase stereotypes and seek authenticity in voice and story. Similar efforts have been tried at the National Museum of the American Indian, Washington, DC, National Museum of Australia, and The Dowse, a small art museum in New Zealand.

BECOMING CENTRAL TO CIVIC LIFE

When the American Association of Museums (AAM) launched its Museums and Community Initiative, it sought to move the conversation about museums as catalysts and partners in social change to a new level. Through a series of six dialogues, held in Providence, RI; Tampa, FL; Los Angeles, CA; Detroit, MI; Wichita, KS; and Bellingham, WA; the project brought civic leaders and museum leaders together to explore the potential of collaboration to strengthen their communities. A wide-ranging set of questions, problems, ideas, works in progress, and thoughtful conversations underscored the need for continuing dialogue and commitment to possibility. The majority of participants in each city were community representatives; to many the idea of the museum as partner was new. The types of relationships suggested varied from city to city. All required that each partner clearly define the assets it brought to well-defined audience needs. And each made it clear that deep institutional self-analysis is a required process before partnership can begin with sincerity and trust.

In its project report, *Mastering Civic Engagement*, participants in the AAM dialogues contribute several important observations. Project writer Ellen Hirzy notes the varieties and character of civic engagement, stating:

> A museum's particular community context anchors it, revitalizes its mission and sense of purpose, and enriches its understanding of what is possible to accomplish. Deceptively simple actions shape and support this connecting; creating and tending a community garden with senior citizens and fifth-graders from a neighborhood school; transforming the museum's imposing entrance into the community's front porch; opening the museum as a place to find comfort after a devastating national tragedy.[20]

For many, enhanced community partnership begins with helping the community to see and use the museum differently. The museum cannot be a recognized community player unless people understand what it brings to their needs. Beverly once initiated a conversation with a group of African American women in a community where she once worked, asking them how her institution might be more meaningful in their lives, noting that specially designed exhibits and programs drew few visitors. They expressed a bit of dismay at the question. One took her hand and said softly, "It's not that we would come to your museum or that we wouldn't come. We would just never think about it. Your place has never been part of our lives." Beverly knew, then, that the museum's ideas about building relationships had been naïve and out of touch. What was most important was that that it find a way to be useful, to meet real needs. Some months later, when an African American organization sought help in documenting a specific community story, the museum was far better prepared to be a partner, bringing its assets in service to the group's goals. The museum offered training in gathering oral histories, equipment to copy photographs, and advice on exhibit installation. The content came from the group. At that point, Beverly clearly realized that the museum could not assume that it knew how to be collaborators without learning first to listen.

If museums are to move from the sidelines of civic life, they will need to change their structure and perspective. Civic engagement is a slow process;

trust is a fragile commodity. Efforts to work within other frameworks cannot afford tokenism. Many institutions do not appear to be as "public" as they need to be. Nonetheless, several of the museum community's potential partners can offer guidance. In her essay in *Mastering Civic Engagement*, Dale Thompson, director of the Providence, Rhode Island, Public Library, cites the long history of libraries as essential community centers.

> For the public library, civic engagement is just part of our nature—the relationships we have with the community and the neighborhoods. The essence of public library service is that each individual's needs are different and each individual's needs are met. People come in, we know their names. We strive to understand the community needs and try to gear our programs and services closely to those needs.[21]

A partnership project between the Providence Public Library and the Museum of the Rhode Island School of Design shared in the public trust established by the library and repositioned the museum as a community-minded institution as well. The joint project took an "art and textmobile"—a transformed bookmobile—to neighborhoods across the state, bringing an artist-in-residence into a community to work with its residents on projects of their choice. Each community designed its own project. With the artist and the museum and library staffs, they worked on murals and gardens, art projects, and various kinds of celebrations and public gatherings. Both the museum and library recognized that what worked for them was not a one-time collaboration, but a deep, ongoing relationship that built new capacities in each organization.

COLLABORATION IS GOOD BUSINESS

The idea of collaboration often raises concerns about competition among institutions. Do museums that work together share smaller slices of the funding pie? Do they steal away one another's visitors and members? How do our visitors view our joint efforts? Do they see them as self-serving, a strategy toward building new audiences, or are they regarded as core to our missions and our respect for others? These are difficult questions that are very much at the heart of the new paradigms for doing business. These questions are also at the heart of our well-being as viable institutions. Cultural anthropologist Cynthia Joba writes:

The ways we choose to relate—to ourselves, to each other, between businesses, between economies, to other species, to the earth itself—drive the outcomes we get more than perhaps any other fundamental assumption. In fact, our very survival may depend on our ability to shift into new ways of relating.[22]

The business of museums in the twenty-first century parallels emerging business models in the for-profit world. If competition was at the heart of the old business paradigm, then the concepts of cooperation and cocreation must now be at the heart of the new paradigm. Both of the latter concepts emphasize doing something together, building on mutual strengths either in parallel activities or in fused, singular approaches. Both relate to new concepts of systems thinking, evoking images of wholeness and interconnectedness.

Applying the idea of cocreation to the museum experience is a dramatic concept. It may apply to our collaborative work with other institutions, or it may describe our changing relationship to our visitors. It challenges the notion of the museum as authority and the visitor as learner and suggests a process through which the strengths of both are the basis for new knowledge—what might be thought of as knowledge creation. It is a powerful metaphor for how the individualized learning experience combines preknowing with new discoveries. The museum as a learning resource takes on new meaning through such dynamic use. Such learning is also stimulated and supported through the connectedness of the museum to the community resources beyond its walls, establishing a learning campus as the ultimate product of collaboration, thinking of the museum as just one, highly integrated piece of a large community-wide learning infrastructure. Whether working toward cocreation as an economic or tourism partnership or a new approach to building more livable communities, clearly the world outside our walls is beckoning us toward participation in dramatic change. As we move more deeply into the Knowledge Age we need to embrace not just new ways of thinking about who we are—both internally and externally—but we must deeply rethink how these changes influence the way we financially support our business.

DISCUSSION QUESTIONS

- Who are your organization's key partners? Have you defined specific goals and objectives with these collaborators? What are they and how are you planning on measuring their accomplishment?

- What *key* audience(s) is (are) currently underserved by your institution? What steps are you taking to include them?
- Does your organization plan to become more engaged in the civic life of your community? If yes, why and how, if no, why not?

NOTES

Epigraph: Daniel Kertzner, The lens of organizational culture, in *Mastering Civic Engagement: A Challenge to Museums,* ed. American Association of Museums (Washington, DC: American Association of Museums, 2002), 30.

1. L. Sasaki, A thing of lasting beauty: The evolution of the Japanese American National Museum's school programs, *Journal of Museum Education* (in press).

2. Ibid.

3. Ibid.

4. J. C. Dana, in *The New Museum: Selected Writings,* ed. W. Peniston (Washington, DC: American Association of Museums, 1999), 3.

5. Marvin E. Bailey and Ruth E. Blakenbaker, The age of the digital paideia, unpublished essay.

6. Cf. K. J. Pittman, N. Yohalem, and J. Tolman, eds., When, where, what and how youth learn: Blurring school and community boundaries, in *New Directions for Youth Development* (San Francisco: Jossey-Bass, 2003).

7. L. D. Dierking and J. H. Falk, Optimizing out-of-school time: The role of free-choice learning, in *New Directions for Youth Development,* ed. K. J. Pittman, N. Yohalem, and J. Tolman (San Francisco: Jossey-Bass, 2003), 75–89.

8. Beverly Sheppard, *The 21st Century Learner* (Washington, DC: Institute of Museum and Library Services, 1999), 3.

9. Thomas L. Friedman, *The World Is Flat: A Brief History of the Twenty-First Century* (New York: Farrar, Straus & Giroux, 2005), xx.

10. C. Marshall, *Engaging a Nation of Learners: The Penn State Conference on Public Service Media* (University Park: The Pennsylvania State University, 2002), 1.

11. Ibid., 3.

12. Ibid., 26.

13. Western Economic Diversification Canada, Softwood Industry Community Economic Adjustment Initiative - British Columbia. http://www.wd.gc.ca/siceai /results_island_e.asp, 2005, accessed July 7, 2005.

14. E. Schlossberg, *Interactive Excellence: Defining and Developing New Standards for the Twenty-first Century* (New York: Ballantine, 1998), 5–6.

15. American Association of Museums, *Excellence and Equity: Education and the Public Dimension of Museums* (Washington, DC: American Association of Museums, 1992).

16. Ibid.

17. Irene Hirano, Changing Public Expectations of Museums, in *Museums for the New Millennium: A Symposium for the Museum Community* (Washington, DC: The Smithsonian Institution, 1997), 42.

18. Ibid.

19. Ron Chew, Community roots, in *Engaging a Nation of Learners*, op. cit., 63.

20. Ellen Hirzy, Exploring museums and community, in *Engaging a Nation of Learners*, op. cit., 9.

21. Dale Thompson, Forging a true partnership, in *Engaging a Nation of Learners*, op. cit., 73.

22. C. Joba, Competition, cooperation and Co-creation: Insights from the World Business Academy, in *The New Paradigm in Business*, ed. M. Ray (New York: Jeremy P. Tarcher/Putnam, 1993), 50.

8

Attending to the Bottom Line

Profitability is a necessary condition for existence and a means to more important ends, but it is not the end in itself for many of the visionary companies. Profit is like oxygen, food, water, and blood for the body; they are not the point of life, but without them, there is no life.
—James Collins and Jerry Porras

The Liberty Science Center, like most science centers, is committed to improving the quantity and quality of science learning in its community. And like most science centers historically it strove to achieve this goal by creating exhibitions and experiences that would wow, entertain, and hopefully educate a large, on-site visiting public. Also like most science centers, these visitors—primarily families and school groups—were counted upon to generate the majority of the institution's income through gate, gift shop, and food services sales. These income streams were supplemented by a mix of government and private grants, the majority of which went into building new exhibitions and developing new programs for visitors. In the mid-1990s the Liberty Science Center decided to take a very different approach to what they did and to how they would be supported. At the core of their decision was a philosophical choice: they decided to make a major commitment to not merely supporting science education in general in their area, but also to step up to the plate and make a commitment to ensuring the quality of the science learning of *all* their region's citizens, including and *particularly* the area's poorest and most underserved children and families.

The museum decided that the single greatest hurdle these poor and underserved children and families faced was access to quality science education. So rather than taking the traditional museum "build-it and they will come" attitude, the institution resolved to reorient its business strategy and specifically focus on ensuring educational access for this most needy segment of the community. In 1997 the Liberty Science Center entered into an agreement with the state of New Jersey to provide science education services to the thirty poorest school districts in the state. New Jersey is a populous state with not an insignificant number of poor students living in it. In excess of 15 percent of the 1.1 million school-aged children living in New Jersey qualify as "Abbott" school districts.

The name *Abbott* comes from a now famous New Jersey court case, *Abbott v. Burke*. Mr. Abbott challenged the "equal and effective" clause of the state's constitution, claiming that because of how tax monies in the state were distributed the state's poorest school districts did not receive an equal share of either the state's opportunities or resources as compared with the state's wealthier school districts. The case went all the way to the New Jersey Supreme Court, where Mr. Abbott won. The result was a statewide commitment by the state government to provide additional support to these poor districts, ranging in size from rural Vineland with 9,000 students to urban Newark with 45,000 students.

No other museum in the United States that we are aware of is as directly involved with such a large, systemic effort to improve precollege student education, particularly for this segment of the population. We say systemic, because the program is designed to fully supplement Abbot district school children's science education, including not only increased school field trip opportunities, but in-school lessons, teacher training, and, equally important, family science learning opportunities, including free passes to the science center. The program currently serves 180,000 students and their families each year, each of which has some contact with the program every single year. Emlyn Koster, president and CEO of the Liberty Science Center, stated to John in an interview, "We decided that rather than just rhetorically say we serve the needs of our community we needed to determine what the community really needed and then make our programs and efforts fit those needs."

The science center has set about creating a vast menu of offerings for the Abbott Partnership program. Prior to the start of each school year, the science center individually negotiates a letter of agreement with representatives from each of the thirty school districts. The result is thirty letters of agreement defining how each district will uniquely participate in the program. This is not a one-size-fits-all program. In collaboration with science center staff, each district selects the mix of onsite, offsite, and online experiences they will utilize in the coming year at all grade levels, pre-K–12. They choose from each of the three areas—school programs, teacher training and family programs—those experiences they feel best meet the needs and interests of their students and their families. All experiences are linked to the Core Curriculum Content Standards for Science and address the science education needs of these traditionally underserved communities.

For example, the science center offers dozens of live and virtual school field trip programs, including their nationally acclaimed Cardiac Classroom program where in collaboration with the surgeons from Mid-Atlantic Surgical Associates and the staff at Morristown Memorial Hospital, Liberty Science Center has created a unique two-way audio and video interactive surgical experience. Participating students have an unprecedented opportunity to become immersed in every facet of a real open heart, coronary bypass surgery. As participants get to talk directly with every member of the operating team, a Liberty Science Center science educator facilitates the powerful learning experience. This signature program of Liberty Science Center has become a mainstay for Abbott participants, as well as thousands of other students throughout the New Jersey area.

All students, grades pre-K–12, who attend public schools in New Jersey's Abbott school districts are eligible for a free Family Pass. The Family Pass provides each student, and up to three guests (which must include one adult) unlimited free visits to Liberty Science Center's Exhibit Floors on weekdays after school, weekends, and holidays and during the summer. The Family Pass is also good for free parking and discounted theater passes to IMAX and 3-D laser shows. As part of this program, the science center provides "Family Friendly Days." These special days are every Saturday, Sunday, and Monday from July 1 to August 31 when a limited number of groups are allowed in the building in order to ensure a more "family-welcoming" atmosphere for visitors. Family Passes can also be used for Community Evenings, which are held after hours at Liberty Science Center from 6 p.m. to 9 p.m., and are scheduled for specific districts at specific times. They provide a special atmosphere for students, teachers, families, and extended families of Abbott school districts to explore Liberty Science Center's exhibit floors, as well as see IMAX films and 3-D laser shows. On these evenings, theater tickets are available free, on a first come, first served basis. The science center offers bilingual demonstrations, special activities, arts and crafts, and a range of special programs available in both English and Spanish.

All Abbott school districts have an agreement with Liberty Science Center regarding the number of teachers who can take part in workshops at no cost. Liberty Science Center is a registered provider of professional development hours, meaning that upon completion of any Liberty Science Center professional development activity, each teacher receives professional development hours. Again, teachers can select from a menu of dozens of workshops, aimed at all grade levels. As part of this program the Liberty Science Center has also established a Teacher Sabbatical program that is open to all K–12 teachers. Sabbatical teachers get involved with educational program development, exhibit design, evaluation, exploration of cutting-edge educational technology, as well as teaching and working with the science center's partner middle school. Each school in the program, of which there are hundreds, selects an "Ambassador." As the official Liberty Science Center representative for his or her school, each Ambassador receives an Abbott Partnership Tool Kit that explains all of Liberty Science Center's programs and how to participate, Family Passes for students in grades pre-K–12, and flyers promoting the science center's numerous free Community Evenings.

These Ambassadors are provided special programs and training, and they in turn serve as advocates for the program ensuring that teachers, students, their families, and communities maximize the opportunities afforded by the program. Ambassadors play a key role in supporting utilization of the Liberty Science Center's innovative learning resources for the lifelong exploration of nature, humanity, and technology. Program staff say that without the commitment of Liberty Science Center Ambassadors and the very important role they play, the Abbott Partnership Program could not succeed.

The Abbott Partnership has not only transformed the programs of the Liberty Science Center, it has transformed finances as well. The Abbott Partnership accounts for more than one-third of the science center's $18 million annual operating budget. And far from being a drain on resources, CEO Koster says the program has been amazingly beneficial to the science center's financial health; the program generates more revenues than it costs to operate. But the benefits according to Koster far transcend the immediate dollars flowing into the institution. The program has benefited virtually every aspect of the science center's business. Because of the magnitude of the project, the institution has needed to add staff and intellectual capacity; these additional human resources have, in turn, contributed to all the other programmatic efforts conducted at the institution. As a consequence of this program, the science center has earned a reputation as a major contributor to the community's well-being, which, according to Koster, has helped to "parlay the brand of the museum into one of larger benefit" for the community. The program has resulted in the institution winning social responsibility awards, which in turn has stimulated increased corporate and private grant opportunities and an increase in individual giving. State support, too, above and beyond the Abbott Partnership has increased. Perhaps the most tangible sign of the benefits this program has reaped according to Koster is that during the museum's recent capital campaign, the state of New Jersey pledged $104 million, $50 million as a direct grant and the balance as an interest-free loan. In short, the Liberty Science Center redefined its entire business strategy from being primarily a general public-centered attraction to being largely a need-focused community resource for a particular segment of their public; in the process they have redirected both their mission and their business model. They have moved from a financial model that was almost totally dependent on unpredictable earned revenues to one with a secure and consistent base, all the while fulfilling their mission and improving their brand.

Money flows to organizations that clearly support and fulfill real needs; in fact, money does not just flow, it runs! Every nonprofit requires financial resources in order to accomplish its mission; the closer the mission is to the perceived needs and desires of the community that organization seeks to serve the more readily those resources will be available. Maybe we're just being nostalgic here, but financial woes did not seem to be the predominant concern of most museums in the first half of the twentieth century. Today, virtually every museum, large and small, old and young, sing the money blues. Why is this? Hanging around the hallways of museums and museum meetings one consistently hears a similar list of culprits, a series of external forces beyond the control of the museum—the events of 9/11, the downturn in the economy, increasing competition, lack of public understanding and appreciation for the importance of the museum's work, and the list goes on. Although few would argue that these events contribute to the financial woes of museums, it is hard to believe that these factors alone can be responsible. Weren't some variations of all of these events present during the first half of the century as well? Why were venerable institutions like the American Museum of Natural History and the Art Institute of Chicago able to survive the Great Depression but now find it challenging to weather a two-year recession? The central tenet of this book is that resources will always be there if your institution is in sync with your constituency. Therefore, it is fair to surmise that what has changed is not just a few volatile external financial factors, but, more important, the fundamental relationship of museums with their current constituencies. It is not sufficient to bemoan the reductions in local and state government funding and blame it on the philistine nature of politicians. As the above Liberty Science Center example and the Boston Children's Museum example from the previous chapter clearly demonstrate, when government feels like your institution is fulfilling what it perceives are fundamental services, it will support you. The same is true for corporations, individual donors, and the public. As James Collins and Jerry Porras discovered when studying some of the most long-term successful corporations in America, the best companies had a core ideology consistent with the desires of their consumers, and because of that they made money. Not the other way around.[1] Companies that set out to make money in the absence of such a core ideology tended to be much less successful—and these were for-profits! We live in a new age and a new age calls for a new approach to building and sustaining financial support.

GOVERNMENT SUPPORT

In the previous chapter we described the new "Agents of Change" initiative at the Ontario Science Centre. The museum projected that this initiative would cost $40 million (Canadian) to complete. It aggressively pitched this new approach to funders and has now raised over $45 million with major gifts from several prominent Canadian funding sources, both private and public. It is telling that the Ontario government was the first to see the promise of the Ontario Science Centre's Agents of Change initiative, committing $15 million through the Ministry of Culture's Infrastructure Renewal program, the ministry that manages the infrastructure and growth in Ontario for personal and economic well-being. The Science Centre's long-term operating business model currently depends upon two financial pillars —government support (approximately 50 percent of revenues) and various forms of earned income from visitor attendance fees, gift shop sales, camps, school groups, facility rentals,

Omnimax sales, concessions, and international exhibition sales and rentals (roughly 50 percent). The center has no reason at the moment to believe that this formula won't continue to work. Lewis expects government support to remain steady and she does not project a decline in revenues from visitors. Perhaps most impressive, the center did not alter its financial model based upon the assumption that this major make-over would swell attendance. Lewis emphasized that the Science Centre had one million visitors per year before Agents of Change and she assumes that it will have one million visitors per year afterward too. "We believe that we must continue to change in order to continue to attract this number of visitors. We don't have all the answers, but we believe that Agents of Change will reinspire our current visitors as well as add a whole new group of visitors that have historically not been part of our regular visitor population."

Since a major percentage of funding comes from the regional government it has ensured that these important stakeholders have bought into their scheme. Embracing a new vision for the institution that seeks to help Canada remain competitive in the twenty-first century is certainly a goal that the Canadian government can embrace. It is no longer satisfactory for a visit to the science center to primarily be a fun, fact-filled leisure experience that results in increased "knowledge and interest" in science. It is ratcheting up its role as an educational institution with a far more serious purpose, albeit still enjoyable. The Ontario Science Centre has told its funders and its public that its goal is for visitors to be sufficiently inspired and energized by their experiences at the museum that they will become Canada's next generation of scientists, engineers, and innovative leaders. Not only has it stated that it will purposefully set out to achieve something as arguably slippery to prove and challenging to accomplish as improving its visitors' innovation and creativity, it has committed to being held accountable for accomplishing this. Says Lewis, "We received government monies in support for our strong commitment to innovation, and clearly what we're doing is innovative." She believes the government will understand that there's a risk involved in this new direction. After all, says Lewis, "the one thing that was clear to us that we couldn't stay the same and expect to continue to successfully achieve our mission. You can't trade forever on 'interactivity'—everyone's interactive now. To progress we needed to evolve and change. I believe that's what we've done. Time will tell how it all works out."

Government monies are inherently political, no getting around that. However, if museums work with their local communities to really understand what the "body politic" values and requires, where the empty niches are, funding can and will follow. Gone forever are the days when museums can expect funding just because they've always gotten it in the past. All organizations, but governments perhaps more than most funders, are increasingly being driven by the twin demands of prioritization and accountability.

In the lower-tax, lower-revenue world in which we now live, every government agency has adopted a more rigorous process for prioritizing funding. These changes have been particularly apparent at the local government level, a source of significant funding for a large percentage of museums. How does what museums do for the public compare with what libraries, fire and police departments, and the sanitation department do? Where do museum services rank alongside the services of the recreation, social service, and economic development departments? If this seems an unfair comparison, think again. Why shouldn't governments weigh the relative pros and cons of what a museum provides the community against the other activities it is asked to support? If your institution doesn't fare well in such comparisons, you have two choices—change what you do or find a different source of revenue. There are numerous examples available of how museums have rethought their roles and responsibilities and repositioned themselves within the pantheon of community needs resulting in increased local government support. There are also plenty of examples where this has not happened and local government support has precipitously declined.

The Government Performance and Results Act (GPRA) of 1993 seeks to "shift the focus of government decision making and accountability away from a preoccupation with the activities that are undertaken—such as grants dispensed or inspections made—to a focus on the results of those activities, such as real gains in employability, safety, responsiveness, or program quality. Under the act, agencies are to develop multiyear strategic plans, annual performance plans, and annual performance reports." The accountability requirements of GPRA have radically transformed all aspects of federal funding. These changes are now filtering down to state and local governments as well. More and more common is the need for institutions to be *measurably* accountable for the monies they receive. The key to accountability is being able to measurably define the public good that will result from monies received. Once again, the criteria for support returns to public good achieved. Institutions need to have a vision, a compelling narrative for how they hope to change the world for the better, and then they need to figure out how they are going to measure it.

An increasingly popular approach to "selling" the museum has been to position the museum as key to economic development. David Chesebrough, president and CEO of the Buffalo Museum of Science, was recently quoted as saying,

> Our role, depending on the situation and community expectations, in returning an economic value for the community investment in our organization [can be substantial]. This can vary from helping to anchor development in a community project such as waterfront development, attracting tourists and/or visitors to a location or region, or helping stabilize a declining inner city neighborhood. Returns to the community can come from direct support for our institution (in lieu of or in addition to government support), tourist dollars expended throughout the community, increased property value or community investment in our proximity, and other indirect means. Outcomes can be measured in economic impact from visitor dollars invested in the area around the [museum], increase in property values in the immediate neighborhood.[2]

A number of institutions have successfully brokered this economic value into tax levies that help to support the institution. For example, the St. Louis Science Center has used a tax levy to guarantee free admission to its exhibit halls. Denver Museum of Science and Nature has successfully negotiated a mileage tax; it has used the proceeds to help support operating expenses. Still other institutions have gone before the voters with bond issues or other forms of debt financing to help them pay for expansions or renovations. The argument that has traditionally been made to the public is that the economic and educational benefits of the museum are worth the taxpayers' subsidy. Some of these efforts have been successful, for example, in Salt Lake City in support of the Children's Museum and others not, for example, a statewide effort in Ohio to support COSI, Columbus. The cautionary tale in all of this is that debt financing, whether from a low-interest government bond or from a more conventional lending source is hazardous. A recent ad hoc task force of the Association of Science-Technology examining "troubled" institutions found that they invariably had overleveraged their capital projects through debt financing. Covering financial shortfalls through borrowing is a calculated risk in the best of times; in the financially uncertain times we now inhabit it is almost always a bad idea.

Government support used to be a mainstay of museum financing, then in the 1980s and 1990s it became increasingly diminished. We believe there is a new future for government support, but it needs to be predicated on legitimate benefit to the community. The Liberty Science Center was able to secure huge state funding through its commitment to satisfying the science learning requirements of New Jersey's most needy students. The Ontario Science Centre received its large federal grant because of the vision they had of building a better future in Canada by providing young people with "the attitudes, skills, networks and tools that will enable them to become the drivers of a sustainable culture of innovation." The Boston Children's Museum has seen its local government monies increase because of its dedication to making Boston a more livable place for all of the city's diverse urban children. What need(s) can your museum, and only your museum, best fulfill in your community? Answer this question and government monies will follow.

CORPORATE SUPPORT

NEWS RELEASE

SAN FRANCISCO, CA, MARCH 18, 2003 The Asian Art Museum today announced a partnership with Target Stores to offer visitors free admission to the new home of the Asian Art Museum every first Tuesday of the month, beginning Tuesday, April 1, 2003. The new museum will open in the city's historic Civic Center on March 20, 2003. Target's generous corporate sponsorship will support free "Target Tuesdays" through the end of 2003. The "Target Tuesdays" program at the new Asian Art Museum represents Target Stores' commitment to community giving, and particularly to the arts and education.

"The 'Target Tuesdays' program helps us open our doors to everyone interested in visiting this world-class collection. We greatly appreciate Target's support," said Emily Sano, director of the museum.

"Target believes that exposure to the arts enriches lives and helps to promote cultural understanding," said Laysha Ward, vice president of community relations, Target Corporation. "We are proud to offer 'Target Tuesdays' so guests can visit the new Asian Art Museum, enjoy its world renowned Asian art collection, and experience its diverse programs and amenities free of charge."

Why should a major, Minneapolis-based corporation such as Target invest so much money in a San Francisco museum? Obviously, the company believes in the mission of this organization, but just as obviously the company hopes to build its brand and extend its customer base by associating with an Asian art museum. It is probably not too much of a stretch to infer that Target's goal in supporting this relationship was to reinforce its marketing position as a retailer that delivers high-quality merchandise at bargain basement prices—Asian art for free! The company has entered into similar partnerships with other museums around the country as well, presumably with similar goals in mind.

Everything and anything seems to be fair game for corporate sponsorship today, from naming rights for exhibitions, building additions, even whole institutions. For example, the Calgary Science Centre just announced that it is changing its name to the TELUS World of Science Calgary. In return for the naming rights, TELUS will invest $9 million over twenty years in the Calgary Science Centre Society. According to the museum, this contribution will be used to build a new and expanded science center and allow for the development of new programs that will encourage lifelong learning in the field of science. According to Karen Radford, president of TELUS Partner Solutions, "This investment is a perfect match for TELUS. We're investing in our children's future and innovation. The TELUS World of Science is about children developing innovative thinking at an early age when natural curiosity makes children excited about and interested in science and technology."

Kevin Matieshin, chair of the Calgary Science Centre Board, says, "The TELUS World of Science is Southern Alberta's premier destination for youth and family learning with more than 256,000 students benefiting from educational programming in the last five years. Together with TELUS we will inspire careers in science, innovation and economic development." TELUS mobile is Canada's top wireless phone company. In addition to this major partnership with the Calgary Science Centre they also are major underwriters of the Ontario Science Centre's Agent of Change initiative. Clearly the company believes these high-profile investments in Canadian science centers will pay off for them too.

Like any fundraising effort, working with corporations is about building relationships. And like any relationship, they work best when they are perceived by both parties as a really good deal—win-win situations. As those who have been around fundraising for years know, you don't raise money by appealing to what you need, but by offering to meet others' needs. Everyone has to end up feeling good about it or ultimately the deal will sour. Money is not the only or necessarily even the best reason to enter into a relationship with a corporate partner!

Good corporate partnerships involve true collaborations, the trading of mutually valued goods and services. Certainly money is one valued gift a corporation can provide, but so too is expertise. Many institutions are finding that corporate gifts of knowledge—business and financial planning, marketing, and subject matter expertise—are equally as valuable as direct cash gifts. For example, as part of its new initiative the Ontario Science Centre has entered into partnerships with universities and corporations. According to CEO Lewis, "We will work with leading-edge academic and corporate researchers, bringing together their research with our proven capacity to make complex subjects accessible. As one example, we have formed a strong partnership with DuPont Canada. As our knowledge partner they have committed over the next eight years to provide us not only with financial support but, even more important, with expertise. DuPont scientists will work with our science communicators in developing innovative programming for our visitors. We anticipate such content partnerships as being key to our success. But we will not relinquish our control over the actual visitor experience; we will not risk our reputation for being trustworthy and unbiased." And that is ultimately the key issue for museums, how to negotiate a relationship with a corporation that is both beneficial to both the industry partner and the museum without compromising the needs of either. There is no magic formula for ensuring that the museum will derive only positive benefits from a relationship with a corporate donor, but healthy doses of good sense, financial and legal diligence, as well as keeping one's eyes open wide are not bad prescriptions. Of course, the same could be said for all fundraising efforts, including contributions from individuals and foundations.

INDIVIDUAL AND FOUNDATION GIVING

Here is a sampling of some recent press releases:

> At the Annual Meeting of the Albany Institute of History & Art in June, Board Chair Nancy Hodes announced a $1 million gift to the museum from trustee Matthew Bender IV. The donation, which will lead the way for the museum's immediate, $5.6 million fund-raising initiative, "Achieving Excellence in the 21st Century," is the single largest cash gift in the Albany Institute's history.
>
> American art collectors James W. and Frances G. McGlothlin plan to bequeath art and give financial support valued at well above $100 million to the Virginia

Museum of Fine Arts. Dr. Michael Brand, VMFA's director, made the announcement in Richmond today, calling the McGlothlins "among the nation's leading collectors of American art." "We have spent the last decade immersed in the world of American art, never suspecting early on that our desire to learn and appreciate this legacy could result in so meaningful a commitment to Virginia," says James McGlothlin, who is the chairman and CEO of the United Company of Bristol [VA], a conglomerate involved in financial services, oil and gas, industrial supply distribution and golf courses. "Fran and I envision a long and creative relationship with the museum's leadership, which in recent years has shown a tremendous level of artistic initiative," he says.

Smithsonian Secretary Lawrence Small announced today that Kenneth E. Behring, a California philanthropist, developer and former owner of the Seattle Seahawks, has increased his support of the Smithsonian to $100 million by making today's donation of $80 million to the National Museum of American History. It is the largest single gift ever to the Smithsonian Institution.

A Rhode Island family foundation and its founders has committed a major gift and bequest to the non-profit USS Saratoga Museum Foundation, Inc. The gift and bequest, representing a combination of cash and personal property having an aggregate value of at least $1,000,000 is by far the largest contribution made to date to support the effort to create a family attraction, educational center and memorial at Quonset/Davisville featuring the aircraft carrier Saratoga as the centerpiece.

The Jordan Schnitzer Museum of Art at the University of Oregon will reopen to the public on Sunday, Jan. 23, 2005. The museum has been closed since September 2000 for a major renovation and expansion project.... The art museum's new facility has been created through a $14.2 million transformation of the 70-year old building, listed on the National Register of Historic Places. The State of Oregon awarded $6.36 million in state-serviced bonds to the construction project. These funds were matched, beyond the requirement, through a combination of grants, estate gifts and contributions from more than 750 individual donors. The single largest private gift came from Portland philanthropist and cultural leader Jordan D. Schnitzer. In recognition of his generosity, the new building will be officially recognized as the Jordan Schnitzer Museum of Art at the University of Oregon.

As these press releases confirm, gifts from individuals remain a major source of funding for many, if not most, museums. Although large contributions from individual donors are always attractive, the reality is that a large percentage of contributed income comes from various fundraising efforts, including events such as auctions and "awards" programs, direct mail solicitations, and contributions from trustees and patrons. Once upon a time, institutions were largely supported by gifts from wealthy patrons.

Virtually all museums created prior to 1960 could count on endowments in place on the day doors opened to the public, largely generated by contributions from a few wealthy patrons. The vast majority of museums created since 1980 are not so blessed. Clearly, being able to count on a few generous souls beats not having them at all. As museums have discovered in recent years, however, when the markets are down, even those with deep financial pockets can be affected. At the beginning of the twenty-first century equity markets saw huge declines and everyone's portfolios, including museums, dropped precipitously in value. With the commitment of the Federal Reserve Board to keep inflation at bay, interest rates during this same period were slashed to record lows, again cutting into any returns that could be expected from a given portfolio. All of this helped to contribute to severe economic pressures on those with wealth, and thus indirectly on museums as well.

All sources of funding come with significant financial and intellectual strings attached, no less so generating money through individual or foundation gifts and grants. As we have previously discussed, securing gift and grant monies is becoming a full-time, exceedingly time-consuming and money-intensive business as the number of nonprofit organizations grows faster than the philanthropic base on which they "feed." Although all fundraising is about cultivating relationships, nowhere is this more important than with individuals and foundations. Good private side development requires time and patience. Historically, individual contributions were primarily about legacy and personal ego. Although we wouldn't want to suggest that this is not still partially true, increasingly individual gifts, foundation grants too, are based on the same criteria as government funding—evidence that the museum is attempting to make a significant and important contribution to society. Good development people understand how to communicate these ideas to potential contributors, clearly emphasizing the important connections that exist between the goals of the institution and the concerns of donor. Good development people also appreciate that these relationships need to be cultivated and that everyone's needs are best met by developing a long-term bond rather than a short-term financial fix.

There are many ways to facilitate communication with donors and contributors, including e-mails, letters, and the good old-fashioned telephone call.

Andree Peek, former president and CEO of Sci-Port Discovery Center, Shreveport, LA, argues that the annual report, too, can and should be a key development tool.

> Beyond setting the right course for advancing our mission each year, keeping our attention on the public we seek to serve and tracking our progress, our most critical factor in sustaining our operations is communicating our success. To quickly and succinctly acquaint granters, donors and the interested public with the progress their support makes possible, we take great care in producing and printing an Annual Report. Without this report, our constituents would be relying heavily on our Form 990 Information Tax Return filed annually with the Internal Revenue Service or fragmented pieces of information they obtain from the media. Neither source shares a full view of our results and the impact of our programs on the people we served during the year.
>
> Our fourteen page Annual Report presents the outcomes of the year more in pictures than words to involve the reader in a comprehensive and enjoyable visual journey of the impact our educational activities have had on the lives of young people and families. Throughout our Annual Report are reprints of comments received during the year from some of our visitors, teachers, donors and children. . . . The Annual Report has become my most valuable tool in building and sustaining relationships with supporters and prospects. Ultimately, communicating our success everyday, with the aid of the tangible results revealed through our Annual Report, keeps the attendance and resource pipeline flowing and the community's passion for our mission ignited.[3]

Obviously, it is easier to talk about raising money from individuals and foundations than it is to do it, but several factors are currently working in the favor of museums, particularly museums in America. The first factor is that the United States has the most dynamic, extensive, and expansive philanthropic system in history. Today, there are over 65,000 grant-making institutions registered with the U.S. Internal Revenue Service. This represents a nearly 5 percent growth since 2001 and includes $435 billion in assets that are being distributed at about $30 billion annually.[4] Of this money, nearly 20 percent is being given for general/unrestricted support and the largest share (22 percent) addresses matters of children and youth.[5] In addition to registered charities, billions of dollars are contributed annually by individuals outside the framework of formal foundations.

A second important factor is that the philanthropic environment has changed dramatically in recent years and is no longer dependent upon large foundations.[6] This reality is reflected in the fact that between 1991 and 2003 family foundations grew by 33 percent, from 20,498 to 30,517, and their assets grew from $9 billion to $25 billion. The priorities of these foundations in order are education, health, human services, and art and culture. [7]

A final important change in the philanthropic world is that today there are 2 million people in the United States who have wealth of more than $1 million to invest.[8] As fundraisers know, people with money will provide substantial support to causes in which they believe. Whereas in the past individual donors with large checkbooks tended to be concentrated in large cities or contributed through large foundations, today these moneyed individuals can be found in large and small communities and are often very amenable to funding smaller organizations.

The point is that even institutions with limited fundraising traditions have opportunities to secure considerable resources today, and the rules of the game of fundraising are changing significantly. All of this is to suggest that museums should not assume that they cannot attract philanthropic support to help fund their institutions. But lest we sound like a broken record, successful fundraising starts with a message. As suggested at the beginning of this chapter, you don't get money just because you set out to get money. You get money because you are doing things that are so important and compelling that individuals and foundations want to give you money.

Of course they won't give you money if you don't ask. And they won't give you money unless they feel that you can actually deliver on what you promise. So always make promises that are worth keeping and, by all means, don't make promises you cannot keep. For example, don't say you will solve all of the world's problems or that you'll achieve outcomes that you can't prove you can accomplish. And never, never make the long-term promise that if you give this once, we'll never ask you again. All sources of funding need to be renewable, both those we dub erroneously "unearned" and those we call "earned."

EARNED INCOME

In a recent chapter on marketing written as part of a book about small science centers, Kim L. Cavendish, president and CEO of the Museum of Discovery and Science, Ft. Lauderdale, writes,

Consider museum birthday parties as a source of earned revenue. Many museums offer a party option for a package price that includes museum admission and use of a private gathering space. But competition is fierce, from other museums, from fast food restaurants, and from entrepreneurial entertainers. So how can a science center compete in this milieu? By offering a complete experience, not just group admission. Think about developing a product that will appeal to today's busy parents by offering a total package. At the Virginia Air and Space Center, a party includes a cake shaped like the space shuttle, a private room with a private science demonstration, an IMAX film, and a personalized exhibit tour. At the Orlando Science Center, the room used for birthday parties has been decorated with fanciful and colorful wall murals and the birthday child gets a special welcome in the theater before the show. At the Museum of Discovery and Science, [Ft. Lauderdale, FL] new party themes are now implemented each year, and parents of the birthday child buy theme-related invitations and party favors from the museum store. The idea is to create one-stop shopping for the event by one call to your reservations number. We have found that, in fact, the "deluxe" options for parties, while more expensive, attract more buyers than those with fewer bells and whistles. When you have developed a quality product that is unique to your institution, it will sell.[9]

As museums have become increasingly dependent upon earned income they have become increasingly creative in how to generate it. Added to the usual suspects of admission sales and sales from gift shops and food services are now birthday parties, facility rental sales, parking fees, tuitions from courses, licensing and merchandising agreements, rental sales of traveling exhibitions, summer camps and overnight camp-ins, films (35mm and large format), and consulting fees for exhibition development and other museum services, just to name a few examples. Many museums have gotten quite good at these ancillary funding strategies; too many museums, though, are pretty hopeless at it. For example, few food service or membership efforts actually generate substantial revenues, yet they often cause substantial management headaches.[10] All earned income efforts require significant financial outlays in order to make money—stores require inventory, courses and camps involve significant preparation, scheduling, and qualified staffing, events require additional set-up and maintenance costs, membership programs involve additional printing and postage costs, and all efforts require professional staff with skills unlike those typically found at museums. In fact, the biggest challenge to most museums trying to generate earned income is that it requires them to be in businesses they are not used to being in.

Take, for example, running the gift shop. Running a retail store, if you want it to be profitable, requires more than convincing a few volunteers you can trust to hang around and ring up sales. Your museum's gift shop is now in direct competition with other retail stores in your community. Once upon a time museums had a near-monopoly on the types of goods they sold in their stores. That's no longer true. Not even counting the Internet where shoppers can find and purchase virtually anything, today even the local mall now has a "museum store" selling similar merchandise. If you want to make more than pocket change off your store, then you need to really approach your store as a serious and separate business.

Unfortunately, few businesses are as cut-throat and demanding as retailing; from buying to pricing to displaying, retailing is both an art and a science. According to retail sales consultant Lisa Duncan of Duncan & Duncan Enterprises LLC, the following are just a few of the things that make up the art of good retailing:[11]

MERCHANDISING AND VISUAL DISPLAY

- Image—defining your store's image and its target customer
- Intention—keeping sales associates abreast of your merchandising plans
- Invitation—enhancing the importance of your store front
- Ingenuity—visually merchandising and communicating your message
- Inspiration—relating trends to your merchandising plans

PROMOTIONS AND ADVERTISING

- Seasonal events
- Vendor relations
- Repetition, the need to constantly plug your business
- Image and intention

And of course successful retailing requires a great sales force, which involves training and management; sales staff need to be friendly, knowledgeable, and customer-focused.

Successful retailing is also a science, a series of tangible sales numbers generated by the interaction of customers with merchandise. According to museum retail consultant Andrew Andoniadis of Andoniadis Retail Services, retail "science" factors include:[12]

- Capture Rate (percentage of visitors making retail purchases)
- Dollars per Visitor (net retail sales/# of visitors)
- Dollars per Customer (net retail sales/# of retail transactions)
- Gross Sales and Dollars per Square Foot
- Inventory Turnover (cost of goods sold/average inventory)

In short, museums should enter into an ancillary income venture with their eyes wide open. To be a successful part of an organization's business model, earned income efforts need to be approached with the same attention, commitment, and expertise as are typically applied to collections and exhibitions.

Earned income efforts should be designed to fundamentally support and if possible totally mirror all other efforts at the museum. In other words, the gift shop should sell items that support and enhance the messages contained in exhibitions. Facility renters should be encouraged to have their events take on the theme of the museum—not only will this be enjoyable but likely more memorable as well. The Boston Children's Museum could have derived rental income from leasing their holdings to any organization that was willing to pay the price, but they opted to rent only to organizations that were consistent with their child and family focus. The restaurant, too, should reflect the museum's mission. For example, the website of Kim Cavendish's Ft. Lauderdale science center highlights the constantly changing themes of their Science Café:

New Science Café demonstrations: Iguanodon Bon Bons, Prehistoric Pasta, Saber-Tooth Soup, Stegosaurus Strudel and T-Rex Bites.

Pasta Fossils

May 28, 29, 30, 2005 from 12 p.m. to 4 p.m.

We can find out many things about dinosaurs by studying their bones. Even millions of years after their extinction, we are able to reconstruct their skeletons, figure out what they ate, where they lived, how fast they might have been, and many other things that—without their bones—would have remained a mystery. In this craft activity, you will get a chance to create a fossil of your very own dinosaur. Perhaps you will create the fossil remains of a lasagnadon, or maybe even a rare linguinisaurus!

Florida Fossils
May 28, 29, 30, 2005 from 12 p.m. to 4 p.m.
Imagine gigantic creatures lounging around your yard, grazing by your pool and chewing on palm fronds. Well, thousands of years ago, some prehistoric animals called Florida home. The Gems and Mineral Society of the Palm Beaches will display their collection of Florida fossils to help guests understand the history of our own backyard.

Dino Match
May 28, 29, 30, 2005 from 12 p.m. to 2 p.m.
Learn about the many adaptations that helped dinosaurs live in a prehistoric world. Then determine if they are related to each other.

Chippin' Away
May 28, 29, 30, 2005 from 2 p.m. to 4 p.m.
Be a paleontologist and dig up a fossilized "chocolate-chip-a-saurus" from your own "dig site."

Such strategic decisions are not only more justifiable under the 501(c)3 tax code but they also make good business sense. A museum's business model should spell out how it will strategically seek to maximize its mission, brand, and products; to be successful in the twenty-first century will require that all three be mutually reinforcing, all the time. As the late Roy Schafer, a museum business "coach," said, "Businesses succeed through a successful combination of the related trinity of factors: understanding your core business and values; knowing what you are best at; and finding the economic driver that works in the marketplace."[13]

DISCUSSION QUESTIONS
- What is the current relationship between your organization's mission, the perceived needs and desires of your community, and your revenue sources?
- What are the current funding priorities of your local government? How well aligned is your organization's financial strategy with these funding priorities? If there's a misalignment, why is this the case?
- What percentage of your organization's funding comes from earned income? How closely aligned are earned income resources with the core mission of your organization? How could they be brought closer into alignment?

NOTES

Epigraph: Jim C. Collins and Jerry I. Porras, *Built to Last* (New York: Harper Business, 1994), 55.

1. Ibid.

2. D. Chesebrough, unpublished ASTC position paper prepared for 2004 ASTC annual meeting session on new business models.

3. A. Peek, Sci-Port Discovery Center—how we operate and position our science center for ongoing success, in *Handbook for Small Science Centers*, ed. C. Yao, L. Dierking, and P. Anderson (Lanham, MD: AltaMira Press, in press).

4. Foundation Center, *Foundation Year Book: 2004 Edition* (Washington, DC: Foundation Center, 2004).

5. Foundation Center, *Foundation Giving Trends: Updates on Funding Priorities* (Washington, DC: Foundation Center, 2004).

6. Center on Philanthropy and Public Policy, *What is New about the New Philanthropy* (Los Angeles: University of Southern California, 2000).

7. Foundation Center, *Key Facts on Family Foundations* (Washington, DC: Foundation Center, 2005).

8. K. Fulton and A. Blau, Trends in 21st Century Philanthropy, Women Funding Networks, URL: http://www.wfnet.org/, 2003, accessed June 12, 2005.

9. K. Cavendish, Marketing basics: Applications for small science centers, in *Handbook for Small Science Centers*, ed. C. Yao, L. Dierking, and P. Anderson (Lanham, MD: AltaMira Press, in press).

10. C. B. Smith, The art of managing a museum—connecting the past, present and future, in *Inside the Minds: The Business of Museums*, ed. C. B. Smith (Boston: Aspatore, Inc., 2004).

11. Lisa Duncan, Lisa Duncan seminars, Duncan & Duncan Enterprises LLC., http://www.lisaduncan.com/retailing.html, 2005, accessed June 13, 2005.

12. A. Andoniadis, The Art & Science of Museum Retailing. MUSE: Western Museums Association, spring 2004.

13. R. Schafer, personal communication, November 19, 2004.

IV

Implementing and Sustaining a Knowledge Age Business Model

9

Strategies for Success

*The key is to get everybody to agree on what "success" means.
Otherwise, the enterprise suffers from dysfunctional pushing
and pulling toward myriad goals, which ultimately result in
customer dissatisfaction.*
—Gordon Bethune, President, Continental Airlines

The Buffalo Museum of Science was built in the geographic center of what in
the 1920s was one of the most prosperous and progressive cities in America.
But like many moderately sized natural history museums built in the first half
of the twentieth century, the museum now finds itself with a decaying physical
plant, located in a decaying section of an economically depressed city while the
majority of its core constituency keeps moving farther and farther away into
outer suburbs—collectively not a great recipe for success. Over the past several
years the institution has been faced with crushing financial realities—declining attendance, huge cuts in government funding, and ever escalating costs in
order to maintain an increasingly decrepit physical plant. New director David
Chesebrough had no choice but to lay off large numbers of staff, reduce hours,
close sections of the building, and generally pull in the belt of the museum so
tightly that most in the museum and many in the community believed that
museum was going to just go belly up and die.

Faced with such dire financial issues the museum began a strategic planning process to try and determine how, if at all, it was going to survive these
new realities. The solution the museum has opted to adopt represents a radically new vision for its future. The Buffalo Museum of Science has decided to
remake its mission, its business strategy, and even its address. The museum has

decided to tie its mission and its bottom line to "building deeper relationships with free-choice learners of all ages through sustained, long-term relationships. . . . To shift the museum's emphasis from attracting casual visitors to converting those visitors into committed learners and engaging them in deeper relationships with the museum." To serve those learners better and to align its service and financial models more closely, it has decided to adopt a distributed approach where better, easier access rather than bigger, fancier exhibitions are the primary draws. Although it will invest resources in restoring and enhancing the quality of its original building, the goal will be to redefine the purpose and role of this original site. Rather than claiming that the museum, like most museums, is defined by a single, grand, one site-serves-all-functions institution, the original building will become the hub of a network of learning centers distributed around the city and suburbs; the main building will no longer be the exclusive destination of the Buffalo Museum of Science. The goal is to reposition the institution as a collections-based discovery center with many sites throughout the region.

The original site will be designed to serve as a catalyst for economic redevelopment and change in Buffalo's economically depressed East Side, while other museum sites serve other areas, fulfilling other needs. The network's new centers will increase the museum's "surface area" within the broader Buffalo community, strengthening its reach and its ability to attract, engage, and support lifelong learners. Chesebrough believes that the combination of a central support facility at the original site plus numerous satellite sites throughout the Buffalo area will provide the museum with new business opportunities, more flexibility, and a better fit between its engagement and business models. The primary business strategy will be to improve significantly the institution's reach to the residents of greater Buffalo through the creation of a series of smaller, more accessible sites. In the process, the museum will also be able to improve significantly the quality and personalization of the services it can provide its publics since most of these new sites will be small enough that individual staff working there will be able to recognize and more individually serve the needs of users.

For many reasons, the new plan includes efforts to revitalize the original facility, which would continue to offer groups of visitors natural history discovery experiences unavailable anywhere else in the region. According to internal documents,

[The original site] would combine the earliest traditions of natural history museums with some of the latest technology, linking visitors to the collections and the scientists working at the museum. Visible labs and collections storage would reveal much more of what goes on behind the scenes at the museum and who is doing it. The building would continue to house collection storage, research labs, and most staff offices. It would continue to serve as a regional destination but it would also become a learning center focused on the needs of the immediate neighborhood.

But equally important, the original site would also be redesigned so that it could serve as the program development center for the rest of the network, creating exhibits, workshop activities, and other programs for circulation to the numerous "Science Spots" the museum will create. The first Science Spot opened in the fall of 2005; eventually dozens of these new satellite venues will be opened throughout the city and region.

With the original BMS building focused on the collections and on large-scale exhibits and events, the Science Spots will provide more individualized experiences such as classes, workshops, camps, and other activities complemented by related retail and convenient food and beverages. These satellites will provide platforms for free-choice learning with a level of convenience and customization that would be difficult to achieve at a single large, centralized site; plus each Science Spot will be designed as a positive revenue generator. Located in leased or purchased commercial space convenient to the museum's various audiences of interest, the Science Spots will be neighborhood learning centers that draw their users primarily from those within walking or easy driving distance. By sharing programs sequentially or simultaneously among them, this distributed network of sites would offer both economies of scale and improved access for users. The Science Spots will also provide a feeder network supporting attendance at programs offered only at the original, central site, which in turn would help boost the original sites attendance and revenues. Of course, in turn, visitors to the original site will be encouraged to partake in the specialized, smaller-scale programs at the satellite Science Spots.

Again, according to internal documents,

By taking the museum to its users, this new approach creates value through proximity and convenience that would be unavailable with the more traditional centralized model. It greatly increases the museum's interface with the community, providing many more opportunities for program experimentation, earned revenue, political support, fundraising, and brand recognition than a more centralized model allows. It maintains a significant commitment to the original facility and its neighborhood, but allows the museum to experiment with new locations, audiences, programs, and partnerships at a relatively low capital cost.

In addition to the Science Spots, the museum is planning on adding some smaller, branded satellites placed in existing venues operated by other organizations. These include sites such as branch libraries, schools, community centers, and perhaps even the zoo. These sites will allow the Buffalo Museum of Science to build partnerships with other like-minded organizations, to recruit crossover users, and to tap new sources of revenue. Where these various satellites do not allow a full range of earned revenue opportunities, they will be funded through grants or contracts. These arrangements make it possible for the museum to extend its services to users who might lack the means to pay for them directly.

As Al DeSena, former director of Wichita's Exploration Place and one of the architects of this new model, said,

> Our industry really needs to take a hard look at the strengths and weaknesses of having a single, large central location. I'm coming to believe that if we want to foster long-term, lifelong learning relationships with the regional population, we need to be much closer to where they live. We need to have a proximate, community presence that is distributed around town where the centers of population are. People need to be able almost to walk to one of these community centers and do it on a regular basis to engage in activities that relate to the core vision and goals of the museum. There is a flow between them and the central location (which is still needed)—of people, ideas, materials, events, etc. These community centers could be new, but that's unlikely. It's probably much more realistic to establish long-term comprehensive relationships and services with organizations that are already distributed around town (YMCA, 4-H Clubs, Girl Scouts, branch libraries, senior centers, etc.).

The Buffalo Museum of Science has made it part of its institutional goal to help build a learning community, which in turn helped push the museum towards a commitment to both attracting new learners and to serving those it already has, which in turn made it realize that its mission was not about exhibitions, but learning. So at both the original site and the satellites, free or low-cost programs are more important than exhibitions and provide attractive entry experiences for those new to the museum. Fee-based programs and specialty retail also serve as opportunities for those learners to pursue deeper relationships and to support the museum proportionately to their use of its resources. The measure of institutional success will no longer be the number of visitors served, but the quality of experiences provided; the financial measure of success becomes not just dollars, but the dollars per visitor over time. The goal is to provide deep, quality experiences that users will be willing to pay for on a fee-per-use basis. The cost of entry experiences will be minimal or free, but deeper experiences will either be fee-based, or subsidized as appropriate. In this way, everyone has access to some measure of what the museum has to offer, but ultimate financial stability is maintained through adequate revenue-generating devices.

This approach attempts to balance the community science and free-choice learning goals of the institution with the political and financial realities of the community. It is a business model that emphasizes access and service over product, quality over quantity. As the museum's director David Chesebrough says,

> Our traditional role of providing social outlets for individuals, groups and family units looking to spend leisure time together was historically marketing, rather than relationship driven. This often placed us in direct competition with amusement parks, malls, festivals, sporting events and other typical choices for spending ever more precious time and family/individual funds. We intend to reinvent this equation so that our institution is competing instead for quality time, for relationship-building experiences, experiences that few of the above "entertainment-focused" leisure experiences can match. We believe this new model will reposition us to be extremely competitive in the changing world in which we operate.

So what does success look like in the twenty-first century? It means providing indispensable value to the public(s) you serve. What we gained during the Industrial Revolution was unprecedented access to products and services; what we lost was value. Value—trust, quality, respect, affordability, honesty, dignity, courtesy, ease, durability, personalization, convenience—these are some of the things that are currently in short supply; the institutions that can return these kinds of value to people will be successful. In today's marketplace "value" is something people will pay seemingly inordinate prices for. That is why people pay more for brand names and designer labels out of all proportion to their apparent worth. According to business experts Shoshana Zuboff and James Maxmin, "this is because value itself is now a subjective, rather than an objective, proposition. It arises from the meanings with which we invest things, not from the things themselves."[1] But as we discussed earlier, it is hard to be all things to all people; to provide all value, all the time. In the crowded, competitive marketplace of the twenty-first century it will be next to impossible, financially or logistically, to provide maximal value to all individuals. The key to success thus requires being strategic, deciding which values are to be emphasized and for whom. Buffalo Museum of Science director David Chesebrough summed up his strategy when he said, "The business strategy of the new Buffalo Museum of Science is to close the distance between the institution and the audience. Instead of expecting people to come to us we intend to come to them. We want to turn our visitors into users and our users into learning partners."

A STRATEGY FOR BEING STRATEGIC

Running a museum is a business, and as we've attempted to highlight, a complex, multifaceted business. In this chapter we talk about the serious question of how a museum should go about deciding what business it should be in. What should the institution's strategy for success be? What should the museum's unique market niche be? And if we can't be all things to all people, what people should we be all things to? It is no mistake that in a book on the business of museums it is only after eight chapters that we finally get to these nitty-gritty questions of business strategies and practices; we believe that the contents of this chapter would have had limited value without first presenting the material that proceeded it. Because it is only within the context of the changing world in which museums now operate that these business strategies make sense. You can't just latch onto a business strategy; it must emanate from a deep understanding of the unique assets an organization possesses and how these assets might be used to serve an audience exceptionally.

A wide variety of business authors have written about how to be strategic in this new business age, including several who have emphasized that you can't be all things to all people; basically a "less is more" approach. As should be clear, we, too, subscribe to this approach. In particular, we will utilize the ideas of two business writers—Fred Crawford and Ryan Mathews.[2] Their ideas derive from years of consumer research, both in the United States and abroad, involving many thousands of individuals and hundreds of companies. Like us, they stress that the goal of any business is to determine how to best use its assets to maximize the value provided to customers. We feel that what sets Crawford and Mathews apart from many other thinkers in this area is their ability to distill out of today's complex marketplace a reasonably simple way to think about various business strategies and frame them into a manageable set of possibilities.

Based upon their research Crawford and Mathews divided value into five separate, though related, categories—*access, experience, price, service,* and *product.* They make the case that no successful business, regardless of type, can financially succeed if it attempts to be great in each of these categories. Their research demonstrated that truly successful companies are selectively striving to be excellent in only one of these categories of values, they are very good in at least one other value category, and remain at industry standards of acceptability in the other three categories. As tempting as it might be to try to be really excellent in all five categories, Crawford and Mathew's research showed that attempting to do so resulted in "leaving money on the table." Although Crawford and Mathews focused exclusively on for-profit companies and their customers, we believe their ideas can be usefully applied to nonprofit companies like museums as well. After all, how many museums can afford to "leave money on the table"? As Crawford and Mathews state:

> The overriding message here is that successful companies understand that value, in consumers' minds, is the intangible "sum total" of a business's performance in all five [value] attributes. There is an aggregate minimum threshold that every company must meet across the board to be successful. This threshold, though, is not the same for all companies. In mature markets or industries, the value threshold is much higher than in emerging industries or among companies with innovative business models.[3]

We believe that museums should now be considered a mature industry. Ironically, museums have only achieved this state of "maturity" relatively recently, despite the fact that they have been around for a long time. Arguably it was only in the last quarter of the twentieth century that they began to blossom in their current manifestation as, first and foremost, public education venues. Because of the changing nature of society at the dawn of the Knowledge Age, museums exploded in popularity. With roughly three times as many museums in the marketplace today as existed in 1975, and more being created every day, museums now represent a mature market, and accordingly, the threshold of value has escalated. Given that by the beginning of the twenty-first century six out of ten Americans were visiting some kind of museum at least once a year and virtually everyone in the country had gone at some point in their life, the expectations for what an in-museum experience could and should be have risen quite high, certainly as compared to what they were twenty years ago. Museum visitors today expect quality exhibitions, service, and experiences. But that still doesn't mean that museums must excel in all five areas of value; rather it means that what constitutes an *acceptable* in-museum experience has, and will continue to change. By contrast, the public is still willing to accept substandard quality in experience, service, and product in a museum's on-line offerings because this is still an emerging area. Make no mistake, though, within a few years these expectations, too, will change.

How does this translate into practical, day-to-day reality? We have taken Crawford and Mathews's five value categories and their ideas about excellence and reinterpreted what these would mean specifically for museums. Table 9.1 summarizes for each of these five key values what we believe a museum in today's marketplace needs to do in order to *dominate*, be *distinguished*, be *acceptable*, or qualify as *unacceptable*. All are stated from the visitor's perspective, not the museum's.

Thus, assuming a museum understands the social, political, and economic context in which it operates and has deeply considered the public it hopes to serve through its internal, external, and financial assets, it should be able to use this simple matrix—five values across and four levels of satisfaction down—to devise a business strategy. Let's look more deeply at each of these five value dimensions, one area at a time. We'll try to illustrate how different museum business strategies emerge from trying to be excellent at one or another of these values.

ACCESS

In the little community of Bemidji, Minnesota, high up at the headwaters of the Mississippi River, there is a small science center. By industry standards, the Headwaters Science Center, a converted storefront with a few exhibits recycled from other institutions, is not much to look at. But for Clarence and Mindy Smith, three-year-old twins who live in Bemidji, and for their mother Florence,[4] the science center is a wonderful place. They love the exhibits, and they love their morning "Tots-In-Science" classes, but what they love most is that it

Table 9.1. **What the public is really saying about what they want from a museum.**

LEVEL	ACCESS	EXPERIENCE	PRICE	SERVICE	PRODUCT
DOMINATE	Always there, whenever and wherever I need you.	Transforms me. I lose all sense of time. Everything feels like it's designed just for me and I get to control what I do and what I learn.	This is me, so price is not an issue— it's all value.	Anticipate my every need because you know me and respect me.	World-class, can't do/see these things anywhere else.
DISTINGUISHED	Easy to access, easy to use.	Everything is truly memorable; I feel like I'm special.	Costs are very fair and consistent.	Helpful, interested in me and take the time to really listen to me.	Best in the region, truly great.
ACCEPTABLE	Convenient with minimum hassles.	Can find things of personal relevance, fun & enjoyable.	Costs honest, comparable to others, similar experiences.	Respectful and courteous, responsive when asked.	Quality good, credible and well presented.
UNACCEPTABLE	My convenience is not your problem.	Can't see myself in this place, nothing here for me. This is about you NOT me.	Pricing seems arbitrary and misleading —not a good value.	Rude, distant, disrespectful, and/or distrustful, of me.	Dirty, quality shoddy, things old, broken or just boring. Same as it's always been.

exists, right there in downtown Bemidji. Bemidji is a long way from anywhere. In good weather, it takes five hours to drive to Minneapolis and the Science Museum of Minnesota—the next nearest U.S. science center (there's also a science center across the border in Winnipeg; it, too, is a many-hour drive). For the 12,000 residents of Bemidji the Headwaters Science Center is a great asset, a true community resource, an organization worth supporting and worth having despite its modest size, programs, and exhibitions. The Headwaters Science Center achieves success by dominating in the area of access; it is the only science center within hundreds of miles in any direction.

We begin with access because this value, more than any other in the past few years, is the value that is changing most rapidly. This is because at the heart of the access value is *time,* and time is something all of us perceive we have in shorter and shorter supply. We have less time to get places and do things, and less time to enjoy those things we can get to and do. Even if we live in a big city surrounded by resources, perhaps especially if we live in a big city, access to resources is important.

Given the increasing cost of time, Americans and other people living in time-starved societies have explored a variety of strategies to stretch or otherwise modify time. The trend is toward increasing the yield on time. The Internet is one such solution, promising to reduce the time it takes to do a wide variety of tasks, including shopping, information gathering, and communicating with people (of course, the reality sometimes lags behind the promise). Other trends include the widespread rise of self-service—although many businesses initially saw this as a cost-saving strategy through reductions in labor costs, its widespread success in the marketplace can mostly be attributed to its time-saving benefits.[5] A third and very insidious consequence of the time crunch has been the tendency for people to try and squeeze as much as possible out of every minute spent, every day. This has led to multitasking strategies, where people now combine what were previously disparate activities. For example, it is common practice these days for people to seek out a place where they can combine the formerly separate leisure activities of eating, shopping, and museum-going within a single experience.[6]

Time saving thus becomes a component of all behavioral decisions, particularly for the individuals who feel most rushed. A pervasive example is found in modern child-rearing, where a new term has crept into our vocabulary— *quality time.* Quality time with a child first and foremost takes for granted that less time will be spent. In effect, being with the child, which is viewed as a means to an end, can be made more efficient so that more positive things can be accomplished.[7] Museum-going, for example, is frequently considered a quality-time activity, particularly for weekend, noncustodial dads. Anecdotal evidence suggests that the number of single dads taking children to museums on weekends is at an all time high.

Historically, leisure was associated with voluntary activity, something that implied a choice between alternatives. Through time deepening, today many people seem to be more able to avoid sacrificing of one activity for another, seeking instead to do it all, see it all, and to accomplish that *now.* We walk for fitness, play golf for contacts, and go to museums to improve our minds. Pass-ing the time in activities that are pleasurable in and of themselves is almost a foreign notion. Efficiency rules our work and our leisure. Speed and brevity are ever more widely admired, whether in serving food, the length of magazine articles, conversations, or museum labels. The emphasis is on cramming more (information, quality, enjoyment, etc.) into less time. Arguably, time is replac-ing money as the most valued resource—the one for which demand has in-creased the most relative to supply. For a long time now, museum-going for most people has been about time, rather than money.[8] A recent study showed that a major reason for the decline in the use of public libraries by more afflu-ent individuals was that the cost of using a library was becoming prohibitive—cost was directly proportional to the time it takes (driving to the library, finding books, checking out books, returning home, and then repeating the process in order to return the book when it's due) and in this reckoning the cost to afflu-ent individuals was significantly greater than it was to less-affluent individuals.[9] Ultimately, if you were affluent, it was cheaper to just go on-line and buy a book at *Amazon.com* than it was to go visit the library and check it out for free. Museums often market themselves as a place that "there is so much to do, you can spend all day." Bill Booth, former director of COSI Toledo (Ohio), told John that their focus groups showed that this made many potential visitors put off their visit until they had "all day," which was almost never.[10] According to Booth, these potential visitors said that they would prefer short, intense expe-riences near the front door, which were packaged in a such a way that there was closure so that they knew that they got what they came for in twenty minutes, at which point they could leave or choose to explore more.

Access is all about availability in time and space. Historically, most museums were located in the heart of the largest cities, and there are many venerable, old institutions that attest to this historic trend. But that is not where most of the newer museums that have sprung up in the past dozen or so years are located; the new museums have followed demographic trends and are being located where the population now lives—it is increasingly common for there to be a host of smaller, more modest museums located in the suburbs surrounding big cities. Over half of all children's museums, a third of all science centers, and even a quarter of all history, art, and natural history museums now exist within small communities.[11] The success of these smaller institutions, many of which have been quite successful, cannot be attributed to their great collections or stellar exhibitions, but rather to their ease of access. Why drive a half day to a larger institution when similar benefits can accrue close to home? This idea is what is motivating the Buffalo Museum of Science to move in the direction of creating a series of satellite facilities in and around the Buffalo area rather than investing huge amounts of money in renovating its existing site in the heart of what has become a challenging location to access, in large part because it is perceived by many in Buffalo as unsafe and undesirable.

Access is about being there when the individual wants you to be there; there is no single method for *being there* for people. In other words, access can be achieved through physical location, by being open longer hours, and by the use of technology. So what would it mean for a museum to dominate in the category of access?

Access can be achieved by making the museum's hours of operation really work for visitors. Many museums still operate as if they are there primarily to serve the convenience of the employees who work there; employees like regular 9:00 to 5:00 jobs, Monday through Friday. Hello! The museum is actually there to serve all those people with those same hours who *do not* work at the museum. Thus, the optimum times to be open are all the evening and weekend hours outside of the regular workday. The Dallas Museum of Art surprised itself and everyone else when it recently experimented with staying open twenty-four hours a day for an entire week. Not only did it have a huge number of visitors; many came in the middle of the night and the wee hours of the morning—in fact many more came in these time slots than came during traditional banker's hours, mid-day, mid-week. Not only did the museum stay open around the clock, but it ran programming at all hours. The results amazed even the most enthusiastic supporters of the idea. Although it created some staffing issues, the museum is now trying to figure out how to create this kind of temporal access all of the time. In the end, it is important to have your operating hours focused on meeting the needs of your target audience, rather than the needs of staff. Anything less would force you into the realm of the unacceptable.

An alternative way to deliver on access would be to create a virtual presence for your institution. One could conceive of creating a virtual presence that was so responsive and so easy to hook into that wherever the individual was and whenever she or he wanted to, that person could connect with the museum. Of course, providing such complete access virtually would change what the nature of the museum experience would be. As we discuss later, this might drive museums to think more broadly about what it is that they deliver in the way of products and services; it is possible that the museum of the future will have no "physical" exhibits.

Access is not just physical though, it is also psychological. Many of the suburban museums referred to above distinguish themselves not just because of their physical proximity but equally because of their psychological access. Often they have a local flavor, an almost "home-made" quality to them. This is not the large, intimidating downtown museum, but the little, home-grown variety that anyone can access and feel competent in when visiting. The search for a level of comfort, community affiliation, and "ownership" is critical to people today. As we rush around ever more frantically, finding ourselves more and more forced to do business with multinational corporations with zillions of units, we increasingly have a soft spot in our hearts for the local, one-of-a-kind business, designed to cater to a local public. This holds equally for nonprofits. Although we all appreciate that the quality of the collections and exhibitions may not be as good as those in the huge, big city institution, there is a quality that might be equally valuable in the small, local institution. Psychological access can be an important business strategy and a way to set your institution apart from the crowd.

Museums that are going to dominate in the area of access will need to truly understand the needs and interests of their target audiences and then relentlessly cater to those needs and interests. Such a museum will have to be open when its audience is ready and willing to visit; it will need to be designed so that the audience can come in (physically or virtually) and easily, quickly, and effectively find what they need and then leave. It will need to cater to the audience's unique social, physical, and psychological desires, whatever those might be. Have many museums historically rated highly on access? No! Can they in the future? Yes! Should they? Well, all museums will need to get significantly better in this area if they want to stay competitive in the leisure marketplace. And a few museums might want to see what it would take to get really, really good at the access game. Because if they can be superior in the area of access it will give them a significant business advantage over the rest of their competition in the museum business.

EXPERIENCE

Hilary Harp had some sense of what to expect on her first visit to the United States Holocaust Memorial Museum in Washington, DC. Of course, she had heard a lot about it, from her Jewish boyfriend Joshua with whom she was now visiting as well as from other friends and family who had visited. But the reality of the visit transcended everything she had thought about. No sooner had she entered the museum and been crammed into that tiny steel elevator along with dozens and dozens of other strangers, that she realized she was in for a very different kind of experience. Hilary was transported to another time and another place, a place that few of us would really wish to have experienced firsthand. She found the horrors of the Nazi regime, the brutality, and the inhumanity just chilling. She had also never known before about the magnitude of the Holocaust, the systematic extermination of not just Jews, but of Gypsies, the mentally challenged and handicapped, homosexuals, and Communists. The piles of shoes and suitcases, of bodies, all left a lasting impression on her. As she left the museum she knew she would never again be the same and would never again think about genocide in the same way. She vowed to never again remain silent if she felt that a group of people were committing genocide; she vowed that such things should never happen again.

It has become all too common to equate *experience* with *entertainment*. What people really want, however, is something more substantive, deeper than the superficial thrill of an emotional jolt or clap of the hands. What people are seeking is a transformation in the way they think, act, and feel. They want to be involved in an experience that helps them transcend the bland, impersonal life that so characterized much of the twentieth century. In some ways, what we're calling experience really gets to the heart of the new transactional quality of what museum experiences need to become in the twenty-first century. Experiences need to help people move to a higher, deeper, and more profound understanding of who they are and how they fit into their world. People also want to have these kinds of experiences in ways that are respectful and considerate of their needs and desires. Experiences can be life transforming, as Hilary's Holocaust Museum visit suggests, but they can also be just life-fulfilling and pleasant, like a really satisfying immersive experience at an aquarium.

Like service, experience is emotional and directed at how a person feels afterward. But service and experience are not the same thing. A good way to distinguish between service and experience is as follows. In every transaction there is an external character to it; it is how you would describe the way you were treated. In other words, service is how you would describe the staff and amenities you encountered. By contrast, experience is the internal character of a transaction. Experience is how you feel about yourself after the transaction.

While great service makes you appreciate the staff and amenities of an institution, great experiences make you walk away with greater appreciation for your own abilities, interests, and intelligence. That's why respect and personalization are such important aspects of experience. While arguably any staff member can smile at people and wish them a good day—good service—it takes a very special staff person to be able to make them feel special and smart—that's good experience.

Yes, a visit to a museum is virtually always a special, out-of-the-ordinary experience, a break from the mundane. There are things you can see only in a museum. Often, but not always, the space is as unique as the objects on display. Our research on visitors confirms this feeling of specialness that the public attributes to museums. And yes, many studies have shown that the public says they go to museums for "entertainment" but don't be misled. The public's concept of entertainment here is not necessarily Madison Avenue's concept of entertainment. The public does not equate going to a museum with going to Disneyland. They understand that there is a core of authenticity and intellectual value underlying what you see and do at a museum, or at least there is supposed to be. That is why the kind of identity-related categories we described in Chapter 3 better capture the motivations of museum visitors than do traditional, marketing-oriented demographic and psychographic categories like age, income, or even "interest in education." Even the *Experience Seekers*, the proverbial tourists, are seeking a different kind of experience than they could get back home; they are seeking a unique opportunity to see things, do things, and learn things that transcend what they can learn on any other day. And they don't want, or expect that their "experience" will be just like everyone else's who visits the museum that day. There is an expectation of uniqueness, a desire for specialness.

Entertaining events—seeing a special large-format film, being part of a demonstration, talking to people in period costumes as they interpret in first person, or getting to wear the period costumes yourself—if unique, are exciting for visitors. But in and of themselves, these events do not suffice. There needs to be substance behind them; some "there," there. When entertainment is the only thing delivered to visitors, they will walk away dissatisfied. The initial success of "entertainment phenoms" such as Planet Hollywood, All-Star Café, and Hard Rock Café has paled. In fact, the entertainment industry as a whole has been in a downturn, which is why Disney and other entertainment companies are increasingly trying to become more museum-like. They know that what the public is really seeking is value-added leisure—enjoyable learning experiences. As Joe Pine and Jim Gilmore describe in their book *The Experience Economy,* what's really important to many consumers today is experience, and they predict that tomorrow experience alone won't be enough. As we move farther into this new age, what will be most important to consumers will be *transformation.*[12]

But more than anything else, what makes the science demonstration that involves you as a participant, the costume-wearing interpreter who talks to you in character, making and tasting food just like your grandmother used to, or getting to actually get into the tank and swim with the dolphins so special is that it is, well, special! These opportunities make you feel like you are not just the average Joe, but someone unique; you're getting to do things that few others get to do. The more special and unique the experience is the better it is. The more unique and customized the experience is to the specific interests and abilities of the individual, the better it is. When these kinds of experiences are working best, they change the visitor; in other words, they transform the visitor.

It is these kinds of transformational experiences that we refer to when we use the term *experience,* and you cannot provide enough of them. What everyone can do without are empty, canned, and mass-produced experiences that seem so common these days. It is like comparing a fresh, whole-grained, handmade, wood-fired loaf of bread with a slice of *Wonderbread;* one is memorable, the other forgettable. The general decline in civility, the growing alienation between those who sell us things and those of us who buy things, mean that all of us are grasping for those special moments when we can directly connect with other humans, or for that matter other living things, in a truly personal and nontrivial way.

This is an area in which museums should and arguably already do naturally excel, but excellence requires commitment. Key to bringing these kinds of internal experiences to the fore resides in knowing who your visitors are, and not demographically, but psychologically. This is where the ideas presented early in this book about identity and self come into play. If we can help visitors affirm the identities they are seeking—whether Explorer, Facilitator, Professional/ Hobbyist, Experience Seeker, or Spiritual Pilgrim—then they will feel that they had a really positive experience. The fact that so many museum visitors currently feel that their museum experience was satisfying, which they do, attests to the natural advantage museums already possess in this area. But like everything else, the bar for satisfying the value of experience is continually being raised as more and more institutions are trying to fill the leisure learning niche currently occupied by museums (including an ever increasing number of new museums). This increasing competition will continually force each museum to work harder just to remain in the same competitive spot. This may not be encouraging news, but it is realistic news.

PRICE

The California Science Center is an immensely popular museum. Despite its location in downtown LA, a stone's throw from the epicenters of both the 1965 Watts and 1992 South-Central riots, it attracts nearly 2 million visitors per year from all over Southern California and from around the world. In fact, the California Science Center attracts arguably the most diverse population of visitors of any major science center in America. On any given day, it is common to see large, multigeneration, recent, and established immigrant Latino/a families strolling through the museum alongside groups of African American youth and Yuppy suburban mothers with their children in space-age strollers. Statistically, 40 percent of the Science Center's visitors are Latino/a, 40 percent are of European extraction, 15 percent are African American, and 5 percent are Asian American—a diversity that comes close to mirroring the amazing racial/ethnic diversity of greater Los Angeles.[13] How, might you ask, do they achieve this diversity? There are likely many reasons, but one undeniable reason is price. The California Science Center has no admission charge. It is one of only a couple of major science centers in America that is free of charge, and, importantly, it has always been so. Compared with the dozens of other major educational leisure attractions in Southern California, the California Science Center stands out as one of the most affordable. The California Science Center has very good exhibits and a wide array of innovative programs, but it dominates its competitors on price. It is not free to run the Science Center, but the institution uses funding from state and local government plus an aggressive fundraising operation to support itself. It has decided that staying free is vitally important to its mission, and to its business model.

Although the California Science Center has gone down the low cost/no cost road, few others in the industry travel the same road. Earned income, particularly through ticket sales, represents an increasingly important revenue source for most museums today. Even institutions that were once free, like Chicago's Museum of Science and Industry and perhaps soon even the Smithsonian Institution, find themselves forced to charge admission. And as we write this book, the $20 adult admission price being charged by the recently reopened Museum of Modern Art in New York City has caused quite a stir. Is it too high a price? Will people really pay this kind of price to go to a museum, even one as great as MOMA?

We are daily inundated with advertising trumpeting the lowest prices in town—absolutely the *lowest price*! We see the rise of "big box" retailers like Wal-Mart, Office Depot, Barnes & Noble, and Home Depot smothering their competition by being so big that they command prices from suppliers that no other retailer can match. And we see more and more jobs going overseas in order to satiate the public's seemingly ceaseless demand for low-cost goods and services—even medical care is now being outsourced to Southeast Asia, where prices are cheaper than in the United States. Is it any wonder that we are convinced that the public's single most important concern is low prices? Well, think again! A wide array of consumer studies reveal that price is indeed an important consuming consideration, but not as much as one might think.[14] In short, low prices are overrated.

Sure, if everything else is equal, people will pick the least expensive option. But rarely is everything else equal. A single, working mother with eight children from Eastpointe, Michigan, summed it up when she said, "If the product is good quality, I will pay the price. If it is poor quality, I don't care what the price is, I won't buy it. If I get [a bad product] you can guarantee I won't go back again."[15] Price is just one factor in people's consuming decisions. It is not that price is irrelevant, but what really matters is honesty and fairness in pricing.

The majority of today's consumers are jaded by all the advertising and hype about low prices. They know that the item being advertised as 50 percent off was never actually twice the current price; the advertised "retail price" is actually a jacked-up mythical price. They know that the rock-bottom priced sale item, which the store only has one or two of left in stock, is just a gimmick to get you into the store. We have all learned these facts the hard way; still the ruse goes on as so many businesses desperately try to lure you into buying from them. And ironically, increasingly consumers don't feel rewarded by the few low prices they may get on the reduced sale items as much as they feel taken advantage of by the abundant higher-priced items that they know somebody else, somewhere, eventually, will sell at a fraction of the cost. The wise course of action seems to be the sane middle road: keep your prices consistent, reasonable, and honest.

Crawford and Mathews believe that "fundamental societal change has taken place when it comes to price. Absolute lowest price may continue to be important to some segment of the population, but it will be just one factor in the purchase-decision process for the vast majority of consumers. And, in many cases, price will actually be a less significant factor than it has been, because people today—and tomorrow—are more rushed and more time-starved than ever before."[16] More and more consumers will find that time, rather than dollars, dictates their buying decisions. Like the example cited earlier about library-goers, access is increasingly a more important "cost" decision. Already, time-pressed consumers find they don't have the time to comparison shop, so they will rely on their chosen vender to be honest. And woe to the business that is dishonest about pricing; it will incur not only the short-term wrath of the consumer, but the long-term curse of bad word-of-mouth. Since word-of-mouth is the primary mechanism by which most businesses, including museums, attract their "customers," one shouldn't even think about messing with anything that will damage good referrals.

For a business like museums, rarely is price the primary reason most people do or don't partake in what is offered. Museums are primarily selling leisure-oriented, life-enriching learning experiences, something that is relatively hard to comparison-shop for; something you either desire or you don't. Yes, there are likely to be other museums and similar, even if not exactly comparable opportunities being offered by other educationally oriented venues (both nonprofit and for-profit) in your community. Thus, it is important to be more or less in line in your pricing with these other experiences, but that still leaves a great deal of latitude in setting prices. Given the mission of most museums, dominating the educational leisure market through price is probably not the strategy that most museums would choose to follow.

Still, it is possible to take this approach. If you live in a community where most leisure educational opportunities are priced beyond the means of a large segment of the public, particularly historically underserved communities, it might make sense to position yourself as a low-cost leader. There might be a number of community leaders and foundations that would welcome a museum that delivered quality learning opportunities at the lowest possible price. In essence, this is the tack that the St. Louis Science Center has taken by virtue of its successful tax levy. However, even if this was your approach, if you could be totally subsidized by a benefactor, we would think you probably would want to charge something since we live in a society where the cost of goods and services tends to mean something. You would want to guard against an association with "cheap," since "cheap" usually means "low quality"—being the cheapest learning opportunity on the block could be perceived as being the poorest learning opportunity too. Low-cost leaders like Wal-Mart and Target are successful because they don't sell shoddy goods. Instead, they work very hard to sell reasonable quality ("brand name") goods at the lowest possible prices.

Smart businesses like these have figured out that price, too, is actually a multidimensioned value. These dimensions include first and foremost honesty and fairness, but also consistency and reliability. Thus, we would recommend that most museums choose to set their pricing at levels that are consistent, reliable, and comparable to the industry norm for what they offer, where they are located, and the length of time most people will avail themselves of the service. Figure out what this price is, let your public know that this is what you are doing, and stick to it. In this way, you will garner a reputation for fair and honest pricing. Again, most patrons aren't looking for "cheap" in a museum, but they definitely are looking for "fair and reasonable." In line with this thinking, a number of major retailers have shifted to what is called *price-led costing* rather than *cost-led pricing*.[17] The old Industrial Age approach to costing a product or service involved determining prices by adding up all your costs and then adding a profit margin on top. An example of this approach was "keystone pricing," which was the practice by retail stores of doubling the wholesale price of an item in order to arrive at the retail price. The new approach begins by determining what price the customer is willing to pay, and then determining what allowable costs will need to be, beginning from design all the way up to the delivered product. This method maximizes prices and minimizes costs. It would be an interesting exercise for museums to use a similar approach.

One final comment on pricing; allow us to gore a favorite ox—the pricing of museum memberships. Currently, we financially penalize ourselves for having visitors come frequently. The typical approach is to deal with frequent visitors by encouraging them to become members. In return for a slightly higher, one-time price (usually something between the cost of two to three visits), members are allowed unlimited entry. The visitor who uses membership wisely can come dozens, if not hundreds of times, and except for the first couple of visits, all subsequent visits are free; the institution loses money every time these members show up. In fact, the national average is that members come between eight and nine times per year. Meanwhile, the majority of our earned revenue projections are based upon maintaining a high level of first-time/one-time visitors—since they pay full freight. What's wrong with this picture? Our best customers provide limited revenues while our worst customers provide the bulk of our resources. Marketing 101 says it's easier to keep a customer than to get a new customer, so why do we constantly build our institutions around creating new customers? Perhaps not surprisingly, the answer is because we are still using an Industrial Age, quantity model rather than a Knowledge Age, quality model. In the latter model, pricing is based upon what you receive—the more you receive, the more it costs (although there are rewards for frequent use).

We need to shift to a strategy that rewards frequent use without penalizing the institution. Frequent flyers don't get cheaper tickets than do one-time flyers, but they do, in theory, get better service. Frequent shoppers at the supermarket don't pay less for their groceries, but they do get access to special deals that less frequent shoppers don't. Frequent customers at other types of institutions earn "points" toward some type of reward—maybe it's every tenth visit free or opportunities to get free gifts—but in the meantime, they pay the same price for their goods and services as everyone else. In essence, we are currently telling our best customers that our product has so little value, that we're willing to functionally give it away. Instead, of encouraging our best customers to spend less, we should be encouraging our best customers to spend more. What would make them spend more? The answer is simple. Our best customers would get the best, most personalized service. This economic model formed the basis of the Alabaster Natural History Museum example we provided at the beginning of this book, a model we challenge museums to think seriously about adopting.

SERVICE

Unfortunately, the following is a true story. The visitor at the large art museum (which for obvious reasons will remain nameless) was visiting from out of town. He had come with his wife, but she somehow had wandered off and he now found himself hopelessly lost somewhere in the seventeenth century. Since he had just spent fifteen frustrating minutes searching for his wife he decided that it was now time to accept that maybe he needed some help. That's when his problems really began.

The first challenge was even finding someone who could help. A few minutes before, it had seemed there were guards everywhere, but right now there were none to be found. So he rapidly moved from room to room searching for a guard. Finally, he spied one at the end of the eighteenth-century period room. Strolling up to the guard he wanly smiled and began to explain his plight. The guard wasn't exactly curt, he just wasn't helpful. He said in a very matter-of-fact way that he was sorry that the man had lost his wife but there really wasn't anything he could do. "I can't just leave my post and help you find her, can I? I've got a job to do." he said. Our visitor tried to find out if there was some likely place that his wife might have to exit, but the guard would have none of this. He suggested the man go to the main guard office and report the problem there. Someone there would probably be able to help him. Of course, the main guard office was several floors down in the basement and on the other side of the building. Without a map, which of course the guard did not have, this too seemed like a daunting task. The guard said getting there was easy, and then proceeded to give the most convoluted and elaborate set of directions imaginable—the kind of directions that even Sherlock Holmes would have found difficult to decipher. Sighing, our hapless visitor thanked the guard and moved on.

Now what was he going to do? He decided to try another guard, but this person too proved to be only slightly more helpful. She suggested going to the front information desk rather than the guard office. At least the directions to the front desk were easier to follow, so Mr. Lost headed for the front desk. As luck would have it, who did he bump into while trying to wend his way back through the various galleries to get to the front hall, but his wife? She of course was oblivious to his plight, having had a marvelous time viewing art. Given his trials and tribulations, the man prevailed on his wife that it was time to leave. So the two, now holding hands so they couldn't get separated, headed off to the exit and departed.

As our frustrated visitor discovered, service is all about people. Service is about humans interacting with humans. Unlike price, product, and even access, service is an emotional attribute. It is about getting solutions, when you need them, in a way that meets your sense of propriety and respect. Service is experienced in a very personal way, one individual at a time. The only way for an organization to provide good service is to have a culture of service permeate the entire organization—top to bottom. It starts with training and ends with rewarding those who actually deliver. Service is *not* about the gratuitous greeting one gets when walking into Wal-Mart, service is about people who go out of their way to make your visit, your program, your time the best, easiest, most enjoyable it can possibly be, and not just when things are going well, but when things are going poorly also.

If you want to get a feeling for what good service feels like you might want to bundle up and take a journey north, far north to Sudbury, Canada, and visit Science North. The moment you walk into Science North you feel welcomed. Everyone in this place seems to be smiling—the visitors and the staff. Everywhere you go there's some fresh-faced young person there to help you discover and explore science. Following Disney's lead, many science centers, zoos, and aquariums these days refer to their visitors as "guests" but in Science North's case this turns out to not just be a label but a reality. Given that so many of Science North's visitors are repeat visitors, individuals who come nearly weekly, many of the interactions between staff and visitor happen on a first-name basis. But this foreigner, John, was treated courteously and respectfully. I was welcomed and truly made to feel like I was being invited into someone's home. The Science North staff acted as if this was their institution and I, the visitor, was there to make it better, not worse. I was made to feel that without me, the institution would not have been complete that day.

How different than most museums. The staff at most museums often seem to act as if the visitors are a necessary evil—they know that these people help to pay the bills, but it would be so much nicer if there weren't so many of them or if we could figure out a way to pay the bills some other way. These attitudes usually start at the top with the most senior staff and then permeate their way down to the bottom, which is where the floor staff reside. As we've pointed out repeatedly, in most museums, the lowest-paid, lowest-status members of the organization are the individuals who work on the floor of the museum and directly deal with the public—the guards, the ticket takers, the coat room clerks. When possible, museums use volunteers at the information desk, because it saves money. What is the message here? What is the message inside the institution? What is the message to the visitor? How many curators of large museums work weekends and help out with the public? Although most museums invest a disproportionate percentage of their budgets in developing exhibitions for the public, they end up squandering much of the benefits of these expenses by skimping on the services provided the visitors who come to see those exhibitions. In our example at the beginning of this section, what is likely to be Mr. Lost's lasting memory of the art museum? We're willing to bet his museum experience was memorable, but his memories are highly unlikely to be related to the museum's quality art collection. He will almost certainly remember how callously he was treated—a displeasure he's likely to share with friends and family when he gets back home.

At the heart of any good service organization is a staff who feels true ownership for the institution. They feel empowered to make decisions and to go the extra mile to ensure that the best interests of the organization are served. Why did the guards feel that it wasn't their job to help this lost visitor? They likely knew that if their supervisor came along and saw them away from their post, they would be reprimanded. Instead, what if their supervisor had trained them that their job was to ensure the safety and well-being of both the objects and the visitors? And even if it really was important to stay and guard that particular spot at that particular moment, there were and should have been things those guards could have done to help that man find his wife—starting with being sympathetic. Again, at the heart of service is emotion. These guards may not have actually been able to help the man find his wife, but they certainly should have comforted him and tried to provide support to an obviously emotionally distraught individual. That's the essence of service.

Great service means giving the public what they want, not some of the time but all of the time. At Continental Airlines, a business that has defined service as a key to succeeding in an industry notoriously devoid of service, all hiring, training, rewards, and measures of success begin and end with service. Continental Airlines turned around its fortunes by adopting a service-first approach to business. It couldn't compete against airlines like American, Delta, and United on the number of flights and it couldn't compete against low-cost airlines like Southwest and Jet Blue on price, but it could and has become competitive on service. As their CEO said, "Customers don't measure winning or losing by our income statement or earnings per share. They measure us by how we get them to where they want to go with their underwear on time."[18]

Since great service begins and ends with employees, desiring to create good service is only the first step in the process; delivering great service day in and day out is the real challenge. People have good days and bad days, they have their varying moods and events at home can conspire to turn even the sunniest person into a grouch. So while it is relatively easy to train an employee to say "Welcome" and "May I help you?" it is much harder to ensure that they communicate a clear and genuine sense of "welcome" and "helpfulness" when they say it. But as Science North and other institutions that have made the commitment to service demonstrate, it is possible. Yet it really does require more than a memo from the director to make this happen. As suggested above with Continental Airlines, it requires a major institutional commitment and change in culture—top to bottom. Rather than investing institutional resources in the trappings of service, such as an extra line for members that doesn't necessarily move any faster or an information desk staffed by volunteers who really don't know that much about the organization, museums would be far better off if they invested in employee screening, training, measuring, and rewards that ensure that *real* quality service is provided to each and every visitor.

Good service, particularly at institutions like museums where the ultimate product is education, is essential. We live in an age where the gap between the service expectations and desires of the public and the service delivery of the business community has become a yawning chasm. More and more people are "voting with their feet." They are choosing to frequent places and organizations that provide them with the service they demand—even at the expense of price and even accessibility, not for all products and services, but for those few products and services of high enough value. Education is likely to qualify for many people as one such product/service worth being selective about. Who can blame people? Why invest a huge chunk of your discretionary time at a place that treats you badly, that acts as if your convenience is your problem, not theirs?

The key to quality service is deeply understanding what the public really wants, and then giving it to them. If you don't understand your public's expectations and needs then it becomes next to impossible to really satisfy those expectations. If you understand that a large percentage of your visitors are primarily seeking to facilitate the experience of another person, then quality service is about making it easy for them to do that. For example, if you are a history museum that attracts a lot of parents with young children, writing label copy that only meets the needs of an adult who is curious about the objects on display will do little to satisfy the needs of a *Facilitator*. Good service, then, can be achieved by providing additional materials, written family guides, or even human guides that make the *Facilitator*'s role easier.

Finally, it is important to appreciate that service is not something you just give to visitors, but something that is embodied in the institution. Service is a way of thinking that permeates the entire experience. For example, it means that a visit to the museum is hassle free from start to finish, that a visitor's every need is anticipated and satisfied, that getting into the museum and out again is easy and without confusion or delay, that restrooms are clean, bright, and "miraculously" just around the corner and easy to find just when the visitor needs them, that food services are affordable and good tasting, that the gift shop has just the things that the public wants to buy at just the right price points, and that there is plenty of seating for tired visitors. And it also means that there is lots of staff available whose only job, or so it seems to the visitor, is to help them satisfy their personal, social, and intellectual needs. It means going the extra mile to ensure that each and every visitor gets what they came for and feels that the museum appreciated them for coming that day for that need, whatever it is. That is great service.

Business writers Adrian Slywotzky and Richard Wise have observed that more and more companies today are finding that the best way to be successful is by focusing on "addressing the hassles and issues that *surround* the product rather than by improving the product itself."[19] In other words, rather than investing tens of thousands of dollars in adding more bells and whistles to your exhibitions, invest the money in making the quality of a visit to your museum more enjoyable. Crawford and Mathews state:

> Based on our research, it's clear that service may actually offer businesses the greatest potential return on investment of any of the five attributes, simply because most companies are doing so poorly at providing good service. In fact, service may represent the richest untapped area for differentiation in the entire consumer goods and services industry. If you're a price or product operator, another company can come along and copy your price or product offering. But it's much more difficult to copy a service offering, as so much depends on employees and company culture. For that reason, service may actually provide a better measure of competitive insulation than the other attributes. So while clearly there are costs involved in terms of employee hiring and training, the potential benefit is significant.

We agree, particularly as it relates to the museum community. Except for the largest museums, institutions with deep pockets and vast collections, competing with other similar institutions on product—the exhibitions and programs offered—is becoming an increasingly tough game. There are just too many museums and museum-like experiences available to the public now. The public is increasingly mobile and can and does visit other museums both at home and when they travel beyond their home town. All of this makes it hard to be the best museum, if the only measure of "best" is exhibitions and collections.

PRODUCT

Bill Hanley[20] said to John, "I knew it was going to be crowded, but I still wanted to come. As I waited for hours in line to get in [to the Smithsonian Institution's Air and Space Museum] I thought about the first time I had visited this museum." Bill had waited in line then, too. It was when the museum first opened. Again, according to Bill, "The wait then was certainly worth it. The Air and Space Museum was an amazing museum; where else could you see, in one place, the entire history of human flight laid out before you—from the Wright Flyer to the *Apollo* capsules?" As a former Navy pilot this place had special meaning to Bill. He said that the exhibit that showed the flight deck of an aircraft carrier was really amazing, he had been back to see that exhibit a half dozen times now over the years. And the exhibit he described to John on this day was another long-past chapter in this historic story of human flight.

Bill was waiting in line so that he could be among the first people on earth to see a real rock from the moon. The rock had been brought back the summer of 1969 by the astronauts who first landed on the moon, and now it was on display right here in Washington. When he finally did get his chance, Bill said he filed slowly by what he discovered was a surprisingly small display. He said he stopped and stared at the tiny little piece of black rock. Although it really didn't look like that much, it didn't matter. Bill knew that he was seeing something historic, something really special and unique, something he would be able to tell his grandkids about. He was glad that there was a place like the Air and Space Museum where he could come and see something like this. As Bill moved on to look, once again at the rest of the museum, he said he thought to himself, "It was worth the wait, I'm glad I came."

Few things make the hearts of museum professionals go pitter-patter more than the "products" they offer—quality art, unique historical artifacts, rare and endangered animals, current science. This, say many, is why they're in the business. But is this why our public seeks us out? Many people say yes, but far fewer than we might hope. There are some institutions and some situations where this is true. For example, in the vignette presented above, Bill's interests and desires probably came very close to matching the expectations of those who curated and built the exhibit. Not only did Bill visit in order to see an object, he came, he looked carefully, and he thought about the object. And because he already knew a lot about the history behind this object, as did most people of his day, he was able to place the object in context and appreciate why it was important and special to human history (despite the fact that there was essentially no interpretive material accompanying the moon rock display). Let's face it, this doesn't happen very often.

There are a few major institutions, Smithsonian Institution, Museum of Modern Art, British Museum, The Louvre, where the public visits with the expectation that they will see things that they can never see anywhere else, ever. It is not that you can't see a Van Gogh, a precious archeological artifact, or a very beautiful diamond somewhere else. It is that there is only *one Starry, Starry Night*, only *one* Rosetta Stone, and only *one* Hope Diamond. And it doesn't really matter if *Starry, Starry Night* is not Van Gogh's best painting or that the Hope Diamond is not actually the largest, most valuable diamond in the world. For the public they are! Large numbers of the public assume that the primary purpose in visiting these institutions is to see these rare and unusual treasurers, and they behave accordingly. For example, roughly a third of all the visitors to the National Museum of Natural History claim the primary purpose of their visit is to see the Hope Diamond and nearly a quarter of all visitors go to see this object first—despite the fact that the Hope Diamond is not the easiest thing to see first when you go to the museum since it is located on the second floor of the building (or third floor, depending upon how you enter the museum). Still, the motivation to see this object drives millions of people to visit, and once they are there, drives how they visit the museum. This is an example of a product-driven institution.

But this is unusual. There is normally not a similar expectation by the public for other museums. Even those large metropolitan museums with arguably world-class collections do not generally attract visitors with this same level of product-focused commitment. The public visiting the Field Museum in Chicago does not come with the same expectations as the public visiting the National Museum of Natural History and, consequently, what they experience is not the same either. Both the Field and the Smithsonian can dominate on "product" but they will need to achieve that dominance in different ways. In both cases it is about satisfying the expectation that this can't be seen anywhere else, ever, but we would argue that, in the first case, it is all about the collection and, in the second case, it's all about how that collection is presented.

The truth is, though, that most museums are neither the Smithsonian nor the Field Museum. An original Winslow Homer or the wheel of the first wagon to traverse the county in 1847 are special objects indeed, but not of the same stature as the *Mona Lisa* or the *Elgin Marbles*. For the latter objects it is not necessary to convince anyone that these items are rare and valuable while in the former case it is only the cognoscenti that truly appreciate their value. Hence the job of the institution with the Homer and the wheel is to contextualize these objects and help the visitor understand why they are important and special. The vast majority of the public goes to the vast majority of museums more for experience than for product. Although it is fair to say that most museum-goers visit with the expectation, even desire, to see interesting art, historical artifacts, animals, and science, they do not, like Bill above, visit primarily in order to see a specific object, and most visitors do not already know so much about the history behind the objects on display that interpretive material is essentially superfluous. Most museum visitors are impressed, but not wowed, by our collections. Most museum visitors are interested in the stories we have to tell, but they do not often enter knowing much about them already. Being truly dominant in the product aspect of the museum business has become increasingly challenging. In an earlier age, every local museum could boast that the majority of its patrons would be unlikely to see objects as rare and valuable as what it had in their collections. And in an earlier age the local citizenry would come to the museum to marvel at these rarities. But with the proliferation of museums, increased mobility, and omnipresent communication technologies, novelty is a characteristic that is becoming increasingly difficult to create. The visitor to the local art museum knows that the museum has nice stuff but she also knows that it doesn't have the *Mona Lisa*—that's in Paris and she's seen pictures of it in books and a special on it on *Discovery*.

The challenge of being product-dominant is not limited to museums. Throughout the developed world more and more companies are finding that they cannot compete on product alone, particularly trying to sell the public on new and novel products.[21] Although during the Industrial Age the path to business growth was through the development and marketing of a continuous stream of new products, today that approach is becoming increasingly difficult as more and more similar products glut the marketplace. As Slywotzky and Wise state, today, at best, "these moves will merely replace revenues and profits lost to commodization and increased competition. They won't represent a platform for driving significant, sustained new growth. . . . Even new-product innovation is a largely depleted avenue for consistent growth."[22] Translated into the world of museums, your museum's objects and exhibits are fundamental to your business, but they can no longer be counted upon to be the exclusive driver of your business strategy.

Still, a large number of museums cling to the idea that to be successful, they must be product-dominant. And the strategy nearly all museums have adopted over the last quarter century for pushing their product-first approach has been the traveling exhibit. For more than a generation, the traveling exhibit has been the wonder drug of the museum industry, the way for even small institutions to have special and unique product. Traveling exhibits provide built-in marketing opportunities, are easier to fundraise for than permanent exhibitions, and are great at generating and expanding audience. Most museums attempt to bring in at least one and sometimes several traveling exhibits each year. The more spectacular the traveling exhibit, the better; blockbuster exhibits are far and away the most spectacular. As a result of this, many institutions are now on the blockbuster treadmill. The museum offers a blockbuster traveling exhibit that brings in large audiences, but then that audience expects another blockbuster, or comparable program, again before it will return.[23] So the museum must offer another blockbuster exhibition in order to maintain its audience. Each new blockbuster involves greater and greater resources to produce, since the easy ones were created first, and so the cost of these traveling exhibits is skyrocketing. Thus, the museum finds itself in a ratcheted situation where there is no going back, only forward since it has convinced its public that the only reason to come to the museum is for the next great traveling exhibit. Implicitly they have communicated, year in and year out, the normal product of the museum, the permanent exhibitions, are not worth coming for in their own right.

In fact, it is particularly the smaller museums in smaller communities that have the most to lose in taking this "New! Now!" at all costs, approach. They are the organizations that can least afford the cost of constantly changing their exhibitions, can least afford the advertising dollars, and, arguably, should find themselves in the best position to get off this merry-go-round. But all too many have not only chosen to stay on this merry-go-round, they've chosen to get on an even bigger one.

Over a one-month period, August 2004, Mac West, a leading museum consultant, recorded more than two hundred museums in the United States in the midst of some kind of renovation, expansion, or new building project; this was in the midst of a significant industry-wide financial slump. Arguably, all these institutions were trying to convince their public that they had changed their product, making it ever greater, better, and new; they were trying to buy their way out of bad times. Nothing wrong with trying to make things greater, better, and new, but achieving product dominance through capital campaigns and expansions is hardly a sustainable strategy, as all too many institutions have discovered. Expansions buy short-term gains in attendance, but not long-term gains in audience loyalty. In fact, like the traveling exhibit game, institutional expansions are often a one-way ticket to financial disaster.

There are many ways for a museum to compete on product, but product dominance is not likely to be the strategy best suited to most institutions. That said, being good or even distinguished is essential. The industry's standards have been consistently raised. And as museum-going becomes an increasingly popular leisure pastime, the public is becoming ever more discriminating about what constitutes a quality museum offering. The majority of Americans now visit some kind of museum at least once a year—most do not visit the same museum twice in the same year. What this means is that visitors coming to your institution have likely been to a number of other institutions like yours before, even if they've never been to your museum before. Your institution's product is being judged against industry standards of quality, diversity, depth, and presentation. All of these dimensions of product are fundamental to your museum's success and it behooves you to make sure that your institution's product measures up. Not only do you need to be concerned with the quality of your objects, but also the quality of how they're presented and how they are interpreted. Today, a typical museum includes more than just objects in glass cases. Exhibitions are increasingly designed as immersive experiences, augmented by surround video, mood-enhancing soundscapes, and even smells. Disappearing are the old-fashioned taped tours, replaced by random-access

CD players and increasingly interactive palm-size computers that can provide audio, video, and GPS-guided "intelligent" information keyed to where you are and what you want to know. Once industry jargon, "hands-on" is now in the public vernacular and has come to represent the visiting public's expectations; "quality" museum exhibitions will be interactive.[24]

Many museums are investing in their websites, extending their product far beyond the four walls of the institution. It is now considered essential for every museum to have a website and because of the newness of the technology everyone seems to think they should invest in this medium. However, it is unlikely that the virtual playing field will long remain level. Much like the physical world of objects and displays, the virtual world will soon be dominated by a few—those who make the largest commitment in this area, and those with the deepest pockets. As everyone rushes to digitize their collections and put them on-line, the time will soon come, if it hasn't already, when the glut of information will demand a level of discrimination by the public, functionally relegating all but a few to second-class status.

We should not forget to include in this discussion of product all the educational programming, classes, and live interpretation that museums do. In many ways, these may prove to be the most enduring and saleable commodities the museum has to offer. In a Knowledge Age, the greatest commodity an organization has to sell is knowledge. Historically, museums have opted to invest their resources primarily in conveying that knowledge through the exhibition medium. The value of this medium is unlikely to diminish any time soon, but like any product its life cannot be projected out to infinity. However, people-driven strategies for conveying knowledge and supporting free-choice learning remain a premium product. Although we've come a long way as a society in our abilities to communicate indirectly—books, television, the Internet, exhibitions and now hand-held devices, just to name a few—quality people-to-people communication remains the most effective and satisfying way to pass along knowledge. Many museums already invest in this form of product, and many more might want to move in this direction. At some point, it is possible to envision a time when the "industry standard" exhibit becomes so prohibitively expensive to produce that only the richest, largest institutions will be able to afford to produce them. When this happens, people-to-people communication may look increasingly attractive. Since the mission of most museums revolves around supporting learning about the arts, history, science, or conservation, using a people-heavy strategy for achieving that mission can be a very cost-effective approach.

Finally, virtually all museums today possess gift shops, most have food services, and increasing numbers also sell parking spaces, rent out rooms for special events, run birthday parties and other events—in general, engage in trying to sell the public a whole range of products and services. The fact that very few museum professionals have any clue about how to run a good retail or parking business doesn't seem to deter museums from thinking that being in these businesses is a good idea. A friend of John's who is in the hotel "recovery business"—the business of taking over the management of hotels that are struggling financially and helping them turn things around—recently told him that the challenge of hotels is that they are typically not in a single business but several (e.g., rooms, food service, bar, parking, etc.) and that this is usually the single biggest reason for their financial distress. He usually begins by trying to figure out which of the hotel's businesses are profitable, and encourages expansion of these, and which are losers, and recommends spinning these off or eliminating them entirely. Museums too need to take a steely-eyed look at their portfolio of businesses and figure out which of these product-oriented businesses make sense for them to try and be in, let alone dominate locally.

PICKING A BUSINESS STRATEGY

So how do you pick a business strategy that works for your specific institution? As we have tried to make clear, you cannot be all things to all people; you cannot be excellent at everything. The game is played by first understanding who your current public is, and what they really want and expect from you. Then you need to look deep and hard at your organization and decide what your major assets are. Which of the five values categories described above—access, experience, price, service, and product—can your museum dominate in? Which other value can you be really distinguished in? And how are you going to ensure that the other three value categories remain at or above acceptable industry standards? And finally, how are you going to design and market those values so that they help you accomplish your mission while matching and exceeding the needs and expectations of your public? That's the game.

There is no single solution that's right for every museum. In fact, there are thousands if not millions of possible "right" solutions. But the answers lie within the information we've presented thus far in this book. It is much like painting your living room. There is no one color that is right for everyone. What is right depends upon the unique needs and realities of your space, your furniture, the mood you're trying to create, and, of course, your unique needs, desires, and aesthetic taste. Taking all of these things into consideration you arrive at a concept. Then you go to the paint store to pick a color. The store has a wall full of paint colors—thousands of colors to choose from. But when you finally make your choice and go to get your paint, there are not thousands of cans of paint, each with a unique color, sitting in the warehouse. All of those thousands of colors derive from just four pigments—red, blue, yellow, and black. From just four basic pigments, mixed in precise quantities, it is possible to produce an almost infinite variety of shades and hues. So, too, is the process of developing a business strategy for your museum. Starting with your audience, driven by your mission as defined by the talents of your staff, the intellectual capacities of your institution, the type and quality of your collections, and the relationships you can create within your community, and ever mindful of the constantly changing realities of community and society, you need to develop a concept for how you want your museum to succeed. Then using the "pigments" of *access, experience, price, service,* and *product,* you need to create just the right mixture of *dominance, distinction,* and *acceptability* to achieve that concept. Figure out how to do it right now, and make sure you keep on doing it right forever and your museum will prosper and thrive. That's the challenge we'll address in the final chapter; how to get it right today and how to keep it right tomorrow.

DISCUSSION QUESTIONS

- Which of the five major business attributes—*access, experience, price, service,* and *product*—does your organization currently strive to excel at?
- How would your rate your organization's success in each of the five value categories—*dominant, distinguished, acceptable,* or *unacceptable*—as compared to your competition?
- What business value category should your institution strive to be dominant in, which distinguished, and in which three acceptable?

NOTES

Epigraph: Quoted in F. Crawford and R. Mathews, *The Myth of Excellence: Why Great Companies Never Try and Be the Best at Everything* (New York: Three Rivers Press, 2001), 73.

1. S. Zuboff and D. Maxmin, *The Support Economy: Why Corporations Are Failing Individuals and the Next Episode of Capitalism* (New York: Viking Press, 2002), 38.

2. Crawford and Mathews, *Myth of Excellence.*

3. Ibid., 32.

4. Pseudonyms.

5. Zuboff and Maxmin, *Support Economy.*

6. M. Schwarzer, Schizophrenic agora: Mission, market, and the multi-tasking museum, *Museum News* 78, no. 60 (1999): 41–47.

7. G. Godbey, The use of time and space in assessing the potential of free choice learning, in *Free-Choice Learning: Building the Informal Science Education Infrastructure*, ed. J. H. Falk (New York: Teachers College Press, 2001).

8. J. H. Falk, The use of time as a measure of visitor behavior and exhibit effectiveness, *Roundtable Reports* 7, no. 4 (1983): 10–13.

9. OCLC, 2003 Environmental Scan: Pattern recognition, http://www.oclc.org/membership/escan/introduction/default.htm., accessed February 27, 2005.

10. Bill Booth, personal communication, June 27, 2005.

11. National Register Publishing, *The Official Museum Directory* (New Providence, NJ: National Register Publishing, 2004).

12. B. J. Pine II and J. H. Gilmore, *The Experience Economy: Work is Theatre and Every Business a Stage* (Boston: Harvard Business School Press, 1999).

13. Cf. J. H. Falk and M. Storksdieck, Using the *Contextual Model of Learning* to understand visitor learning from a science center exhibition, *Science Education* 89 (2005): 744–778.

14. Crawford and Mathews, *Myth of Excellence*; M. Treacy and F. Wiersema, *The Discipline of Market Leaders* (New York: Basic Books, 1995); P. F. Drucker, *Management Challenges for the 21st Century* (New York: Harpers Business, 1999).

15. Crawford and Mathews, *Myth of Excellence,* 41.

16. Ibid., 43.

17. Drucker, *Management Challenges for the 21st Century.*

18. Crawford and Mathews, *Myth of Excellence,* 73.

19. A. Slywotzky and R. Wise, *How to Grow When Markets Don't* (New York: Warner Business Books, 2003), 15.

20. Pseudonym.

21. Slywotzky and Wise, *How to Grow When Markets Don't.*

22. Ibid., 5.

23. A. Mintz, That's edutainment! *Museum News* 73, no. 6 (1994): 33–36.

24. J. H. Falk, C. Scott, L. D. Dierking, L. J. Rennie, and M. Cohen Jones, Interactives and visitor learning. *Curator* 47, no. 2 (2004): 171–198.

10

Putting It All Together
Thriving in the Knowledge Age

So long as a dedication to public service is its driving force, a museum can be a good one in an almost infinite number of ways. The constructive ways in which museums can innovate and explore new dimensions are almost endless. In everything museums do, they must remember the cornerstone on which the whole enterprise rests: to make a positive difference in the quality of people's lives. Museums that do that matter—they matter a great deal. And their crowning glory is that they can matter in so many marvelous ways.
—Stephen E. Weil

Imagine a museum . . .

with priceless, one-of-a-kind objects that allows its users to borrow them and use them as part of their everyday life.

that has no building, no exhibitions, and no objects—just a virtual presence on the Web that is accessible 24/7, worldwide.

committed to supporting underserved children, but rather than directly serving those children at its building, it goes out into the community and trains community leaders so that those leaders can better work with children.

built with a coffee and wine bar at its center; a museum designed primarily
to enable young, single adults to have thoughtful and engaging conversations about science issues in the evening.

helping to revitalize a local indigenous language and share cultural lessons
by collaborating with local media outlets in broadcasting the "Alutiiq Word
of the Week."

working with the local police department to create job training in the arts
for juveniles charged with graffiti vandalism.

These are all museums that currently exist. In order, the museums are the
National Museum of the American Indian; the Virtual Museum of the City of
San Francisco; Pacific Science Center and Franklin Institute Science Museum;
the Dana Center of the Science Museum, London; Alutiiq Museum and
Archaeological Repository, Kodiak, Alaska; and Nevada Museum of Art, Reno.
As the director of Public and Legislative Affairs for the U.S. Institute of
Museum and Library Services recently said to us, "The museum of tomorrow,
the museums that are being created by so many innovative institutions today,
bear little resemblance to the public's now dated concept of 'museum.'"[1]
Museums all over the world are rethinking what it means to be a museum.

As this book has tried to emphasize, every museum must rethink how it does
business if it wants to thrive in the radically altered marketplace of the twenty-
first century. Surviving, let alone thriving, in the Knowledge Age, is already a very
challenging task for all museums, in large part because the rules of the game
have changed. It would be wonderful to think that the successful strategies of the
past quarter century could just be applied forever, but sadly this does not seem
likely. As never before museums must consciously and deliberately develop business models that make sense for the new age in which we now live. As one of our
colleagues quipped, "This isn't just going to happen by accident anymore."
Those in the vanguard of the Industrial Age one hundred years ago pioneered a
revolutionary new way of doing business that ended up being amazingly successful. The model they created did not come with an instruction manual. And
so it is now. Although we and others can provide some guidance for how to
thrive in the Knowledge Age, no one can tell you exactly how to do it. All of these
new ideas and all of the changes we've been advocating are for a purpose. That
purpose is to create a successful museum. But what does it mean today to have a

successful museum? And once a museum obtains that elusive thing called "success," how can it be sustained? In fact, how does the whole field move forward in the Knowledge Age, how can all museums contribute to the success of the entire community? These are the issues we address in this final chapter.

SUCCESS IN THE KNOWLEDGE AGE

Although museums come in many shapes and sizes, a generation ago it would have seemed a doable task if you asked a group of museum professionals to list the most successful museums and enumerate the characteristics that made them really good. Although individual professionals might have quibbled over which institution should or should not make the short list and in which order, they certainly would have gravitated toward a list that included institutions such as the Smithsonian, Metropolitan Museum of Art, British Museum, Louvre, and American Museum of Natural History. The characteristics of "greatness" would have primarily focused on the quality and size of the collections and the curatorial staff, and secondarily on the size and extent of exhibitions. But today, how would we decide? These larger museums might still make the list, but perhaps not. Vying for top billing today would be many smaller museums, including some with minimal, if any collections, and some without permanent exhibitions. In fact, we would postulate that a comparable collection of museum professionals today would find such a task extremely daunting. For example, in the United States, the Institute of Museum and Library Services annually makes awards for museum excellence. Their guidelines state:

> The principal criterion for selection is the museum's commitment to public service through exemplary and innovative programs and community partnerships. Nominations should describe the institution's goal in serving its community, the target population served, the community partnerships and efforts undertaken to achieve the goal, the outcome of these efforts during the last two to three years, and projections for future efforts in this area. Achievements that might be highlighted include programming that demonstrates how the institution has attracted new audiences; innovative programming that addresses current educational, social, economic, or environmental issues; and positive effects of the institution's collaboration with other organizations in the community.[2]

Not much in these guidelines relates to size, collections, curatorial staff, or even exhibitions! The point is, at the beginning of the twenty-first century, our criteria of quality, our ideas of what constitutes a successful museum, are still evolving.

Take size, for example. Like so many things related to the Industrial Age, museums in the twentieth century were judged by size. Small museums aspired to be medium-sized museums and medium-sized museums longed to be large. Bigger and larger were always better—bigger buildings, larger staffs, bigger collections, larger exhibitions, bigger budgets. The trend in the twentieth century was always toward bigger. That's because in a mechanical age, greater performance could be achieved by being bigger—economies of scale and scope. The biggest institutions always seemed to command the lion's share of the resources; they had the richest donors and received the largest grants. In the twenty-first-century Knowledge Age, those assumptions no longer work. In the Knowledge Age optimum size depends upon the function that needs to be achieved. As Peter Drucker states, "The characteristics of information imply that the smallest effective size will be best. 'Bigger' will be 'better' only if the task cannot be done otherwise."[3] In other words, no longer are the world's biggest museums automatically positioned to be the most successful. Words like *innovative, community-relevance, responsive,* and *flexible* are increasingly being used as criteria of museum excellence and as the basis for support.

Given the rapidly changing landscape, all successful museums in the future will need to be responsive and nimble. In the past, museums were run through a slow, but meticulous process of command-and-control, top-down management. Increasingly, museums will need to adopt more flexible communications systems, systems that permit multidirectional communications internally and externally. They will also come to rely increasingly on technology to support their communications. As is often the case, Drucker is right on target when he states, "Technology is not [machinery], but humanity. It is not about tools; it is about how people work. It is equally about how they live and how they think."[4] In order to be successful, twenty-first-century museums will need to maximize the creativity, flexibility, and ingenuity of their relationships, both inside and outside the organization. Increasingly, a measure of an institution's success will be how well it supports the continued learning and growth of its staff, board, and volunteers. Another equally important measure of an institution's success will be how well it builds long-lasting and meaningful collaborations and associations externally.

New Criteria for Success

As we've already emphasized, successful institutions will be those that create indispensable value to their publics. Successful museums will also create dynamic workplaces that support and develop their staff. Successful museums will be institutions that create and sustain meaningful community relationships. These are all becoming key criteria of museum success in the Knowledge Age. But at least one additional measure of success will be common for museums and other nonprofits in this new age. We are witnessing a greater and greater erosion of the boundaries that distinguish the nonprofit and for-profit worlds. Just as more and more for-profits are now being judged by the traditional nonprofit criteria of social and environmental responsibility, increasingly nonprofits are being judged by the traditional for-profit indicator of financial success. For years many people assumed that being a "nonprofit" meant that you didn't need to make money, or in some cases shouldn't make money. Today nothing could be further from the truth. Nonprofit leadership is now held highly accountable for budgets, and nothing will get a museum director fired quicker than red ink in the balance sheet. In the twenty-first century, a museum's financial status will be a major criterion of institutional success.

Creating public good, building a learning organization, fostering community collaboration, and generating financial surpluses—these are the new standards of twenty-first-century museum success. Not one, but all four of these areas will need to be great for an organization to be judged successful. As we laid out in Chapter 2, to be successful in the Knowledge Age every museum will need to focus on and devise ways to answer four key questions:

1. Why do you exist? Whom are you serving? In other words, who is your public and what are the specific needs they have that you are uniquely trying to satisfy?
2. What assets do you bring to the table? What are the internal assets your institution brings to its business such as its human resources of staff, board, and supporters; also the assets of intellectual property, collections, building, and brand?
3. How will you forge and maintain partnerships and collaborations with like-minded organizations in the community in order to leverage your impact?

4. How will you support your business? What is your business strategy? What is the unique combination of products and services you will provide to the public in order to satisfy specific public needs and generate sufficient revenues to keep your doors open?

Collectively, these questions form the foundation of a Knowledge Age business model. At the core of this new business model are the Knowledge Age attributes of understanding and relationships, all of which need to be personalized to meet the unique and ever-changing needs of all involved—board, staff, collaborators, funders, and communities. But the most important understandings and relationships museums will need to possess revolve around the shifting needs and values of the publics they hope to serve. As we have emphasized repeatedly, no longer can the museum dictate, top down, what the public should receive; no longer can the museum expect that one approach, one label, one type of experience, will satisfy all. In the Knowledge Age, successful museums will be those that figure out how to develop long-lasting, meaningful transactions with their publics; that means thinking of those we serve as assemblages of individuals and not as some undefined, mass "public." In the Knowledge Age, resources will flow to organizations that focus their attention on deeply understanding the needs and priorities of those outside of the institution; resources will be spent developing internal and external strategies for meeting those needs and priorities. This approach is in stark contrast to the way things were done in the past, when priorities were set on the inside by a small group of individuals who felt they knew what the public needed without the benefit, of course, of ever actually communicating with the consumers they claimed they were serving.

Arguably the museum community's strongest public role in this new age is as educator. Museum work inevitably encompasses people who come to learn in some capacity—whether to wonder, to consider, to question, or to discover. Collectively, museums have an unfathomable number of resources—points of connection of unlimited possibility. Individually, they are found in all kinds of communities, proudly embraced as community assets. The ultimate mission, then, may be to use the institution's assets to create the richest learning environments possible for as many people as possible.

While the museum's collections, scholarship, and educational expertise provide content and experience, the museum's greatest strength may be its capacity to cater to different ways of learning within a single institution—to invite and respond to the multiple styles and interests of so many kinds of visitors. If museums are to succeed at being truly relevant twenty-first-century educational resources, they need to find new ways to respond to individual interests. New ideas will come from many sources. Many in the museum community have turned to the entertainment industry for new models, while others have found inspiration in the practices of libraries, health care facilities, and other kinds of nonprofits. For example, when the Institute of Museum and Library Services first merged libraries and museums into a single entity, opinions were divided about the efficacy of the new partnership. The institutions were different in so many ways. Yet, there were lessons to be learned by all. One of the most striking—and potentially instructive—differences between the two was in the delivery of services. To libraries, their customers are *users;* to museums they are *visitors.* This difference in nomenclature alone switches the power and process of learning from the individual to the institution. Library services are designed to respond to the individual's specific quest; the learner dictates the journey. By contrast, museums are rarely responsive to the individual quest, but create the learning journey through predesigned exhibition experiences. Thinking about one learner at a time may be a useful model for the future work of museums.

The library model also challenges the museum's position on authority—especially as it strives to build new partnerships. By practice, librarians do not question the motives or sophistication of each user. Each quest is a private and personal one—a dictate much respected by trained librarians. Librarians put their expertise to work providing guidance, trusted references, and useful tools in service to the user. In contrast, museums occupy a more difficult space in terms of their relationship to the learner by virtue of their efforts to more tightly control the learning experience. Exclusive authority has long been the province of the museum curator, whose expertise has been earned through long periods of research and study. Yet each visitor, too, possesses knowledge and expertise; the museum that recognizes the potential authority of each visitor would be a very different type of institution. Such an institution establishes a sense of trust and respect with its audience. It both listens and informs and creates new information from the results. In many ways, it takes on the characteristics of a "forum"—long held up as an admirable role. It has often been said that museums should be forums—not attics, not temples. The forum image is dynamic, suggesting a variety of voices and opinions, debate and discussion, discovery and disagreement. It suggests purpose and an intention to share and clarify, learn and teach. The forum is foremost a place for people—unlike either an attic or a temple, both of which suggest a place where only the few and the privileged can access what is contained there. In the museum as forum, objects can still play critical roles, but they become mediators of learning rather than silent vessels of truth, beauty, or history.

In the Knowledge Age, the center of economic power will increasingly shift to the individual customer, rather than the producer, manufacturer, or distributor. No longer will institutions be able to decide unilaterally what is good or bad for the public. In this new age museums will need progressively to shift their focus away from passively and paternalistically serving "visitors" to more actively engaging and facilitating "users." Museums must increasingly become true partners with the public, supporting learners in their personal journeys. The best news of this new age is that the core museum business as outlined above, the learning business, is going to be the fastest-growing, most dynamic part of the economy. Individuals, corporations, and governments will spend ever increasing sums of money in support of learning; education, broadly defined, will be valued like never before in human history. The bad news, though, is that there will be many others vying to get a slice of this ever-growing economic pie. In an increasingly competitive environment, only the best free-choice learning providers will succeed; only the best museums will be successful.

Ah, so much rhetoric about success! How do you know if you've achieved it? How do you measure success? It is not just the criteria for success that are changing, so too are the metrics of success. In the past it was sufficient for museums to use what proponents of outcomes-based assessment call "outputs"—the opening of a new exhibition, the printing of a catalogue, or even the numbers of individuals who visited—as evidence of success. In the Industrial Age, it was all about outputs! But as we've emphasized throughout this book, that is not the way it will be in the Knowledge Age. Although these Industrial Age indirect measures of success are still accepted in some circles, those circles grow smaller every day. As the Knowledge Age fully comes to maturity, only *direct* measures of success—outcomes—will be acceptable. An outcome is how well you have actually served your audience, whether you have delivered the services, the experiences, the transformations this public came to you for. Have you measurably influenced the *quality* of people's lives? An outcome is a documented change in a target population's attitudes and behaviors. Examples of outcomes include definable changes in the public's knowledge and under-standing, evidence of a long-term commitment on the part of individuals to continue exploring an idea after they leave your institution, measurable in-creases in the attitudes or productivity of key staff and volunteers, and even outcomes attained through the mutually reinforcing programs of two or three collaborating public education organizations. An example of an outcome might also be a 20 percent increase in the museum's endowment or a 15 percent in-crease in net revenues from earned income. In the twenty-first century both the process and product of sustainability will be based upon the metrics of impact. Success in this new century will require that museums not only achieve excel-lence in each of the four areas we've specified; it will require that they achieve lasting, measurable excellence in each area.

CREATING AND MEASURING SUSTAINABILITY

In 1999 the Institute for Learning Innovation completed a major study at the National Aquarium in Baltimore (NAIB).[5] The study was designed to assess the overall impact of an NAIB visit on the conservation knowledge, attitudes, and behaviors of the general visitor, both in the short term and the long term. Within the framework of the NAIB's stated goals and approach, this study was designed to assess four key aspects of the NAIB visitor experience:

1. Incoming conservation knowledge, attitudes, and behavior of NAIB visitors
2. Patterns of use and interaction with exhibition components throughout the NAIB
3. Exiting conservation knowledge, attitudes, and behaviors of visitors
4. Over time, how the NAIB experience altered or affected individuals' con-servation knowledge, attitudes, and behaviors

Over three hundred randomly selected aquarium visitors participated in the study, which involved a mix of quantitative and qualitative methods. Per-haps not surprisingly, the study revealed that visitors to the NAIB were a self-selected group that were generally more knowledgeable, more concerned, and more inclined to be involved in conservation-related issues than the general public. Yet despite being more knowledgeable and concerned than the general public, NAIB visitors were far from experts or conservationists.

The typical visitor spent a long time in the NAIB, about two hours on average, and generally attended to and became engaged with most of the key exhibit components during this time. Although attraction and engagement with exhibit components throughout the NAIB were generally high, visitor interaction with direct and specific conservation-related signage and exhibition components was surprisingly low—less than 10 percent of the visitors were attracted to exhibit components with specific conservation information.

Nonetheless, virtually all visitors (93 percent) understood the fundamental conservation message at the NAIB. Visitors upon leaving the aquarium, without prompting, were able to describe the institution's main message—which was to "preserve/protect/save" the environment and nature.[6] Although most visitors did not engage with the specific exhibit components that contained direct conservation messages, visitors perceived that a pervasive conservation message permeated the aquarium. Upon exiting, visitors most commonly talked about conservation with greater emotion than when entering and showed significant gains in their appreciation that conservation involved complex interconnections between animals and their environment and humans and the environment, as well as the need to balance the coexistence of people and nature.

Changes in visitors' conservation knowledge, understanding, and interests after visiting the aquarium by and large persisted over several months. Overall, the NAIB affected positive short-term and long-term change in visitors' understanding and awareness of conservation issues in their lives. Not only did the NAIB visit increase visitors' general knowledge related to topics addressed at NAIB, but it provoked a greater sense of awareness and appreciation for conservation issues and the connections between their own lives and conservation issues. For instance, after six to eight weeks, two-thirds of visitors persisted in more prominently discussing conservation in terms of complex interconnections and a need to balance the coexistence of people and nature. Interestingly, in the long term, visitors were also more likely after entering the NAIB to relate conservation issues to social/political/cultural/economic factors and root causes, such as overpopulation.

The NAIB experience also connected to visitors' lives in a variety of ways following their visit. In particular, almost a quarter of visitors (24 percent) specifically noted that the NAIB visit had inspired or motivated them to visit other aquaria, zoos, museums, and parks. These visitors talked about how things they had seen at these other institutions reminded them of things they had seen or heard at the NAIB. About one in five (21 percent) visitors made connections between their recent visit and their personal and family lives and a comparable number (18 percent) made connections between their NAIB visit and subsequent things they had seen on television or read about in the print media. These personal connections rarely related to inspired conservation action, however.

An important long-term finding was that, in the absence of reinforcing experiences, the general enthusiasm/emotional commitment visitors expressed for conservation-related experiences upon exiting the NAIB generally waned back to entry levels. Visitors to NAIB left the institution very excited and committed to the conservation cause, but there was no evidence that this short-term enthusiasm translated into long-term action as the NAIB hoped it would. Overall, the findings revealed a successful institution, an institution capable of both satisfying the needs of a diverse visiting public as well as successfully fulfilling the major part of its educational and conservation mission. The NAIB provided visitors an opportunity to see and experience the diversity of aquatic life, translating and portraying complex subject matter in ways that appealed to all audiences. Given its conservation mission to effect change, however, the challenge remained how best to translate the excitement of the NAIB experience into conservation-related actions after a visit. This is a challenge the NAIB has accepted. The NAIB was pleased with what it was doing well, but also concerned about its shortcomings. Five years later it has begun to implement programs and exhibitions designed to address directly the issue of sustaining visitor commitment and influencing long-term conservation-related behaviors. It has also secured funding to conduct another round of research to test how successful this new effort will be.

The critical question for any organization is not what can it do to get through these next few years, but how it can build an organization that will thrive long into the future, how it can do better tomorrow than it did today. As business gurus James Collins and Jerry Porras say in *Built to Last*, great companies "institutionalize these questions as a way of life, a habit of mind and action."[7] The best organizations don't get that way because they're lucky, they work at it. Success, particularly in the rapidly changing world in which we now live, requires a continuous commitment to improvement and investment in the future. There is no finish line, no point at which success is "achieved." Bob Waterman wrote in *The Renewal Factor* that excellent organizations ". . . have

made curiosity an institutional attribute. They seek a different mirror, something that tells them that the world has changed and that, in the harsh light of
the new reality, they aren't as beautiful as they once were. The mirror also tells
them that unless they change, they're in for a crisis."[8]

Using Knowledge to Manage Success

According to Collins and Porras, "[Great] companies, we learned, attain their
extraordinary position not so much because of superior insight or special
"secrets" of success, *but largely because of the simple fact that they are so terribly
demanding of themselves.*"[9] That said, demanding success is in and of itself not
a strategy for success any more than determination alone is what it takes to be
great. Great athletes possess determination, but they also develop tremendous
skills. Great scientists possess great determination, but they also possess above
average intelligence. To create and run a great museum requires determination
and it requires great insight and knowledge—insight and knowledge of the
present and the future. To create a sustainable museum requires continually
updated understanding of your current and potential markets, comprehen-
sion of your successes and failures, and awareness of the business you are in
and what the next great innovations in your business might be. Although there
truly are no "secrets" for how to make your museum great and sustainable,
there are a few "tricks" that successful organizations can and do use to stay
ahead of the curve. It should come as no surprise that all of these "tricks" have
something to do with knowledge.

The key to keeping the beast of change at bay is being able to know what
change looks like; where it's coming from and where it's going. The goal is not
to fight change, but anticipate it and go with it; not to control it but to manage
it. The key to managing change is knowledge; not information, but knowledge.
Information today is certainly plentiful; in fact all of us are inundated by information. What we lack is *quality* information—the right kind of information,
presented in the right format, at the right time. What we continually crave is
knowledge. One of the hallmarks of the Knowledge Age is that we recognize and
value knowledge like never before. Accordingly, today we have systematized and
refined the process for acquiring knowledge. One such process is evaluation.

In the future more and more museums will be doing evaluation. We'd like
to believe this will be because museums understand the value of evaluation,
but the reality is that these changes will be driven more by necessity than good

intentions. An increasing number of both public- and private-sector funders already require evaluation as part of the granting process, and soon all will move in this direction. Boards, too, are increasingly moving toward a more evidence-based approach to governance. In the twenty-first century, not only will evaluation become mandatory, the scope, scale, and complexity of what is assessed will increase significantly. Ten years from now, we predict that what museums will consider as an "acceptable" evaluation will bear little resemblance to what is considered standard today.

Institutional Accountability—The "THRIVE Assessment" Approach

In the twentieth century, institutional assessment was rarely, if ever, the purpose to which museum evaluation was directed. Even as of this writing, the vast majority of museum assessment studies are based upon the asking of little questions and by design provide little answers. Did the public enjoy this program? Did this exhibition successfully teach the concept of Plate Tectonics? What is not being asked are the big questions! For example, most zoos and aquariums today claim that their mission is to protect and conserve biodiversity, but few of these institutions have ever attempted to actually measure how much biodiversity protection occurred as a direct result of their public education programs. As was discovered during the NAIB study described above, this is a tough question to assess, and the answers may not always be totally satisfactory. However, these are the kinds of questions twenty-first-century evaluations will need to address. Not to ask these questions, not to know whether or not your institution actually fulfills its mission, is a recipe for placing yourself in the position of being judged by policy makers, funders, and public alike as, at best inadequate, and at worst disingenuous.

Clearly it is far more difficult to measure the success of an organization than it is to measure the success of a particular exhibition or program; but just because it is more difficult does not mean that it is any less important. Just as the trend in philanthropy in the past decade has been for funders to require more and better evaluation of newly funded exhibitions and programs, the future trend will be for these same funders to demand evidence of institutional success across all dimensions of the institution. Managers and funders will increasingly want to shift their focus onto the broader and more significant collective, long-term impacts of an institution's work rather than, as presently happens, merely focusing on the short-term, narrowly defined, and limited outcomes of each individual effort. Ultimately, assessing mission will become fundamental and standard, but so too will become assessing internal development, external relationship building, and finances.

Currently, there are no accepted standards for how nonprofit institutions like museums should be institutionally evaluated, and no accepted methods for providing those assessments. That does not mean that no one has any ideas about how this might be accomplished. A wide variety of efforts have been invented and tried over the past fifty years.[10] The approach we advocate using is based upon a technique that has become popular in the for-profit sector and has begun to be experimented with in the nonprofit world as well—the balanced scorecard approach. Although we don't subscribe to the specifics of the balanced scorecard approach, we do appreciate its holistic nature.

The balanced scorecard approach has the advantage of being both an institutional assessment and a strategic management technique. The approach was developed in the early 1990s by Robert Kaplan and David Norton.[11] They named their system the "balanced scorecard" because it attempted to consider more than the traditional financial bottom line as the basis for assessing an organization. According to its advocates, it enables organizations to clarify their vision and strategy as well as translate them into action and provide feedback in order to improve strategic performance and results continuously. Kaplan and Norton describe the innovation of the balanced scorecard as follows:

> The balanced scorecard retains traditional financial measures. But financial measures tell the story of past events, an adequate story for Industrial Age companies for which investments in long-term capabilities and customer relationships were not critical for success. These financial measures are inadequate, however, for guiding and evaluating the journey that Information Age companies must make to create future value through investment in customers, suppliers, employees, processes, technology, and innovation.[12]

The traditional balanced scorecard involves viewing the organization from *four* perspectives: (1) Learning and Growth; (2) Business Processes; (3) The Customer; and (4) Finances. Metrics are created and data collected and analyzed relative to each perspective. We have taken these ideas and developed a significant modification that better dovetails with the framework presented in this book. We call our new approach the "THRIVE Assessment," where THRIVE is an acronym standing for "*T*ools for *H*elping maximize *R*esources, *I*nternal learning and growth, public *V*alue, and *E*xternal relationships. We believe this approach to institutional assessment better accommodates the needs and realities of nonprofits like museums. We recommend that every museum develop visions, initiatives, targets, and measures around the following four areas:

- Public Value
- Internal Learning and Growth
- External Relationships
- Resources and Finances

Public Value

This perspective refers to the effort of a museum to define and measure how effectively it accomplishes its goals of creating public value. Metrics based on this perspective allow all within the museum to know how well their institution is meeting its mission—whether the specific products and services it creates actually support the public good it seeks to achieve. In other words, whom is the museum trying to serve and how well it is actually serving that audience. These metrics have to be designed carefully by those who know these processes most intimately; although outside consultants can help tremendously, ultimately each institution needs to invest in determining for itself how it will define and measure success. These measures need to be framed in terms of specific changes in the public, starting with the public's motivations for visiting. For example, a measurable outcome statement might read as follows: increase to 60 percent the number of visitors who enact an Explorer motivation and through that process learn about conservation-related behaviors and practices that they can and do implement at home within sixty days of visiting the aquarium. Eighty percent of these visitors will not only accomplish this outcome but attribute it to their aquarium experience and express positive feelings about it.

We would also suggest that in addition to defining and measuring mission-oriented outcomes that each museum also document its "support processes." Support processes are all the things that make accomplishing mission possible, such as exhibitions mounted, publications produced, and programs run. These "outputs" are not evidence of accomplishing one's mission, but they are easy to measure and benchmark and they help to provide a tangible way to gauge the process by which the museum is trying to accomplish its mission. Therefore support processes represent indicators of "how" an institution is setting about accomplishing its outcomes and can gauge progress accordingly. In at least some small way, a number of museums are attempting to monitor systematically and regularly their public value; examples include the Children's Museum, Indianapolis; Glenbow Museum, Calgary, National Postal Museum, Washington; and National Aquarium in Baltimore.

Internal Learning and Growth

For this perspective, our approach comes close to the ideas of Kaplan and Norton. They suggest that this perspective includes employee training and institutional cultural attitudes related to both individual and institutional self-improvement. Where our approach deviates is that we believe that each individual employee is motivated by a work-related identity, similar conceptually to the museum-related identity described in Chapter 5. The basis for assessment needs to be predicated on understanding these worker identities and helping to ensure that they are positive and maximally enacted. As we have pointed out repeatedly in this book, in the Knowledge Age, people—the most robust repository of institutional knowledge—are an organization's most valuable asset. In the current climate of rapid societal and technological change, it is becoming necessary for knowledge workers to be in a continuous learning mode. Museums often find themselves unable to hire new employees with the mix of skills and backgrounds they need, the aging of the Baby Boom generation threatens many institutions with the imminent retirement of their most knowledge-able employees, yet at the same time there is a decline in training of existing employees.

Metrics can be put into place to guide managers in focusing training funds where they can help the most; however, remember that in the workplace as in the leisure world, free-choice learning is the predominant mode in which individuals gain their knowledge and foster innovation. So in addition to traditional training, employees need mentors and tutors, as well as the encouragement to develop and support informal "knowledge-sharing" groups. Each individual associated with the organization should be encouraged to understand his or her work-related identity needs, to set annual learning goals and have these goals monitored and supported. To help foster a learning organization, all members of the organization, from floor staff to trustees, should be empowered to act as both learners and teachers, as both trainees and trainers.

The bottom line is that staff, board, and volunteer learning and growth constitute the essential foundation for success of any Knowledge Age museum. This is a dimension in which rhetoric currently far exceeds reality in most museums. A few museums are making major efforts to pioneer ways of creating a more reflective and empowered workforce; good examples include the Fort Worth Museum of Science and History, Denver Museum of Art and the Boston Museum of Fine Arts.

External Relationships

We believe that no museum, no nonprofit for that matter, can long exist in the twenty-first century that does not develop meaningful long-term external relationships—relationships with the whole community, with strategic partner organizations, and with key individuals. This perspective is thus designed to ensure that the museum develop clearly articulated goals and objectives for how it intends to build and sustain these various relationships and then monitor and measure its success at satisfying those goals and objectives. As with the previous categories, identity comes into play. Not just visitors and employees have identity-needs, but institutions too! What is the identity your institution wishes to project into the community, and how can you build and support that identity? What are the identity needs of your partner organizations? Is it reasonable to support those?

The key to successful monitoring of success is to be as specific and concrete as possible. If, for example, your museum has a partnership with the local school system you should define annual benchmarks of success for this partnership. These benchmarks should not just be numbers of students served, though these might, as above, represent a useful indicator of "support processes." Rather, the benchmarks of success should be measurable outcomes that indicate what you, the museum, hoped to gain from this partnership (e.g., community awareness and appreciation, revenues, return visits by families, changes in students' attitudes toward art, history, or science) as well as what your partner, the local school system hoped to gain (e.g., greater interest in school art, history, or science, improved test scores). Poor performance from this perspective would be a strong indicator of future decline, even in the face of current mission success. Developing, maintaining, and successfully fulfilling relationships is ultimately as fundamental to institutional success and vitality in the years ahead as are the other three target areas listed in this model. Sadly, great examples of museums regularly and systematically assessing their community relations are hard to come by. However, some institutions have at least appreciated the need and made some small steps in this direction, including the Buffalo Museum of Science; Museum of Fine Arts, Houston; Walters Art Gallery, Baltimore; and the Japanese American National Museum, Los Angeles.

Revenues and Finances

Here, more than in the previous three areas, we borrow liberally from Kaplan and Norton's ideas. Every museum needs to attend to proper financial planning, tracking, and analysis. Timely and accurate funding data are always fundamental to a well-run business and managers of museums should do whatever is necessary to provide such data. It was the tendency of for-profit businesses to be overly focused on this part of the scorecard that prompted Kaplan and Norton to emphasize the importance of the other perspectives in order to create more of a "balanced" view of an organization's performance. That said, some museums can be faulted for tilting too much in the other direction, hence the need to keep this perspective equally front-of-mind when thinking about how to run and manage the organization.

Most museums already are required by their boards to develop annual budgets and to track income and expenses monthly, quarterly, and annually. Relatively few institutions tie their financials directly to their goals and outcomes, however. If they don't already, we would encourage museums to benchmark and track the sources and allocations of all revenues and expenses. Much as a good retail store tracks a wide range of financial indicators, museums too should create indicators of the financial costs and returns from all parts of its operations—from administration and fundraising to exhibitions and programs and how these specifically interact with and contribute to the outcomes specified in the other three categories above. Good examples of museums with thorough financial tracking procedures include The Field Museum, Chicago; The Bronx Zoo, New York; and Science Museum of Minnesota, Minneapolis–St. Paul.

Despite the additional challenges this "THRIVE Assessment" approach to institutional accountability is likely to engender, the costs of not being accountable, of not even trying to measure one's impact, are likely to be far greater. For years, museums have managed to skate along under the radar of accountability; those days are increasingly numbered, unless of course museums want to slip into total anonymity and obscurity. If museums aspire to be recognized as important players in society, to play on the education stage with the "big dogs," then they can expect the scrutiny that comes with being an important player; the higher the profile, the higher the funding, but also the higher the demands for accountability. Accountability promises to become one of the largest challenges of this new age, a challenge that can be met through implementation of institutional evaluation, as we have broadly defined it. In the end, though, it is about measuring what is important and not just what is easy to measure. In other words, like everything else, the challenge of institutional assessment is to think both strategically and pragmatically. One final note: if museums are not proactive about accountability, if they do not seize the initiative and define for themselves the criteria of success, then it can be expected that external forces will sooner or later impose criteria upon them. One need look no further than the mess the public schools are in with "No Child Left Behind" to appreciate what the consequences of that scenario might look like.

There's no doubt that the road ahead will be full of challenges. Every museum will face setbacks; even the best organizations have both good times and bad. But the great organizations will have more good than bad times; over the long haul, they will generate consistently excellent results for their publics, employees, community partners, and bankers! Although the needs and values of a museum's constituencies may change, and even the definition of what constitutes a constituency may change, great organizations will always meet, in fact, exceed their constituency's needs. As it has been in the past, the great museums of the twenty-first century will not just be leaders within their local communities; they will be leaders within the larger community that is the museum field. Perhaps, then, the ultimate challenge of this new age will be what it takes to be a leader in the museum field because that definition too will continue to evolve and change. As the free flow of information forces all of us to think more globally and broadly, both in terms of the publics we serve and in how we define the business we're in, we can look forward to not only the definition of "museum" morphing and changing but so too what it means to be a contributing member of the "museum community." In the coming years, the learning landscape will become increasingly crowded, and increasingly competitive, so much so that the success of individual museums may lie beyond the capabilities of individual actions.

THE MUSEUM BUSINESS AS A SHARED RESPONSIBILITY

The aquarium study described above is an example of a research study that provided useful information to not just a single institution, the National

Aquarium in Baltimore, but to the entire zoo and aquarium community. We could have easily picked several other studies to cite as such an example but we could not have cited hundreds of other studies; that just would not have been possible. To date, we would be hard pressed to cite even one hundred comparably rigorous, systematic, and empirically sound investigations of museums; not in the United States, not even worldwide. Although the number of museum-learning researchers and evaluators has grown tremendously in recent years, still only a limited number of individuals do this kind of work. Despite considerable effort on the part of a number of people in the field, worldwide, there are only a handful of graduate programs supporting research on learning in museums and only a handful of institutions that support deliberate experimental development work.

This is not just a little problem, it is a huge problem. Every day, the museum community is falling farther behind in its efforts to generate the knowledge that it can use to map out the business strategies of tomorrow. The goal of research and development is to ask bigger questions, to take risks, to ask questions in ways that push the boundaries of knowledge and practice. Research and development, as opposed to market or evaluation research, is intended to create new ideas and open new doors; it is fundamental to helping us understand something about the world we are about to enter. Good research and development helps us ask questions we didn't even know we needed to ask. Unfortunately, there is still relatively little research and development in the museum world. Such efforts tend to be risky and exploratory and they tend to be expensive and often unproductive in the short term. But that's the cost of staying ahead of the curve; there's no easy way to look into the crystal ball! Currently, the museum community invests the tiniest fraction of one percent of its annual collective budget in research and development. By contrast, the pharmaceutical industry invests about 40 percent of its annual budget in research and development; the tech world invests about a third of its revenues on research and development as do energy companies. Is the future of the museum industry that much more secure and predictable than that of the pharmaceutical, technology, and energy industries? If museums, as a community, are to thrive in the coming years they will need to invest in research and development; they will need to reorient their priorities so that a greater share of resources goes to supporting efforts to understand and predict the future of business. How else will museums, individually and collectively, manage to stay ahead of the curve and keep one step ahead of the competition? There just isn't any other way for this to happen.

Future research and development will need to not only dig deeply into the specifics of how people learn in and from museums, but investigate fundamental questions about the very nature of learning, particularly free-choice learning. Other lines of research and development will need to ponder non-learning related aspects of museums—museums as social institutions, museums as businesses, museums as economic drivers in a community. It is all well and good to say that museums are fundamental parts of the learning and economic infrastructure of society, but to what end and to what benefit? The community needs to understand how museums fit into the total lifelong learning, social, cultural, and economic trajectory of citizens. It needs to understand what museums do really well, so well that others need not try to compete. Museums also need to better understand what they do not do well, and either improve or opt not to compete in these arenas.

Knowledge is truly the key to future success of the industry, and as an industry museums must make a commitment to supporting knowledge acquisition. It is unlikely that many institutions, even the wealthiest institutions, can independently support a full-blown research and development effort. And even if they did, the community would run the risk of creating the kinds of competitive and proprietary wrangling over knowledge that is rampant in the for-profit world. One of the real assets of the museum community has always been its willingness to share ideas and openly cooperate with each other. To maintain that spirit, even in the face of increased competition, needs to be an industry-wide commitment. National foundations like the National Science Foundation and the Institute of Museum and Library Services have already stepped up to the plate in this regard. Both of these foundations have in recent years significantly increased their commitment to only funding research and development efforts that will make a difference to the whole community. But even if every dollar these foundations spent in support of the museum community were directed toward research and development it would still be a drop in the bucket.

All museums, and all the organizations that represent them, need to lobby for a greater emphasis and financial support for research and development. Incumbent upon organizations like the American Association of Museums, the Association of Science-Technology Centers, the Association of Children's Museums, the American Association of Zoos and Aquariums, and others is that they not only provide encouragement and guidance for research, as many currently are beginning to do, but money as well. It is not an outlandish idea that a percentage of the dues of all these professional associations be directed to supporting industry-wide research and development efforts. If the museums that make up the membership of these organizations are not willing to help support the basic research enterprise, an enterprise designed to benefit directly all parts of the industry, who then should be expected to support such efforts? If it is always someone else's responsibility, then it is no one's responsibility. And so it seems at the moment. Museums are delighted to eat at the table of others' research and development, but paying for the banquet often seems to be someone else's responsibility.

The maturation of the museum community demands a stepping up to the responsibility of doing what every other mature industry has realized. In order to survive in the Knowledge Age, the museum community needs to invest in itself. Each institution will need to make its own personal investments; investments in institutional marketing and evaluation represent one such important contribution. But the investment in exploratory studies and efforts to develop new and innovative strategies and ideas transcend the capabilities of most individual institutions. That investment will need to come from the collective whole.

So we conclude this book by saying that thriving in the Knowledge Age will require both individual and collective actions. Each museum must do its part to develop a robust and appropriate business model for succeeding in its own unique community with its own unique suite of publics that it serves. Equally, though, each museum must help contribute to the greater good, by collaborating on generating the knowledge necessary for the museum industry as a whole to succeed. The ultimate recipe for thriving in the Knowledge Age is for each museum to look out for its own interests but also to work collectively to sustain and grow a vibrant museum community.

Thomas Kuhn astutely observed in his classic book *The Structure of Scientific Revolutions* that existing paradigms are extremely hard to dislodge.[13] Even in the face of disconfirming evidence and supreme challenge, people tend to cling to old ways of doing things. According to Kuhn, only a new and better alternative is sufficient to turn the tide. We understand how hard it will be for museums to let go of their Industrial Age business models that have worked so well for so many years. We also understand how critically important it is for museums and other nonprofits to embrace a new paradigm. We hope the framework we've provided will be that new and better alternative that allows museums to build new business models appropriate to the realities of a Knowledge Age. With new models, museums can continue to thrive. Let the thriving begin!

DISCUSSION QUESTIONS

- How does your institution define success? Is today's definition of success the same as it was ten years ago? Can you envision what success in your organization will need to look like in five to ten years?
- Has your organization developed benchmarks for measuring success in all four key areas—*Public Value, Internal Learning and Growth, External Relations,* and *Resources and Finances*? If not, which areas require benchmarks, what would those benchmarks be, and what strategies should be put in place to evaluate them on an on-going basis?
- What are key community-wide questions that you think need investigating? How can your organization play a role in encouraging the professional community to investigate these questions?

NOTES

Epigraph: S. E. Weil, From being *about* something to being *for* somebody: The ongoing transformation of the American museum, *Daedalus* 123, no. 3 (1999): 229.

1. M. Bittner, personal communication, July 25, 2005.

2. Institute of Museum and Library Services, National Award for Museum Service, http://www.imls.gov/grants/museum/mus_nams.asp, (accessed August 17, 2005).

3. P. F. Drucker, *The Essential Drucker* (New York: Harper Business, 2001), 341.

4. Ibid., 343.

5. L. Adelman, J. Falk, A. Schreier, H. O'Mara, and J. De Prizio, *Conservation Impacts Study: National Aquarium in Baltimore. Technical Report* (Annapolis, MD: Institute for Learning Innovation, 1999); also L. M. Adelman, J. H. Falk, and S. James, Assessing the National Aquarium in Baltimore's impact on visitor's conservation knowledge, attitudes and behaviors, *Curator* 43, no. 1 (2000): 33–62; and J. H. Falk and L. M. Adelman, Investigating the impact of prior knowledge, experience and interest on aquarium visitor learning, *Journal of Research in Science Teaching* 40, no. 2 (2000): 163–176.

6. Visitors' perception of the main messages at the NAIB were not affected by their initial conversation with data collectors before their visit (something we took pains to measure).

7. J. Collins and J. Porras, *Built to Last* (New York: Harper Business, 1994), 185.

8. R. Waterman, *The Renewal Factor: How the Best Get and Keep the Competitive Edge* (New York: Bantam, 1987).

9. Collins and Porras, *Built to Last,* 186.

10. For example, S. P. Osborne, Performance and quality management in VNPOs, in *Managing in the Voluntary Sector—a Handbook for Managers in Charitable and Nonprofit Organizations,* ed. S. P. Osborne (London: International Thomson Business Press, 1996); V. Murray and B. Tassie, Evaluating the effectiveness of nonprofit organizations, in *The Jossey-Bass Handbook of Nonprofit Leadership and Management,* ed. R. D. Herman and Associates (San Francisco: Jossey-Bass, 1994).

11. R. S. Kaplan and D. P. Norton, *The Balanced Scorecard: Translating Strategy into Action* (Boston: Harvard Business School Press, 1996).

12. Ibid., 5.

13. T. Kuhn, *The Structure of Scientific Revolutions* (Chicago: University of Chicago Press, 1962).

References

Adams, M., J. H. Falk, and L. D. Dierking. (2003). Things change: Museums, learning, and research. In *Researching Visual Arts Education in Museums and Galleries: An International Reader*, ed. M. Xanthoudaki, L. Tickle, and V. Sedules. Amsterdam: Kluwer Academic Publishers.

Adelman, L. M., J. H. Falk, and S. James. (2000). Assessing the National Aquarium in Baltimore's impact on visitor's conservation knowledge, attitudes and behaviors. *Curator* 43, no. 1: 33–62.

Adelman, L., J. Falk, A. Schreier, H. O'Mara, and J. De Prizio. (1999). *Conservation Impacts Study: National Aquarium in Baltimore. Technical Report.* Annapolis, MD: Institute for Learning Innovation.

Albert S., and D. Whetten. (1985). Organizational identity. In *Research in Organizational Behavior*, vol. 6, ed. L. L. Cummings and B. M. Straw. Greenwich, CT: JAI.

Albrecht, K., and R. Zemke. (1985). *Service America: Doing Business in the New Economy.* Conyers, GA: Irwin Professional Publications.

American Association of Museums. (1992). *Excellence and Equity: Education and the Public Dimension of Museums.* Washington, DC: American Association of Museums.

Anderson, D. (1999). *A Common Wealth: Museums in the Learning Age.* London: Department for Culture, Media and Sport.

Anderson, G. (ed.). (1998). *Museum Mission Statements: Building a Distinct Identity.* Washington, DC: American Association of Museums.

Andoniadis, A. (Spring 2004). *The Art and Science of Museum Retailing*. Oakland, CA: Western Museums Association.

Archibald, R. (2004). *New Town Square, Museums and Communities in Transition*. Walnut Creek, CA: AltaMira Press.

Bailey, M. E., and R. E. Blakenbaker. *The Age of the Digital Paideia*. Unpublished essay.

Bakke, D. (2005). *Joy at Work: A Revolutionary Approach to Fun on the Job*. Seattle: PVG.

Bateson, M. C. (2004). *Willing to Learn*. Hanover, NH: Steerforth Press.

Busenitz, L. (1999). Entrepreneurial risk and strategic decision making. *Journal of Applied Behavioral Science*, September, 325–340.

Caplow, T., L. Hicks, and B. Wattenberg. (2001). *The First Measured Century: An Illustrated Guide to Trends in America, 1900–2000*. Washington, DC: The AEI Press.

Cavendish, K. (in press). Marketing basics: Applications for small science centers. In *Handbook for Small Science Centers*, ed. C. Yao, L. Dierking, and P. Anderson. Lanham, MD: AltaMira Press.

Center on Philanthropy and Public Policy. (2000). *What is New about the New Philanthropy*, Los Angeles: University of Southern California.

Chesebrough, D. (2004). Unpublished ASTC position paper prepared for 2004 ASTC annual meeting session on new business models.

Collins, J. C., and J. I. Porras. (1994). *Built to Last*. New York: Harper Business.

Council of Economic Advisors. (1999). *Economic Report of the President*. Washington, DC: U. S. Government Printing Office.

Crawford, F., and R. Mathews. (2001). *The Myth of Excellence: Why Great Companies Never Try and Be the Best at Everything*. New York: Three Rivers Press.

Cross, R., and S. Brodt. (2001). How assumptions of consensus undermine decision making. *Sloan Management Review*, Winter, 86–94.

Dana, J. C. (W. Peniston, ed.). (1999). *The New Museum: Selected Writings*. Washington, DC: American Association of Museums.

Davis, D. F. (1988). *Conspicuous Production: Automobiles and Elites in Detroit, 1899–1933*. Philadelphia: Temple University Press.

Dempsey, B. (2004). The Library Journal, Reed Business Information. www.libraryjournal.com.

Dierking, L. D., and M. Adams. (1996). *Spirit of the Motherland Exhibition: Summative Evaluation*. Annapolis, MD: Science Learning, Inc.

Dierking, L. D., and J. H. Falk. (2003). Optimizing out-of-school time: The role of free-choice learning. In *New Directions for Youth Development*, ed. K. J. Pittman, N. Yohalem, and J. Tolman, 75–89. San Francisco: Jossey-Bass.

Dierking, L., V. Kaul, and J. Stein. (2005). *DINOSPHERE: Now You're In Their World: Summative Evaluation Report*. Annapolis, MD: Institute for Learning Innovation.

Dierking, L. D., and W. Pollock. (1998). *Questioning Our Assumptions from the Start: An Introduction to Front-End Studies in Museums.* Washington, DC: Association of Science-Technology Centers.

DeLong, J. B. (2000). *Cornucopia: The Pace of Economic Growth in the Twentieth Century.* Working Paper no. 7602. Washington, DC: National Bureau of Economic Research.

Drucker, P. F. (1992). *Managing the Non-profit Organization: Principles and Practices.* New York: Harper Business.

Drucker, P. F. (1995). *Managing in a Time of Great Change.* New York: Truman Talley Books/Plume.

Drucker, P. F. (1999). *Management Challenges for the 21st Century.* New York: Harper Business.

Drucker, P. F. (2000). *The Discipline of Innovation.* Boston: Harvard Business Review.

Drucker, P. F. (2001). *The Essential Drucker.* New York: Harper Business.

Duck, J. D. (2001). *The Change Monster: The Human Forces That Fuel or Foil Corporate Transformation and Change.* New York: Crown Business.

Duncan, Lisa. (2005). Lisa Duncan seminars, Duncan & Duncan Enterprises LLC., http://www.lisaduncan.com/retailing.html.

Ernst & Young. (1998). *Measures That Matter.* Boston: Ernst & Young, Inc.

Faber, C. S. (2002). U.S. Census Bureau Current Population Report: Geographical Mobility, March 1998 to March 1999. Washington, DC: U.S. Government Printing Office.

Falk, J. H. (1983). The use of time as a measure of visitor behavior and exhibit effectiveness. *Roundtable Reports* 7, no. 4: 10–13.

Falk, J. H. (1995). Factors influencing African American leisure time utilization of museums. *Journal of Leisure Research* 27, no. 1: 41–60.

Falk, J. H. (1998). Visitors: Who does, who doesn't, and why. *Museum News* 77, no. 2: 38–43.

Falk, J. H. (2000). Assessing the impact of museums. *Curator* 43, no. 1: 5–7.

Falk, J. H. (2002). The contribution of free-choice learning to public understanding of science. *Interciencia* 27, no. 2: 62–65.

Falk, J. H. (2003). Personal meaning mapping. In *Museums and Creativity: A Study into the Role of Museums in Design Education,* ed. G. Caban, C. Scott, J. Falk, and L. Dierking. Sydney, Australia: Powerhouse Museum Publishing.

Falk, J. H. (2006). The impact of visit motivation on learning: Using identity as a construct to understand the visitor experience. *Curator* 49, no. 2: 151–166.

Falk, J. H., and L. M. Adelman. (2003). Investigating the impact of prior knowledge, experience and interest on aquarium visitor learning. *Journal of Research in Science Teaching* 40, no. 2: 163–176.

Falk, J. H, P. Brooks, and R. Amin. (2001). Investigating the long-term impact of a science center on its community: The California Science Center L.A.S.E.R. Project. In *Free-Choice Science Education: How We Learn Science Outside of School*, ed. J. Falk, 115–132. New York: Teacher's College Press, Columbia University.

Falk, J. H., and L. D. Dierking. (1992). *The Museum Experience*. Washington, DC: Whalesback Books.

Falk, J. H., and L. D. Dierking. (2000). *Learning from Museums*. Walnut Creek, CA: AltaMira Press.

Falk, J. H., T. Moussouri, and D. Coulson. (1998). The effect of visitors' agendas on museum learning. *Curator* 41, no. 2: 106–120.

Falk, J. H., C. Scott, L. D. Dierking, L. J. Rennie, and M. Cohen Jones. (2004). Interactives and visitor learning. *Curator* 47, no. 2: 171–198.

Falk, J. H., and M. Storksdieck. (2005). Using the *Contextual Model of Learning* to understand visitor learning from a science center exhibition. *Science Education* 89: 744–778.

Firestone, Bruce M. (2002). Business model—a definition. www.dramtispersonae .org/BusinessModel

Foundation Center. (2004). *Foundation Giving Trends: Updates on Funding Priorities*. Washington, DC: Foundation Center.

Foundation Center. (2004). *Foundation Year Book: 2004 Edition*. Washington, DC: Foundation Center.

Foundation Center. (2005). *Key Facts on Family Foundations*. Washington, DC: Foundation Center.

Friedman, Thomas L. (2005). *The World Is Flat: A Brief History of the Twenty-First Century*. New York: Farrar, Straus & Giroux.

Fulton, K., and A. Blau. (2003). *Trends in 21st Century Philanthropy, Women Funding Networks*, http://www.wfnet.org/

Godbey, G. (2001). The use of time and space in assessing the potential of free choice learning. In *Free-Choice Learning: Building the Informal Science Education Infrastructure*, ed. J. H. Falk. New York: Teachers College Press.

Goldstein, M. (2004). The global age wave. Presentation developed for Voka-Vlaams (www.vola.be).

Goodwin, R. N. (1974), The American condition. *The New Yorker*, January 28, 38.

Gore, L., M. Mahnken, J. Norstrom, and D. Walls. (1980). *A Profile of the Visitors: The Dallas Museum of Natural History*. Unpublished manuscript, University of Dallas, Irving, TX.

Gozdz, K. (1993). *Building Community as a Leadership Discipline: The New Paradigm in Business*. New York: Jeremy P. Tarcher/Putnam

Graburn, N. H. (1977). The museum and the visitor experience. In *The Visitor and the Museum*, 5–32. Prepared for the 72nd Annual Conference of the American Association of Museums, Seattle, WA.

Gurian, E. H. (2001). Function follows form: How mixed-use spaces in museums build community. *Curator* 44, no. 1: 87–113.

Haas, Robert D. (1993). *The Corporation Without Boundaries: The New Paradigm in Business*. New York: Jeremy P. Tarcher/Putnam.

Harris, N. (1999). The divided house of the American museum. *Daedalus* 128, no. 3: 33–56.

Heimlich, J., J. Falk, K. Bronnenkant, and J. Baralge. (2005). *Segmenting Visitors to Zoos and Aquariums by Self. Technical Report*. Annapolis, MD: Institute for Learning Innovation.

Hirano, I. (1997). Changing public expectations of museums. In *Museums for the New Millennium: A Symposium for the Museum Community*. Washington, DC: The Smithsonian Institution.

Hood, M. (1983). Staying away: Why people choose not to visit museums. *Museum News* 61, no. 4: 50–57.

Institute for Museum and Library Service. (2005). National Award for Museum Service. http://www.imls.gov/grants/museum/mus_nams.asp.

Joba, C. (1993). Competition, cooperation and co-creation: Insights from the World Business Academy. In *The New Paradigm in Business*, ed. M. Ray. New York: Jeremy P. Tarcher/Putnam.

Kagan, Ron. (2002). Civic engagement starts with the board. In *Mastering Civic Engagement: A Challenge to Museums*, ed. American Association of Museums. Washington, DC: American Association of Museums.

Kaplan, R. S., and D. P. Norton. (1996). *The Balanced Scorecard: Translating Strategy into Action*. Boston: Harvard Business School Press.

Kaplan, R. S., and D. P. Norton. (2001). *The Strategy-Focused Organization*. Boston: Harvard Business School Press.

Kertzner, Daniel. (2002). The lens of organizational culture. In *Mastering Civic Engagement: A Challenge to Museums*, ed. American Association of Museums. Washington, DC: American Association of Museums

Knowles, M. S. (1970). *The Modern Practice of Adult Education*. New York: Association Press.

Kotler, N., and P. Kotler. (1998). *Museum Strategy and Marketing: Designing Missions, Building Audiences, Generating Revenue and Resources*. San Francisco: Jossey-Bass.

Kubey, R., and M. Csikszentmihalyi. (2002). Television addiction is no mere metaphor. *Scientific American* 284, no. 2: 76–83.

Kuhn, T. (1962). *The Structure of Scientific Revolutions.* Chicago: University of Chicago Press.

Lach, J. (1998). Boomers breaking through. *American Demographics* 25, no. 8: 37–42.

Laermer, R. (2002). *Trend Spotting.* New York: Perigee.

Lewin, K. (1945). The research centre for group dynamics at Massachusetts Institute of Technology. *Sociometry* 8: 126–135.

Lewis, D., and D. Bridger. (2000). *The Soul of the New Consumer.* London: Nicholas Brealey Publishing.

Lowry, G. D. (1999). The state of the art museum, ever changing. *New York Times,* January 10, Arts and Leisure, 1.

Lusaka, J., and J. Strand. (1998). The boom—and what to do about it. *Museum News* 77, no. 6: 54–60.

Lydecker, Kent. (1996). Interview with Sherene Suchy. In *Leading With Passion: Change Management in the 21st Century.* Walnut Creek, CA: AltaMira Press.

Marshall, C. (2002). *Engaging a Nation of Learners: The Penn State Conference on Public Service Media.* University Park: Pennsylvania State University.

McGuigan, C., and P. Plagens. (2001). State of the art. *Newsweek,* March 26.

McKendrick, N. (1982). The consumer revolution of eighteenth-century England. In *The Birth of a Consumer Society: The Commercialization of Eighteenth-Century England,* ed. Neil McKendrick, John Brewer, and J. H. Plumb. Bloomington: Indiana University Press.

Merriman, N. (1991). *Beyond the Glass Case.* Leicester, UK: Leicester University Press.

Miles, R. S. (1986). Museum audiences. *International Journal of Museum Management and Curatorship* 5: 73–80.

Mintz, A. (1994). That's edutainment! *Museum News* 73, no. 6: 33–36.

Moussouri, T. (1997). *Family Agendas and Family Learning in Hands-on Museums.* Unpublished doctoral dissertation, University of Leicester, Leicester.

Murray, V., and B. Tassie. (1994). Evaluating the effectiveness of nonprofit organizations. In *The Jossey-Bass Handbook of Nonprofit Leadership and Management,* ed. R. D. Herman and Associates. San Francisco: Jossey-Bass.

National Register Publishing. (2004). The Official Museum Directory. New Providence, NJ: National Register Publishing.

OCLC. (2003). 2003 Environmental Scan: Pattern recognition, http://www.oclc.org/membership/escan/introduction/default.htm.

Oldenburg, R. (1989). *The Great Good Place: Cafes, Coffee Shops, Bookstores, Bars, Hair Salons, and Other Hangouts.* New York: Marlowe & Co.

Osborne, S. P. (1996). Performance and quality management in VNPOs. In *Managing in the Voluntary Sector—a Handbook for Managers in Charitable and Nonprofit Organizations.* London: International Thomson Business Press.

Packard, V. (1978). *The People Shapers*. Bucks: Futura.

Packer, J., and R. Ballantyne. (2002). Motivational factors and the visitor experience: A comparison of three sites. *Curator* 45: 183–198.

Paris, S. G., and M. Mercer. (2002). Finding self in objects: Identity exploration in museums. In *Learning Conversations in Museums*, ed. G. Leinhardt, K. Crowley, and K. Knutson, 401–423. Mahwah, NJ: Lawrence Erlbaum & Associates.

Patton, M. Q. (1990). *Qualitative Evaluation and Research Methods*. 2nd ed. Newbury Park, CA: Sage.

Peek, A. (in press). Sci-Port Discovery Center—how we operate and position our science center for ongoing success. In *Handbook for Small Science Centers*, ed. C. Yao, L. Dierking, and P. Anderson. Lanham, MD: AltaMira Press.

Pekarik, A. J., Z. D. Doering, and D. A. Karns. (1999). Exploring satisfying experiences in museums. *Curator* 42: 152–173.

Pines, J., and J. Gilmore. (1999). *The Experience Economy*. Boston: Harvard Business.

Pittman, K. J., N. Yohalem, and J. Tolman (eds.), (2003). When, where, what and how youth learn: Blurring school and community boundaries. In *New Directions for Youth Development*. San Francisco: Jossey-Bass.

Prentice, R., A. Davies, and A. Beeho. (1997). Seeking generic motivations for visiting and not visiting museums and like cultural attractions. *Museum Management and Curatorship* 6, no. 1: 45–70.

Robert, P. (2003). *Enhancing Volunteerism among Baby Boomers*. Washington, DC: AARP.

Rosenfeld, S. (1980). *Informal Education in Zoos: Naturalistic Studies of Family Groups*. Unpublished doctoral dissertation, University of California, Berkeley.

Rossi, P. H., and H. E. Freeman. (1993). *Evaluation: A Systematic Approach*. Newbury Park, CA: Sage.

Sagon, C. (2004). Formerly known as Sutton Place. *The Washington Post*, April 7, F1.

Sasaki, L. (in press). A thing of lasting beauty: The evolution of the Japanese American National Museum's School Programs. *Journal of Museum Education*.

Schlossberg, E. (1998). *Interactive Excellence: Defining and Developing New Standards for the Twenty-first Century*. New York: Ballantine.

Schwarzer, M. (1999). Schizophrenic agora: Mission, market, and the multi-tasking museum. *Museum News* 78, no. 6: 41–47.

Senge, P. M. (1990). *The Fifth Discipline*. New York: Doubleday.

Sheppard, B. (1999). *The 21st Century Learner*. Washington, DC: Institute of Museum and Library Services.

Sherman, H. J., and R. Schultz. (1998). *Open Boundaries: Creating Business Innovation through Complexity*. Reading, MA: Perseus Books.

Skramstad, H. K. (1997). Changing public expectations of museums. In *Museums for the New Millennium*, 38. Washington, DC: Smithsonian Institution.

Slywotzky, A., and R. Wise. (2003). *How to Grow When Markets Don't*. New York: Warner Business Books.

Smith, C.B. (2004). The art of managing a museum—connecting the past, present and future. In *Inside the Minds: The Business of Museums*, ed. C. B. Smith. Boston: Aspatore, Inc.

Storksdieck, M., and J. H. Falk. (in prep.). An investigation of the long-term impact of a science center visit experience. *Science Education*.

Thurow, L. (2003). *Fortune Favors the Bold: What We Must Do to Build a New and Lasting Global Prosperity*. New York: Harper Business.

Treacy, M., and F. Wiersema. (1995). *The Discipline of Market Leaders*. New York: Basic Books.

Trescott, J. (1998). Exhibiting a new enthusiasm: Across U.S., museum construction, attendance are on the rise. *The Washington Post*, June 21, A1.

Van Allan, P. (2004). Long name replaced with "Penn Museum." *Philadelphia Business Journal*, April 9.

Wageman, S. (in press). How to foster innovation within your science-technology center: Observations from under the seat cushion. In *Handbook for Small Science Centers*, ed. C. Yao, L. Dierking, and P. Anderson. Lanham, MD: AltaMira Press.

Waterman, R. (1987). *The Renewal Factor: How the Best Get and Keep the Competitive Edge*. New York: Bantam.

Weil, S. E. (1999). From being *about* something to being *for* somebody: The ongoing transformation of the American Museum. *Daedalus* 128, no. 3: 229–258.

Weil, S .E. (2002). *Making Museums Matter*. Washington, DC: Smithsonian Institution Press.

Wells, M., and R. J. Loomis. (1998). A taxonomy of museum opportunities—adapting a model from natural resource management. *Curator* 41: 254–264.

Zuboff, S., and D. Maxmin. (2002). *The Support Economy: Why Corporations are Failing Individuals and the Next Episode of Capitalism*. New York: Viking Press.

Index

Note: Page numbers in italics refer to figures.

60 Minutes, 62–63

Abbott Partnership, 162–66
Abbott v. Burke, 162
acceptability, 218
access, 191, 192–97
accountability: legislation for, 168; political context of, 71–73, 239; THRIVE assessment, 233–35
acquisition, 18
admission fees, 7–8, 42
adults, 119
advertising: future of, 59–60; self-fulfillment and, 56
African Americans, 68–69, 101–2, 201
age: reaching various, 100–102
Alabaster Natural History Museum (model), 3–12, 205
Albert, S., 130
Amabile, Teresa, 122
Amazon.com, 59–60
American Association of Museums, 153, 154–55

American Council on Family Relations, 36
American Museum of Natural History, 223
ancillary services, 177–78; dining, 5–6, 113, 217; gift shops, 42, 43–44, 113, 178–79, 217; merchandise, 43–44, 178
Anderson, David, 64–65
Anderson, Rob, 73
Andoniadis, Andrew, 179
annual reports, 175
aquariums, 97–98
architecture: approval of eco-friendly buildings, 73–74; as cause of isolation, 66–67
Armstrong, Neil, 60
art, 17–18
art museums, 40
Asian Art Museum, 170–71
assessment, *23*, 232–35. *See also* THRIVE assessment
assets, 20; financial, *23*; in Industrial Age, 22; intellectual, 126–29; in Knowledge Age, 110–11

attendance: declining, 30
audiences, 17–18, 41, 42, 86–87, 227–29;
    about, 87–90, 228; building
    collaborations with, 150–52;
    expectations of, *193*; Experience
    Seekers, 93, 100, 199; Explorers,
    91–97, *95*; Facilitators, 92, 94–97, *95*,
    99, 100, 209–10; meeting the needs
    of, 98–100; Professional/Hobbyists,
    92–93; reaching young and old,
    100–102; selection of, 19
audio-guides, 42; future use of, 3–4, 5,
    6–7
Australia, 96–97
authority, 154
Ayers, Edward, 147

Baby Boomers, 60–61, 69
Bailey, Marvin, 144
Bakke, Dennis, 121–22
balance scorecard, 234
Bender, Matthew, IV, 172
BHAGs (Big, Hairy, Audacious Goals),
    19–20
birthday parties, 217
Blankenbaker, Ruth, 144
blockbuster exhibitions, 31, 44, 214
board of directors, 115–18, 233
Booth, Bill, 195
Boston Children's Museum, 135–40, 170,
    179
Boston Museum of Fine Arts, 237
bottom line: corporate support, 170–72;
    earned income, 176–80; government
    support, 166–70; individual and
    foundation giving, 172–76
bottom-up models, 22
Bouge, Don, 58
Bowling Alone, 68

Brand, Michael, 173
branding, 129–32
Bridger, Don, 56
British Museum, 212, 223
The Bronx Zoo, 238
Brooklyn Children's Museum, 146
Brooklyn Expedition, 146–47
Brooklyn Museum of Art, 146
Brooklyn Public Library, 146
Buffalo Museum of Science, 185–90,
    196, 238
building: of museums, 40–41
*Built to Last: Successful Habits of
    Visionary Companies*, 20, 231
Burke, Abbott v., 162
business models, 225–26; changing,
    22–25; defined, 18–22; in Industrial
    Age, *21*, 21–22, 38–39; making a
    difference, 102–3; need for, 13–14,
    17–18, 125

Calgary Science Center, 171
California Science Center, 90–98, 201–2
Campbell River, 148–49
capital, 110–11
Casagrande, Lou, 135–37, 139
The Catcher in the Rye, 48–49
Cavendish, Kim L., 176–77, 179
Census Bureau, U. S., 54
center: need for, 65–66
change: financial pressures and, 42–43;
    museums and, 74–76; need for new
    business model, 13–14, 22–25; search
    for identity and, 65–67; staff and,
    14–15
Chesebrough, David, 169, 185, 186, 189,
    190
Chew, Ron, 155
children, 92

The Children's Museum, 83–86, 119–20
choice: restriction of, 122
CityACCESS, 138
City Celebrations, 138–39
Cleveland Museum of Art, 17–18, 24
collaborations, 20, 43; becoming central
    to civic life, 154–55; Boston
    Children's Museum and, 138;
    building with visitors, 150–52; as
    good business, 157–58; within the
    organization, 123–25; with schools,
    140–45, 146–47, 162–66; success of,
    237–38; supporting lifelong learning,
    145–48
collections, 127–28, 148, 211–17
Collins, James, 20, 166, 231, 232
Colorado Digitization Project (CDP),
    128, 147–48
Command Audio Corporation, 58
Common Ground (exhibit), 140–41
A Common Wealth: Museums in the
    Learning Age, 64–65
communications, 36–37
community: as goal of organizations, 60;
    leadership for, 137–40; museums
    reaching out, 152–55; within the
    organization, 123–25; third places, 67
compassion, 73–74
competition, 53, 59–60, 122
computers, 42, 55, 59–60
connecting, 153
consolations, 115
Consumer Revolution, 32
consumers and consumerism: behavior
    of, 52; business response to, 56–57;
    individual-centered economy, 50–54;
    individualized services, 57–58; in
    Industrial Age, 38–39
Continental Airlines, 207, 209

Corporation for Public Broadcasting,
    146
corporations and corporate support:
    collaborations with museums, 44–45,
    170–72; compassion and, 73–74;
    distrust of, 71; success of, 232; in the
    twentieth century, 37–38
Crawford, Fred, 190–92, 203, 210
creativity, 120–22
curators, 112
curiosity, 91–92
customers. See audiences
customer service, 56–57, 114–15, 191,
    209–10
customization, 52–53, 57–58, 103

Dallas Museum of Art, 196
Dana, John Cotton, 142
DeLong, J. Bradford, 32, 54–55
demand: creating, 35–37
demographics, 135–36
Denver Museum of Art, 237
Department of Commerce, 146
DeSena, Al, 188
development, 123, 240–42
digital libraries, 147
Dinosphere (exhibit), 83–86
The Discipline of Market Leaders, 86
Disney, Walt, 35, 36
Disneyland, 35
distinction, 218
diversity, 117–18, 136, 152–55. See also
    ethnicity
dominance, 218
donations: corporate support, 44–45,
    170–72; foundations, 172–76;
    government support, 166–70;
    individual, 172–76
The Dowse, 155

Drucker, Peter, 120, 125, 224
Duncan, Lisa, 178

earned income, 176–80, 201–2
e-Bay, 58
Echo Boomers, 60, 62–63
Economic Context: business response to, 56–57; competition, 53, 59–60; consumer behavior, 52; growth of individual-centered economy, 50–52, 57–58; new consumers, 53–56; product customization, 52–53
economic development, 169, 186
education, 41, 216; as key mission, 39
educators, 112, 226
endowments, 174
entertainment, 198–200
Environmental Scan, 25
ethnicity, 68–69, 101–2, 113–14, 154–55, 201. See also diversity
evaluations, 23, 232–34. See also THRIVE assessment
Evers, Tom, 51
evidence, 233–34
Excellence and Equity, 153
exhibitions, 31, 41–44, 214
expectations, 93, 193
experience, 191, 197–201
The Experience Economy, 55–56
Experience Seekers, 93, 100, 199
Exploratorium, 150
Explorers, 91–92, 93–97, 95
external assets, 23
external learning, 118–20
external relationships, 237–38

Facilitators, 92, 94–97, 95, 99, 100, 209–10
Falk, John, vii–viii, 195, 207, 211

families: centering on, 84–85, 99–100; group identity and, 68; improving family friendliness, 107–8; isolation of, 66–67
Family Learning Initiative, 119–20
The Field Museum, 212–13, 238
field trips, 39, 142–43
The Fifth Discipline, 124
financial planning, 238–39
Firestone, Bruce M., 19
floor staff, 45–46
food services, 5–6, 113, 217
Ford, Henry, 34, 37, 51
Ford Motor Company, 34
formality, 121
Fort Worth Museum of Science and History, 237
Foundation for the Arts and Humanities, 146
foundations, 72–73, 172–76. See also specific foundations
Franklin, Benjamin, 43
free-choice learning, 70–71
Freed, Sylvia, 83–84
Freud, Sigmund, 67
funding, 42–43, 238–39; corporate support, 170–72; earned income, 176–80; government support, 166–70; grants, 139, 174–76; individual and foundation giving, 172–76
fundraising, 45, 174

genealogy, 68
General Motors, 38
gift shops, 42, 43–44, 113, 178–79, 217
Gilmore, Jim, 55–56, 200
Gissing, Andie, 62
globalization, 52

Golin Harris, 73
Goodwin, Richard, 67
government: distrust of, 71; legislation, 72, 168; support from, 42, 166–70
Government Performance and Results Act (GPRA), 72, 168
Gowen, Richard J., 146
Gozdz, Kazimierz, 123
Graburn, Nelson, 70
Gracyalny, Jim, 51
grants, 139, 174–76
Great Depression, 36
group identity, 68–69

hands-on activities, 108
Hanley, Bill, 211
Harp, Hilary, 197–98
"have-nots", 64–65
"haves", 64–65
Headwaters Science Center, 192–93
Hirano, Irene Y., 154–55
Hirzy, Ellen, 156
Hodes, Nancy, 172
hours of operation, 196
Howe, Neil, 63
human resources, 111–12; as asset, 110–11; fostering creativity and innovation, 120–22; opportunities for learning, 118–20; staff, 14–15, 45–46, 112–15, 118–20; trustees, 115–18; volunteers, 118

IBM, 55
identity: branding and, 130–32; categories of, 91–98; changing, 89–90; customer service and, 209–10; experiences and, 200–201; group identity, 68–69; as visit motivation, 90–98

Independent Sector, 72
Industrial Age: business in, 29–30; business model and, 21, 21–22, 32–39, 45–46; corporations in, 13, 37–38; effects of, 51–52; mass production and consumption, 33–34; success of museums in, 224
Industrial Revolution, 33–34, 54–55
informality, 121
Information Age. See Knowledge Age
innovation, 120–22
inputs, 42
Institute for Learning Innovations, 229–31
Institute of Museum and Library Services, viii, 40, 223; call for action from, 145; collaborations with, 227, 241; collections of, 126–27; technology and, 146
intellectual assets, 126–29
intellectual property rights, 128
Interactive Excellence, 152
internal assets, 23
internal learning, 118–20, 236–37
Internet, 194
interpretation, 18

Japanese American National Museum (JANM), 140–45, 238
Joba, Cynthia, 157–58
Joy of Work, 121–22

Kagan, Ron L., 117
Kaplan, Robert, 234, 236
King Tut Exhibition, 31, 43
knowledge: success and, 232–33, 241
Knowledge Age, 49–50; business model and, 13–14, 23, 23–25; descriptions of museums in, 221–23; distribution of

wealth in, 64–65; Economic Context, 50–60. *See also* success
Knowles, Malcolm, 119
Kosta, Pam, 129–30
Koster, Emlyn, 162, 164–65
Kroc, Ray, 35, 36

land, 110–11
Latino Community History Project, 154
leadership, 124, 137–40
learning: internal, 236–37; as motivation, 88–89; as museum's greatest strength, 226–27; opportunities for staff, 118–20; quest for, 69–71; supporting lifelong, 145–48
Learning from Museums, vii
Learning Societies, 64–65, 70
Lee, Sherman, 17–18
leisure, 70, 194–95
Levine, Mel, 62
Lewis, David, 56
Lewis, Lesley, 150–51, 167, 172
Liberty Science Center, 161–66, 170
libraries, 157, 227; digital, 147
lifelong learning, 145–48
living history, 106–10
The Louvre, 212, 223

management, 120–22
Managing in a Time of Great Change, 125
marketing, 36, 43–44, 56, 59–60
Mashuntuckett Pequot Museum, 155
mass communications, 36–37
mass customization, 57–58
mass marketing, 36
mass production, 33–34, 56
Mastering Civic Engagement, 156
Mathews, Ryan, 190–92, 203, 210

Matieshin, Kevin, 171
Maxmin, D., 190
McDonald's, 35
McGlothlin, Frances G., 172–73
McGlothlin, James W., 172–73
memberships, 9–10, 204–5
merchandise, 43–44, 178
metrics, 235–36
Metropolitan Museum of Art, 31, 40
micro-management, 122
mission statements, 19, 41, 102–3, 150
Missouri Historical Society, 149–50
mobility, 66
motivation: identity types and, 90–98, 100–102; for visiting museums, 88–89
Museum of Fine Arts, 40, 238
Museum of Modern Art (MOMA), 202, 212
Museum of Science (Boston), 43
museums: brief history of, 39–46; building of, 40–41; business as shared responsibility, 239–43; change and, 74–76; community and, 148–50, 152–55; compartmentalization of, 45–46; competition and, 19; expectations of, 75–76; as external and internal learning organizations, 118–20; growth of, 30; making a difference, 102–3; motivations for visiting, 87–90; partnerships with schools, 140–45; value in, 191–92. *See also* bottom line; collaborations; success
Museums and Community Initiative, 155–56

National Aquarium in Baltimore (NAIB), 229–31, 239–40

National Museum of Australia, 155
National Museum of Natural History, 212–13
National Museum of the American Indian, 155
National Science Foundation, U. S., 90, 97, 146, 241
The New Paradigm in Business, 123
niche marketing, 59–60
No Child Left Behind, 145
nonprofits, 72, 197, 225, 234
North African Muslims, 68–69
Norton, David, 234, 236

Oldenburg, Ray, 66–67
Old Sturbridge Village (OSV), 106–10, 125, 129, 151–52
Ontario Science Center, 150–51, 166–67, 170, 172
Ordan, Mark, 50–51
outputs, 42
outreach staff, 113

Packard, David, 120
parents, 99–100
partnerships. *See* collaborations
Patchen, Jeffrey, 84–85, 99–100
Peek, Andree, 175
Penn Museum, 129–30
Perseus Digital Library, 147
personalization, 52–53, 103
Philadelphia Museum of Art, 40
philanthropy, 40, 42, 233–34
Pine, Joe, 55–56, 200
Political Context, 50, 71–76
Porras, Jerry, 20, 166, 231, 232
poverty, 64–65, 161–62
Powerhouse Museum, Sydney, 96
pressure, 122

price, 50–52, 191, 201–5
price-led costing, 204
prioritization, 168
product, 52–53, 191, 211–17
Professional/Hobbyists, 92–93
profitability, 161–66
promotions, 178
Providence Public Library, 157
public value, 235–36
Pulleyn, Chris, 131, 132
Putnam, Robert, 68

quality, 50–52
quality time, 194
quest culture, 69

Radford, Karen, 171
Reid, Katherine Lee, 17–18, 24
religion, 69
The Renewal Factor, 231–32
research and development, 123, 240–42
retailing, 178–80
revenues. *See* funding
rewards, 122
Rhode Island School of Design, 157
Rodriquez family (fictional case study), 3–7
Roof, Wade Clark, 69

Sabloff, Jeremy A., 130
Salinger, J. D., 48–49
Sanderson, Steven E., 126
Sano, Emily, 170
Sarbanes-Oxley Act (SOA), 71–72, 117
Sasaki, Lisa, 140–42
Schafer, Roy, 180
Schlossberg, Edwin, 152
schools: collaborations with, 140–45, 146–47, 162–66

Science Museum of Minnesota, 238
Science North, 207
Science Spots, 187–88
Scitech Science Centre, Perth, 96
security: need for, 65–66
self-fulfillment, 55–56, 69
self-identity: branding and, 130–32;
   categories of, 91–98; changing,
   89–90; customer service and, 209–10;
   experiences and, 200–201; within
   groups, 68–69; as visit motivation,
   90–98
Senge, Peter, 124
September 11th, viii, 7, 30
service, 56–57, 114–15, 191, 205–11
services: mass production of, 34–35
Sheppard, Beverly, 106–7, 129
signage, 108, 230
60 Minutes, 62–63
Skramstad, Harold, 102
Sloan, Alfred, 38
Slywotzky, Adrian, 210, 214
Small, Lawrence, 173
Smithsonian Institute, 39, 211–12, 223
social class, 53–56
Social Context, 50, 60–71
The Soul of the New Consumer, 56
specialization, 123
spirituality, 69
Spiritual Pilgrims, 93–94, 100
Spock, Michael, 137
sponsorship, 171
staff: floor staff, 45–46; need for change,
   14–15; needs of museums, 112–15;
   utilizing, 118–20. See also customer
   service
stakeholders, 112
Star Wars (exhibit), 43

strategic plans, 19–20; for Old
   Sturbridge Village, 109–10; picking,
   217–18; strategy for, 190–92
Strauss, William, 63
subject expertise, 109
success: access, 192–97; Buffalo Museum
   of Science, 185–90; customer service,
   205–11; experience, 197–201; in the
   Knowledge Age, 189–90, 223–29; new
   criteria for, 225–29; price, 201–5;
   product, 211–17; strategies for,
   190–92, 217–18; sustainability,
   229–32; using knowledge to manage,
   232–33
Suchy, Sherene, 124
Summers, Nick, 62
support processes, 235–36
sustainability: creating and measuring,
   229–32
Sutton Place Gourmet, 50–51

Target, 170–71
teamwork, 63, 124–25
technology, 146–48, 216, 224; future of,
   3–4, 5, 6–7
teenagers, 62–63
TELUS, 171
terrorism, 66
third places, 67, 137
Thompson, Dale, 157
Thompson, J. Walter, 36
THRIVE assessment, 233–35; external
   relationships, 237–38; internal
   learning and growth, 236–37; public
   value, 235–36; revenues and finances,
   238–39
Thurow, Lester, 128
time saving, 194

TiVo, 58
tokenism, 157
top-down models, 22, 38
Treacy, Michael, 86
triage, 107–8
trustees, 115–18
twentieth century, 54–55, 68; industrial
    business model, 38–39

United States, x, 49; distribution of
    wealth in, 64–65; mobility of
    citizens, 66
United States Holocaust Memorial
    Museum, 197–98
urban mission, 135–37
users. *See* audiences

validating, 153
The Valley of the Shadow, 147
value: access, 192–97; experience,
    197–201; meaning of, 191–92;
    picking a strategy, 217–18; price,
    201–5; product, 211–17; service,
    205–11
Vincent, Clark, 36

Virginia Museum of Fine Arts, 101–2,
    172–273
vision statements, 19
visitors, 228. *See also* audiences
visual display: of merchandising, 178
volunteers, 45–46, 118

Wageman, Susan, 120–21, 122
Walters Art Gallery, 238
Waterman, Bob, 231–32
Watson, J. B., 36
wealth, 64–65
Weil, Stephen, 102
West, Mac, 215
Whetten, D., 130
Wiersema, Fred, 86
Wildlife Conservation Society, 126
Wing Luke Asian Museum, 155
Wise, Richard, 210, 214
word-of-mouth, 60, 63
work, 70
World of Life (exhibit), 90–91

zoos, 97–98
Zuboff, S., 190

About the Authors

John H. Falk, president of the Institute for Learning Innovation, is internationally recognized for his leadership, research, and writings in the area of free-choice learning. Prior to founding and directing the Institute, he held senior positions at the Smithsonian Institution, including associate director, Smithsonian Environmental Research Center; director, Smithsonian Office of Educational Research; and special assistant for education to the assistant secretary for research. He has written more than a hundred scholarly articles and book chapters, as well as written or edited more than a dozen books, including, with Lynn Dierking, such classics as *The Museum Experience, Learning from Museums*, and *Lessons without Limit*. Falk is adjunct professor of Science Education at the Oregon State University, serves on the national board of the Smithsonian's National Postal Museum, is on the editorial board of the journals *Curator, Journal of Museum Education*, and *Science Education*, and is a member of several national and regional advisory commissions.

Beverly K. Sheppard assumed the position of president and CEO of Old Sturbridge Village in June 2002 after serving as the deputy director, and then acting director of the Institute of Museum and Library Services, the federal agency focused on supporting museums and libraries. She has honed strong leadership skills and a vision of a twenty-first-century Learning Society through her work in the museum profession for more than twenty years, developing award-winning education programs and building educational and community partnerships at the Chester County Historical Society in West Chester, Pennsylvania, and as president of the Pennsylvania Federation of Museums and Historical Organizations. Sheppard is well known in the museum field for her longstanding leadership in pushing institutions to embrace partnerships and the needs of twenty-first-century learners; two of her widely read publications —*Building Museum and School Partnerships* and *Museums, Libraries and the 21st Century Learner*—speak to these issues.